CLAIRE McCARDELL

The Designer Who Set Women Free

Elizabeth Evitts Dickinson

SIMON & SCHUSTER

*New York   Amsterdam/Antwerp   London
Toronto   Sydney/Melbourne   New Delhi*

Simon & Schuster
1230 Avenue of the Americas
New York, NY 10020

For more than 100 years, Simon & Schuster has championed authors and the stories they create. By respecting the copyright of an author's intellectual property, you enable Simon & Schuster and the author to continue publishing exceptional books for years to come. We thank you for supporting the author's copyright by purchasing an authorized edition of this book.

No amount of this book may be reproduced or stored in any format, nor may it be uploaded to any website, database, language-learning model, or other repository, retrieval, or artificial intelligence system without express permission. All rights reserved. Inquiries may be directed to Simon & Schuster, 1230 Avenue of the Americas, New York, NY 10020 or permissions@simonandschuster.com.

Copyright © 2025 by Elizabeth Evitts Dickinson LLC

All rights reserved, including the right to reproduce this book or portions thereof in any form whatsoever. For information, address Simon & Schuster Subsidiary Rights Department, 1230 Avenue of the Americas, New York, NY 10020.

First Simon & Schuster hardcover edition June 2025

SIMON & SCHUSTER and colophon are registered trademarks of Simon & Schuster, LLC

Simon & Schuster strongly believes in freedom of expression and stands against censorship in all its forms. For more information, visit BooksBelong.com.

Grateful acknowledgment is made to the McCardell, Harris, and Orrick families for permission to quote from archival materials.

Excerpts in this book have been adapted from a *Washington Post Magazine* article, "A Dress for Everyone," by Elizabeth Evitts Dickinson, published on December 12, 2018.

For information about special discounts for bulk purchases, please contact Simon & Schuster Special Sales at 1-866-506-1949 or business@simonandschuster.com.

The Simon & Schuster Speakers Bureau can bring authors to your live event. For more information or to book an event, contact the Simon & Schuster Speakers Bureau at 1-866-248-3049 or visit our website at www.simonspeakers.com.

Interior design by Carly Loman

Manufactured in the United States of America

1 3 5 7 9 10 8 6 4 2

Library of Congress Cataloging-in-Publication Data has been applied for.

ISBN 978-1-6680-4523-7
ISBN 978-1-6680-4525-1 (ebook)

*For all those in search of their true calling,
and to Matt and Nola for encouraging me to pursue mine.*

Contents

Introduction: Dressing for a Revolution   1
Author's Note About the Usage of Names in This Book   7

PART I: RICK

1: The Practice House   11
   1905–25
2: An Army of Brave Women   29
   1925–26
3: This Clothes Business Certainly Is a Gamble   41
   1926–27
4: This Town Doesn't Pity a Soul   59
   1928–29

PART II: SOME DAMNED WEIRD STUFF

5: Let the Girl Do It   77
   1929–33
6: Everyone Deserves Pockets   91
   1933–34
7: Abdication   101
   1934–37
8: Hanger Appeal   113
   1938
9: Gushing Nitwits   129
   1938–39
10: The Specter of War   147
   1939–40

PART III: CLAIRVOYANT CLAIRE

11: Shooting Craps — 157
Fall 1940

12: We Admit This Line Is Different — 169
1941

13: It's Rather Fun to Have a Limit — 181
1941–43

14: Mr. Claire McCardell — 193
Spring 1943

15: Make of It What You Will — 201
Spring and Summer 1943

16: The American Look — 207
1944–45

PART IV: WOMEN ARE WHAT THEY WEAR

17: Stay Out of Topeka, You Bum — 221
1946–50

18: Society Is an Awful Chore, Isn't It? — 233
1950–52

19: Ah, Men — 243
1953–55

20: McCardellisms — 253
1955–56

21: The Quiet Genius — 261
1956–58

Epilogue — 273
Acknowledgments — 277
Notes — 281
Selected Bibliography — 309
Index — 313

INTRODUCTION

Dressing for a Revolution

It was after six o'clock on a June evening in 1955, and Claire McCardell sat in her Manhattan apartment with an eager young journalist. McCardell, age fifty, had recently made the cover of *Time* magazine, only the second fashion designer to achieve the honor. *Life* was readying a story about outfits she'd made using fabric designs by the artists Pablo Picasso and Marc Chagall. McCardell had granted hundreds of interviews during her twenty-seven-year career. But in all that time, she'd never allowed a journalist inside her apartment. Somehow, she'd been disarmed by the energetic reporter, whose dogged curiosity she'd come to admire over the several days the woman had shadowed her at work.

The journalist was equally surprised to have gained access to McCardell's Upper East Side home. She'd been warned that McCardell protected her personal life. The writer, though, was Betty Friedan, and she was on a mission. The thirty-four-year-old mother would later write that "something is very wrong with the way American women are trying to live their lives today." She was already forming the ideas that would become her 1963 feminist cri de coeur, *The Feminine Mystique*. On that evening, she wanted to take a peek inside the life of one of the most influential women in America.

Friedan had told her editor at *The Town Journal* that a profile on Claire McCardell would provide the story of American fashion coming into its own. McCardell had ushered in a new era of modern design and pioneered what was widely known as the American Look: casual, stylish, ready-to-wear sportswear that was also affordable. In doing so, she had become one of the first designers to successfully join high fashion with mass production.

Equally important to Friedan was the story of a woman advancing her ambitions in a culture that prioritized men. McCardell was born and raised in the small town of Frederick, Maryland, far from the centers of fashion. When she had arrived in New York in 1925, clothing labels had carried the name of the manufacturer or the department store, not the designer. McCardell had wanted to create her own brand, and she'd wanted her name to be stitched on the label. What she'd envisioned didn't yet exist, so she'd set out to build it. Her aspirations outpaced what was allowed in the dressmaking industry, let alone by a woman.

Friedan now sat in one of McCardell's armchairs, pen poised over her open notebook. McCardell didn't look anything like a famous fashion designer. She wore an understated ankle-length dress made of navy wool jersey. Her long, wavy hair was caught up in a casual knot, her natural blond shot through with streaks of silver. Tendrils framed an angular face free of makeup.

McCardell opened a wardrobe filled with clothes she'd made over the years. She walked Friedan through some of her innovations. She'd developed leotards and leggings, brought hoodies, denim, and leather into womenswear, ushered the swimsuit into its contemporary form, included pockets in her clothes, and made the wrap dress a wardrobe staple. In the early twentieth century, women had been restricted to wearing sports clothes in private, female-only spaces. McCardell had brought those clothes out into the open and transformed them into everyday street wear.

"I've always designed things I needed myself," McCardell liked to say. She thought of herself as a "continuous experiment, a testing ground for ideas." Clothes, for her, were more than a way to cover and protect the human body or to peacock one's personal style; they were a physical manifestation of a woman's ideas, identity, and desires. McCardell eschewed the male-dominated vision of fashion, preferring to create clothes that fit women's bodies as well as their growing ambitions. Conventional dressmaking often dictated that women force themselves into structured clothes to achieve the idolized hourglass shape, but McCardell cut her garments to fit a woman's natural body. She'd forsaken high heels and introduced ballet flats. She'd shocked retailers when she invented the capsule wardrobe composed of mix-and-match separates in the early 1930s. The women who wore McCardell—from housewives to Hollywood stars, from artists and activists to hardworking professionals—tended to be confident, accomplished, and, most of all, comfortable.

Now the freedoms McCardell had advocated and advanced for herself and for other women were under attack. That was what Friedan really wanted to discuss. Women, like McCardell, had increasingly pursued higher education and built careers in the years between the world wars. They'd entered the workforce in droves during World War II, but as soldiers came home, many women were pushed to stop working and return to domesticity.

The fashion world reflected the postwar change. The French designer Christian Dior had introduced a hyperfeminized style replete with padded shoulders, tightly cinched waists, and high heels. He wanted to "save women from nature," and he squeezed his models into clothing with an eighteen-inch waist. The press had dubbed it the "New Look." In fact, it was a regression to the old ways of manipulating a woman's body by putting her in restrictive clothing.

McCardell was having none of it. Her creative mission was unapologetic and her position unwavering: She wanted to set women free. "You can't go back," she told Friedan. "You have to design for the lives American women lead today."

Friedan's profile ran under the attention-grabbing headline "The Gal Who Defied Dior." The article named McCardell as the progenitor of America's national fashion, as well as a courageous rule breaker who had fought bias to build her career. "She changed the world's meaning of fashion," Friedan wrote.

Friedan's statement is undeniably true. We owe much of what hangs in our closets to Claire McCardell. Yet it's Dior's name that we all remember.

This book corrects the record by telling the story of Claire McCardell and the feminist genesis of the clothes she designed. Drawing on McCardell's personal letters and work notebooks, archival documents, interviews with her family and those in the fashion industry, as well as newly discovered source material, the chapters ahead show how McCardell became an internationally renowned inventor and designer in her lifetime.

McCardell did not realize her success in isolation. Rather, she was at the center of a constellation of women who worked diligently to create the fashion industry in New York amid the turbulent political and cultural turmoil of the Great Depression and World War II. In just three decades, Claire McCardell helped revolutionize what women had been wearing for the past three hundred years and simultaneously built the business model for the modern-day fashion designer. She achieved that success by taking herself and her novel ideas seriously, even when many people around her did not.

In this never-before-told story of Claire McCardell, we meet someone who rose to the heights of her industry because she made tough choices and set boundaries. At a time when the median age of marriage was twenty, McCardell chose not to have children and to remain single until she was nearly forty years old. She instead built her empire, a decision that didn't gel with society's ideals. She embraced her artistic self and questioned traditional gender roles, all while designing clothes meant to support a woman's life and individual circumstances.

The filaments of McCardell's fashion ideas can be traced back to the nineteenth century, when suffragists argued that a woman's freedom began with her clothes. Unencumbered bodies meant unencumbered lives. The crucial connection between clothes and liberty became ever clearer as more women entered the public realm and civic life, as McCardell did. She joined a long line of women advocating for agency and independence through dress, and she cleverly and diligently chipped away at prevailing dress codes.

McCardell's approach earned her a loyal international fanbase of customers and fellow designers in her lifetime. And it earned her the ongoing loyalty of the fashion industry, which still reveres Claire McCardell, even as she has been forgotten by the world at large. Designers from Tory Burch to Anna Sui to Michael Kors, among many others, extol her ingenuity and credit her designs and her business acumen as inspiration.

Seventy years ago, two pillars of female empowerment—McCardell and Friedan—met in New York. What they discussed remains deeply relevant today. The status of womanhood, like the tides of fashion, is always in flux. Women remain embroiled in many of the same battles that McCardell knew all too well. Her ideals continue to resonate as we live in a head-spinning time that tells women to be anything they want while simultaneously dismantling the progress made for equity and autonomy. Stitching Claire McCardell's name back onto the apparel she pioneered is not merely a history lesson in provenance; it is a vital and timely reminder of a designer, and a movement, that was always about far more than clothes.

AUTHOR'S NOTE ABOUT THE USAGE OF NAMES IN THIS BOOK

There's an interesting debate when it comes to naming a woman in a biography. Should an author reference her by the more informal and intimate first name or use the last name? The decision is complicated by the reality that a woman's surname often changes to that of her spouse after marriage. There's rarely such debate in biographies of men, where it's long been standard to use the last name. In fashion, it's frequently the last name that identifies the designer. It is a *Chanel* suit, not a *Coco*. It is a *Dior* dress, not a *Christian*. Similarly, it is a *McCardell*, not a *Claire*. In her lifetime, she was known professionally as McCardell or Claire McCardell. She went by her maiden name even after she married later in life. In the pages ahead, you'll learn how she fought to be recognized by that name on the clothes she designed. I take my lead from McCardell herself and refer to her as McCardell throughout. I give the same consideration to McCardell's fashion industry contemporaries. I identify each woman by the last name she chose for her professional life, which was not always her legal married name.

PART I

Kick

(1905–29)

CHAPTER ONE

The Practice House

1905–25

The neighborhood kids called her Kick, and the nickname was well earned. In 1912, at age seven, Claire McCardell's booted toe rarely missed the thin-skinned bone of a boy's shin. Her aim was as precise as it was painful. She delivered her swift kicks only after words had failed. Of course, when you were the only girl joining in the boys' games, words often fell on deaf ears.

The trouble usually began when the boys changed the rules. Rockwell Terrace, the street where McCardell lived, was their playing field. The wide, oak-lined boulevard made a perfect backdrop for Run, Sheep, Run. The boys liked to say that a girl couldn't lead the game of chase. Enter McCardell's boot.

McCardell's mother, Eleanor, would sit on the front porch, keeping one eye on her daughter, the other on her crocheting. Her daughter usually bounded up the steps after playing, grass staining her white cotton pinafore dress and mud clotting the knees of her stockings. She never managed to come home as clean as when she'd left.

It had been three years since the McCardell family had moved to the new garden suburb a mile outside the historic town of Frederick, Maryland. McCardell's father, Adrian LeRoy McCardell, who went by Roy, had been able to afford the small corner lot at 301 Rockwell Terrace thanks to his salary at the Frederick County National Bank. He and Eleanor had built a three-story brick Dutch Revival with a broad porch overlooking a swath of green lawn. Inside, fireplaces warmed cozy parlor rooms filled with books and art, and the dining room was big enough to host the extended family. McCardell's paternal ancestors had left County Antrim, Ireland, in the early 1800s and settled in Maryland's fertile Piedmont Plateau. Her grandparents and many of her aunts, uncles, and cousins lived within walking distance.

Eleanor, meanwhile, came from a long line of Southerners. Born in 1880 in Jackson, Mississippi, she was the daughter of a former Confederate officer. In her early twenties, she visited a friend in Frederick, where she met and fell in love with the quiet, handsome Roy, seven years her senior. They married in 1902. Baby Claire arrived three years later, on May 24, 1905. She had the classic McCardell nose, a retroussé pug that would, in adulthood, give her angular face a childlike softness. Her vivid blue eyes shifted from a stormy hazel to a steely blue gray, depending on the light. Her brother Adrian arrived three years later, followed in 1913 by Robert, who went by Bob, and in 1916, by John, who was nicknamed Max.

On Sunday mornings, the family attended the Evangelical and Reformed Church, where her devout father was an elder. Women kept their gloves on, men removed their hats and straightened their ties, and Kick left her boisterous outdoor energy at the door, adopting the role of obedient daughter in her starched dress. The society pages of the local paper chronicled the lives of the white middle and upper classes. A quarterly article named those with perfect attendance at Sunday school, and the McCardell siblings always made the list.

After church, the family gathered at her paternal grandfather's house in town. McCardell sat among her many aunts and uncles and cousins, her plate overloaded with her grandmother's fried pork and beaten biscuits, and later, if she was lucky, a dessert of orange slices topped with freshly shredded coconut that her grandmother called ambrosia.

In the afternoon hours before bedtime, Kick was free to roam outside with her friends. She'd change from her Sunday finery into a pinafore dress and blouse, pull on black wool stockings, and lace up her leather boots. She'd braid her long honey blond hair and twist the two plaits into a chignon. The last thing you wanted when climbing trees was a free-flowing plait hooking a limb. As she scrambled into the branches of an oak, she sometimes wondered why her clothes were so impractical. Her brothers' sturdy pants were made for climbing and running. They had pockets for carrying apples from the nearby orchard or stashing the coins their father gave them for ice cream. Why didn't her outfits have pockets? Why couldn't a girl's clothes be both pretty and practical? Like most children, McCardell questioned the world around her, and from an early age, clothes became the focus of her inquisitive mind.

On rainy afternoons, McCardell sometimes entertained herself with a game she called Playing Lady. She sneaked into her parents' bedroom and opened the inner sanctum of her mother's wardrobe. Eleanor was as fashionable as the small town of Frederick and the family's budget allowed. She was also fastidious about her possessions and didn't like them to be disturbed, but McCardell would rather play now and ask for her mother's forgiveness later.

McCardell sometimes ran her hands along her mother's clothes, feeling the watery silks, the nubby wools, the starchy laces. She would free a dress from its hanger and step into it, the frock swimming on her small body. She couldn't reach the tiny buttons marching up the back. Getting dressed as a woman required having someone to help you. She'd pose before the mirror, miming the manners and postures she observed on the adults.

Dress codes of the era dictated that middle- and upper-class women like her mother wear different outfits depending on the time of day and the event. Unstructured dressing gowns were reserved for the bedroom. Housedresses were meant for chores and home life. To go outside, a woman had to truss herself into a corset and a day dress. Eleanor's day dresses had high lace collars and reflected the demure sensibility of a lady of her station. She wore them with stockings, gloves, and a hat when running errands in town or attending volunteer committee meetings for the Civic League and Red Cross. Tea dresses, a bit fancier, were required when playing bridge at the nearby country club or attending an afternoon tea dance.

Then there were the evening gowns. Frederick was rural, but it wasn't remote. Equidistant from the cities of Baltimore and Washington, DC, by about fifty miles, Frederick had a robust cultural scene. It had long been a stop for politicians, artisans, and performing artists, who traveled through using one of the country's first nationally funded roads. Eleanor reserved those finer gowns for the nights she and Roy went dancing or to performances at the National Theatre in Washington. They routinely attended Frederick's arts events, and they made certain that their children did so as well. By elementary school, McCardell was going to the theater with her parents, visiting museums, and participating in literary clubs for girls her age. Eleanor encouraged her daughter, who had an innate shyness, to take the stage in a children's theater production of *Little Women*. McCardell played the lovable but doomed character Beth March.

McCardell had heard many stories of her maternal grandmother, who had lived in the same Civil War era in which *Little Women* takes place. McCardell's grandmother had been a decorous woman who loved fine silk. To get dressed in the 1860s, she first had to hook a corset onto her midsection that ran from her breasts to her hips and could be tightened by laces in the back. Rigid with steel stays, it laced tightly up her back, pushing her bust up and cinching her abdomen to create the ideal hourglass curves. Then she fastened onto her waist a cage crinoline, a birdcage-shaped undergarment constructed of steel rings and cotton tapes that expanded her skirt into a wide bell.

Next came the dress itself. The bodice had whalebone sewn into the seams for further contouring of her torso. Eleanor said these dresses had been so big and stiff from all the structuring used to shape them that they could stand on their own without a hanger, as if inhabited by a ghost.

The burden of all those layers was only one of the challenges a woman faced when wearing such attire. It was difficult to walk without catching her enormous skirt on a table or under a carriage wheel. The hem dragged on the ground, collecting dirt and grime and necessitating arduous hours of handwashing in tubs of boiling soapy water. Even just sitting in a cage crinoline required careful positioning, as society mandated that a woman keep her ankles covered by fabric.

Corsets, meanwhile, could be punishing to the body. In the 1860s, Mary Walker, one of the country's first female surgeons, dubbed them torso prisons because they put enormous pressure on a woman's internal organs. Walker freed herself by adopting an outfit of trousers, vest, and a coat and was promptly arrested on New York City's Canal Street for impersonating a man. Starting in the mid-1800s, so-called decency laws made it illegal in some states to appear in public wearing clothes not matching your assigned birth gender. In some cities, those arrested could face up to six months in jail, and a woman also risked being sent to a psychiatric institution. "I don't wear men's clothes," Walker had argued. "I wear my own clothes." Walker continued to wear gender-defying dress and she faced ongoing public harassment. One person pelted her with eggs. A deeply offended woman set her dog on her.

By the time McCardell's mother was born in 1880, the fashionable silhouette of women's clothes had morphed to include a bustle. The understructure beneath a dress had a stiff shelf at a woman's bottom so that her skirt protruded at her low back. At the turn of the century, the shape of dresses changed yet again. They were slimmer, the cage crinoline now a memory. Eleanor next followed the popular Gilded Age silhouette, where a woman's breasts and backside were lightly padded and her body shaped by a corset into an "S" shape. To achieve that fashionable figure, Eleanor wore a new style of corset that forced her hips down and her bust forward. Such a health corset, as it was called, claimed to avoid placing dangerous pressure on the abdomen and internal organs. But the goal was to forcibly transform the body into an idealized form, which at that time made women look, in the words of one observer, an awful lot like pigeons. In 1912, when McCardell played in her mother's wardrobe, the basic premise of women's dress—multiple garments layered over restrictive undergarments—had not radically changed in more than three hundred years.

◆

McCardell's fascination with clothes evolved into an obsession with paper dolls. The ten-cent packets of dolls sold in the general store were made of thin card stock, and they came with a woefully limited selection of outfits. So McCardell began making her own. She took her mother's back issues of *Vogue* and *Harper's Bazaar* and squirreled them away in the attic. One afternoon, a friend came over to play, and McCardell led her upstairs to her secret stash. Dormer windows pierced the slate roof and flooded the space with sunlight, and there in the corner towered a stack of magazines nearly as tall as they were.

The girls sat on the floor, and McCardell fanned out the magazines. She opened one and flipped through the pages until a fashion illustration caught her eye. She picked up her scissors and cut. She lopped the top off a dress and combined it with the skirt of another. She sliced the sleeves off a shirt and added them to a dress. Then she guillotined a woman wearing a pretty hat and placed the head atop a different body.

Her friend stared, confused. "What are you doing?" she asked.

"I'm making them better," McCardell replied.

Rarely satisfied with what she saw, she invented new outfits. As she cut her custom paper dolls, she worked her way through years of her mother's fashion magazines, observing how silhouettes shifted with the seasons.

Twice a year, McCardell also got to see firsthand how garments were constructed. The McCardells, like most other people, made their own clothes using patterns sold through books. In rural Frederick many also worked from memory, using the handed-down knowledge of previous generations. The general store offered a few ready-to-wear items that they could buy off the shelves, including gloves, coats, and men's pants. Jeans and overalls were available for working-class men. McCardell's mother could buy her stockings and McCardell's tights from the local

Union Manufacturing company, but women still needed to custom make many of their clothes. Those who could afford it, such as the McCardells, hired a dressmaker to help.

Eleanor selected her new clothes from the *Vogue Pattern Book* because its designs always copied the latest trends from Paris. She went to town to buy fabric and often took McCardell with her. They walked along Market Street, filled with the smell of hay and the musk of horses pulling passenger wagons and the more appealing aroma of cinnamon and yeast emanating from Garber's Bakery. Carroll Creek flowed through the center of downtown Frederick and provided the hydropower for the nearby textile mills. McCardell's grandfather owned one of the town's oldest businesses, a candy warehouse and shop called A. C. McCardell, Confectioner. There he made homemade confections using patented candy molds and exotic fruits.

Eleanor liked to collect gossip along with her supplies, so the walk to the general store was slow as she stopped to chat with friends and neighbors. Before marrying Roy, Eleanor had been wooed by a lawyer back in Jackson, Mississippi. The man had believed that Eleanor's gregarious nature would help secure him a political future, but he quickly wearied of having to keep his hat in his hand as they strolled downtown because Eleanor greeted everyone.

Inside Hendrickson's General Store, McCardell walked among shelves stacked with thick bolts of colorful fabric and bins filled with rolls of ribbon. Samples of fine imported lace stretched like cobwebs for shoppers to examine, and all manner of poor birds had been denuded of plumage, their colorful feathers taken for hats and dress trim. The frugal Eleanor took her time choosing fabric. The store clerk unfurled her selected bolts and measured the required yardage against brass tacks set at intervals on the countertop.

Once the supplies had been secured, McCardell's father hauled the family's treadle sewing machine to the front room of the house. When the sewing machine was placed, McCardell knew that Anna Koogle was coming.

A sought-after dressmaker, Anna Kate Koogle lived in Middletown, a short trolley ride from Frederick. She was born in 1891, a few decades after the invention of the Singer sewing machine forever transformed clothes making. She had learned to sew as a child on her mother's Sears model. When Miss Annie, as McCardell called her, mounted the steps of Rockwell Terrace, McCardell was eagerly waiting.

Koogle took Eleanor's selected dress patterns and material, and she carefully measured and cut each piece, altering patterns as needed to best fit Eleanor's body. Next it was time for Koogle to settle in behind the sewing machine. She placed her foot on the treadle that powered the needle, as though she were readying herself to play a piano. McCardell sat on the other side of the machine and watched.

At age seven, McCardell was finally allowed to help make her own dress. Eleanor and Koogle walked her through the many considerations when deciding on a style: Where should the waist be? What should the sleeves look like? Where should the hem land on the leg? McCardell decided on a drop-waist white cotton shift dress that hit just below her knees. She thought a pretty grosgrain would be nice for a sash at the hips, and she convinced her mother to buy enough for her to make a matching bow for her honey-colored hair.

Koogle asked if she wanted to add ruffles. McCardell shook her head. Ruffles are pretty, her mother chimed in, but McCardell wanted no embellishments. Even as a child, her aesthetic sensibility was strong.

◆

By the time McCardell entered high school in 1919, she preferred sketching clothes and sewing over doing schoolwork. She struggled to maintain good grades, much to her parents' chagrin. The McCardells were unique among parents of the time in that they placed a premium on formal education for their daughter, not just for their three sons. Their house was filled with books and magazines, and they subscribed to newspapers from Frederick, Baltimore, and DC. Over dinner, they discussed politics, current events, and the latest novels. In 1893, McCardell's grandfather had cofounded Hood College, one of the first women's-only schools to offer bachelor's degrees. The fifty-acre campus sat less than a mile from their house, and the presumption was that McCardell would enroll there one day. Her father, who served on the local school board, imagined that his daughter might become a teacher, one of the few careers open to women at the time. Eleanor was traditional, and she believed in her role as a homemaker, but she was progressive when it came to her daughter's potential. She encouraged McCardell to dream big about her future.

Each semester, McCardell took her report card home for her father's signature, and he frowned at so many Cs and Ds. She struggled in the classroom and was reserved in her academic contributions. People seemed to speak in different languages. Her banker father was most fluent in the concrete language of numbers, her garrulous mother in the semantics of domesticity and social life. McCardell's language was clothes. She could conceive outfits in her mind, really see them. Designing "is just my way of expression," she once explained, "as speaking is not."

Geometry was one academic subject that made sense to her. She had no problem visualizing 3D and 2D shapes, how angles and lines intersected and related to one another. All those hours making clothes had taught her about spatial relations, pattern making, and dimensional problem solving. Two-dimensional shapes became three-dimensional objects, held together by seams and buttons.

Apart from geometry class, McCardell felt most alive in the hours she spent outdoors. She was competitive and possessed a natural athleticism, sharpened by the sibling rivalry with her three younger brothers. She joined Adrian on the golf links to see who could hit the ball the farthest and participated in her brothers' pickup baseball and football games on Sunday afternoons. She competed to see who could swim the fastest across the neighbor's pond.

Sporting events had become an important part of the social life of American teenagers, including those in Frederick. Tailgates before football and baseball games were often followed by mixers featuring orchestras bused in from Baltimore. At her first school dance, she wore a favorite angora sweater. She noticed that its fine threads shed on her date's navy blue suit, and she never forgot it. Boys took McCardell to the movies, and they went to Rockwell Terrace for dance parties in the living room, the music playing from the family's Victrola. But McCardell never settled into going steady with one boy the way some of her friends did.

She counted down the days until June, not just because it marked the end of the school year but because it meant going to the YMCA's sleepaway camp in Big Pool, Maryland, an hour from Frederick. The camp's wooden cabins hugged the lakeshore and were surrounded by miles of pine forest. In 1920, when McCardell was fifteen, she got to share a cabin with her best friends. Even after lights out at 9:30 p.m., her jubilant laugh carried across the still evening. McCardell, who was once described as "full of slang and laughs," had an infectious humor. But over breakfast, a girl in the neighboring cabin complained about all the "queer noises" coming from their cabin at night.

One afternoon, after a morning of scheduled activities with the counselors, the campers were left to their own devices. Some napped; others played cards or wrote postcards. McCardell and her friends sat on the shore in the heat of a humid afternoon. Sweat pooled on their necks as they baked inside their heavy black wool bathing costumes.

The bathing suit, as its name implies, had originally been designed for outdoor bathing. In the nineteenth century, women wore a full dress with pantaloons and wool swim stockings. Showing bare legs on a public beach constituted nudity and could lead to arrest. As more female swimmers took to the water at the turn of the century, however, they contested the cumbersome design. Every unnecessary thread added drag against the water. In 1902, an intrepid male writer put on an outfit like those that women were required to wear. He wrote that the "pounds of apparently dead weight seemed to be pulling at me in every direction." He could handily swim a mile in his own suit, but swimming just a hundred yards in female garb exhausted him.

One of McCardell's childhood heroes was an Australian swimmer named Annette Kellerman. She'd scandalized society in 1907 when she had begun wearing a body-hugging wool jersey swimsuit that looked a bit like an acrobat's leotard with swim trunks. The skirtless one-piece had freed her for swimming—even as she still wore the requisite black swim stockings—but the tightly fitted suit led to police fines and public harassment.

In 1920, the emerging flapper trend raised hemlines, revealing more leg than ever. Fashion rebellion was in the air, even in rural Frederick. Dresses were shorter, and girls bobbed their hair. Most American women kept with the socially acceptable bathing costume, but others started rolling their stockings down to below their knees and exposing their bare thighs on public beaches. Some brave souls ditched the swim stockings altogether. The Nineteenth Amendment to the Constitution, which had given white women the right to vote, had been passed the previous summer, but a woman showing her bare legs was a bridge too far. Not even America's Olympic athletes were immune. That year, the women of the swim team had to fight to compete without stockings. National competitiveness eventually won out over moral fears, and they raced with bare legs. But for most women, stockings remained a requirement.

At camp, McCardell wore a one-piece bathing suit with trunks and stockings that resembled Kellerman's costume. She had loved swimming since she was little, but the stockings diminished the pleasure of being in the water. Sitting at the edge of the lake, McCardell and her friends sweated in their hot suits, the mosquitoes making a meal of their bare arms. The sun glinted off the cool water like an invitation.

It took all of them to push the boat off the shore and into the water. Camp rules prohibited taking a boat without permission, but why ask a counselor if the chance was that they'd say no? When pressed on a matter she felt strongly about, McCardell would often respond that she "didn't give a deuce." And today she didn't give a deuce about the rules. They reached the center of the lake where McCardell rolled off her stockings and left them in the boat.

She leapt into the water. Her bare legs met the cold, dark depths beyond the reach of the heat. She rose to the surface, her body buoyant and strong as she sliced a line through the water. The mineral smell of the lake in her nose, her body in motion: what a feeling to go barelegged! No pond muck getting caught in the stocking thread, no extra fabric to slow you down.

McCardell had a rebellious streak, particularly when it came to rules that she deemed unfair. She was testing her limits now, learning to walk the line between having her way and staying in the good graces of her parents and her community. She and her girlfriends were navigating between the strict moral codes their mothers had been raised on and a new freedom that seemed to be just on the horizon. They yearned to ride bicycles, play tennis and golf, and to swim and fish and captain their own boats. They longed to race and run and hike through the mountains of western Maryland with the same abandon the boys enjoyed. They wanted to partake in outdoor adventures and competitive sports, even as some doctors warned that women should avoid exertion when menstruating.

Their desire for freedom was inextricably linked to fashion. As early as the 1890s, *Vogue* equated physical recreation, sports, and the emergence of sportswear with autonomy. "The result of all this activity being that we have become as proud of our muscles and nerve as our dear mothers and grandmothers used to be of their delicate constitutions," one editorial proclaimed.

McCardell and her friends headed back to shore, where they found a male camp counselor waiting for them. Their punishment for taking the boat and for swimming without stockings was a half hour of carrying heavy axes over their shoulders while walking in a circle.

As high school progressed, McCardell created most of her clothes. Ideas came faster than she could sketch, and she tried them out in harried spurts at the sewing machine. Anna Koogle scolded her restless impatience. "I didn't sew very well, but I managed to get an 'effect,'" McCardell later said. When she wasn't allowed money to create something new, she altered her existing clothes, changing the hemlines, the sleeves, and adapting them to the new trends.

She experimented on anything and everything. When she saw a dress or coat or skirt in front of her, she also envisioned a garment that didn't yet exist. She pictured a version of the physical object manipulated to her liking, and then she made it a reality. Hers was a family of inventors, after all, her grandfather having patented his unique candy molds. You imagined something, designed it, and then you made it. She'd observed that process her whole life, the way "our lives are tuned to ingenuity—in inventions, gadgets," she said. She delighted in experimenting.

Her love of clothes had matured into a calling. She was "determined to save the world from ugliness and dreary clothes," she joked to a friend. After high school, she wanted to study clothing illustration at the Parsons School of Design, known as Parsons (at this time, it was still called the New York School of Fine and Applied Art). Going to college in New York would require her parents' blessing and their financial support for tuition and living expenses. With her high school graduation swiftly approaching, she informed her parents of her aspirations. Her father's response was swift and definitive. His only daughter would not travel 250 miles north to live alone in a city as large, as debauched, as New York. That city was, he said, a "den of iniquity." McCardell needed to stay put and enroll in Hood. The college didn't offer a costume design program. The closest McCardell could get was a major in home economics. McCardell graduated from Frederick High in June 1923. The occasion was bittersweet.

That summer, instead of creating clothes that would save women from dreariness, she was forced to sew the bleakest of all garments: a uniform. Hood sent instructions to buy Butterick sewing pattern number 2838 to make the required dress, which she would wear in the school's chemistry lab and test kitchen. And she had to make three of them.

◆

On September 20, McCardell descended the porch steps of her house and walked to her first day of college. The commute took all of six minutes.

She was among a handful of locals in the freshman class. Most of their classmates hailed from other states, some from as far away as the Midwest and California. They lived on campus and enjoyed the camaraderie of dorm life. Those classmates got to reinvent themselves away from the watchful eye of their families. As a day student living at home, McCardell missed out on such joys and felt the added pressure of being the granddaughter of a school founder.

Still, a sense of great possibility energized the campus in the fall of 1923. Hood was a microcosm of the larger shifts happening in women's lives around the country. The Great War had unleashed women into the workplace, expanding the possibilities of what they could do and achieve. The outspoken students of Hood were enthusiastic about their education. "The real purpose of a college education is to arouse a desire to understand life in the whole," one of McCardell's classmates wrote in the student newspaper that September. Their studies were meant to foster an intelligence and curiosity that "will carry us further than the lessons assigned us," she wrote, and lead to a lifetime of achievement.

Hood was one of the first colleges to offer a bachelor of science degree in home economics. The discipline, conceived in the mid-nineteenth century, was seen as a back door for women to gain access to higher education and the sciences. Students hoped to stoke their intellectual engagement and even enter jobs outside the home that catered to the new domesticity. Women were becoming dietitians, professors of home economics, scientists working in textile labs and test kitchens. Two months before McCardell began college, President Warren G. Harding established the Bureau of Home Economics within the US Department of Agriculture. A female chemist took the helm, and her department swiftly became the largest employer of female scientists in the country.

McCardell's home ec curriculum required courses in English composition, algebra, organic chemistry, bacteriology, and spoken English, a class that taught proper elocution and debate. In addition, she had to take electives, such as physiology, zoology, and a foreign language. She chose French, to bring her closer to the language spoken by the world's greatest fashion designers at the time.

A healthy diet, exercise, and fresh air were seen as vital to the modern woman, and physical education was a part of the curriculum at women's colleges. Decades prior, Catharine Beecher, an early founder of home economics curricula, had advocated for women's education and physical health. She'd lobbied against corsets, arguing that their distortion of the body prevented proper exercise. As more women participated in athletics, what to wear became a pressing concern. Sports clothes didn't yet exist. One 1880s manual on women's exercise cautioned that high-heeled boots had no place in the gymnasium. Popular women's magazines took up the discussion, offering tips for making clothes that would cover the arms and legs as propriety required but not impede movement.

The Western fascination with the East around that time led to the adoption of Turkish-style trousers. The poofed legs resembled a skirt when a woman stood still but allowed her to move more freely. In 1893, Butterick released a pattern for gymnasium bloomers. But when women began playing intercollegiate sports in public arenas, only female spectators were allowed to watch. In 1923, trousers on women, even bloomers, were still largely forbidden in public.

In Frederick, baffled clothiers began to correlate the rise in sports with an increase in the average height and size of American women. "Due to their indulgence in athletic sports," the male owner of a local glove shop warned his colleagues, "women now have larger hands and feet than formerly."

Those were the same clothiers who advertised in the Hood student newspaper. As McCardell's classmates wrote of their intellectual and athletic pursuits, the local shop of Thomas H. Haller ran an ad assuring students that "if every lady who reads this most interesting and progressive paper . . . will wear a Gossard Corset, she will secure more comfort for her body, more style for her attire, and surely a lot of peace for her mind." The Gossard Corset's claim to fame was that it would shape a woman's figure to be pleasing to the male eye while not disturbing her internal organs. Be progressive. Be smart. But also, be painfully pretty.

McCardell refused to wear such undergarments. They "push you out of any resemblance to the way nature made you," she said. The purpose of clothes, she believed, was to support a person's lived experience. "I don't hate crinolines as such," she once joked. "I hate them when they try to get in elevators."

McCardell's pursuit of a home ec degree would culminate in a semester spent in a campus building known as the Practice House. Inside that ersatz home, students partnered to plan meals, care for and maintain the house, sew, decorate, cook, and entertain. Practice Houses were a new and integral part of home economics curricula across the country. They became the living labs of learning, where the chemistry of food, the science of textiles, and the mechanics of mass-produced machinery worked in tandem with the intelligent application of human skill and creativity. Or so the colleges said. McCardell didn't give a deuce about being a housewife. Marriage and children didn't occupy her mind the way clothes did. Nor did academics.

Student grades were sent to parents directly. McCardell's were abysmal. The chemistry professor told her parents that the only thing their daughter had learned was that acids shouldn't come in contact with human skin. "The burns on my hands were proof that I had permanently memorized that one fact," McCardell later said.

If McCardell's first year at Hood was a slog, her sophomore year was worse. She simply couldn't pretend to care about the path she'd been set on. She wanted to make clothes, and she wanted to go to New York. A few weeks after McCardell had completed another academically dismal year at Hood, Roy announced over supper that he'd come to a decision. McCardell would be allowed to apply for the 1925–26 academic year at Parsons. He would pay her tuition and basic expenses. He looked his stunned daughter in the eyes and told her that she had to work hard and make good grades, or she would have to come home.

McCardell's brothers believed that their mother had changed their father's mind. Eleanor saw her daughter's talent. It's also possible that Roy McCardell, a banker attuned to good and bad investments, understood that a traditional college education offered diminishing returns for his daughter.

Eleanor suggested that they bring Anna Koogle in one last time to send McCardell off in style. McCardell declined. She couldn't possibly know what her life in New York would entail, so how could she know what she should wear? Instead, she asked for a pair of good sewing scissors and a modest budget to buy fabric when she got to the city. On a cool September morning in 1925, she boarded a train with her trunk, her scissors, and a bit of pocket money. Finally, she was speeding north to Manhattan.

CHAPTER TWO

An Army of Brave Women

1925–26

McCardell's train pulled into Grand Central Station just after noon on Wednesday, September 2, 1925. She exited onto the streets of midtown Manhattan and was met by the frenzied speed of a city teeming with over six million people. Exhaust, horse manure, the feral honk of cabs. Harried pedestrians shouldered past her on the crowded sidewalks.

The six-story building at 340 West 85th Street, by contrast, sat on a serene tree-lined street near the Hudson River. A brass plate affixed to the exterior read "Three Arts Club." McCardell's school had no dorms, so the all-women boardinghouse would be her home for the academic year.

Inside, gilt-framed oil paintings lined the walls, and sprays of fresh flowers adorned end tables. There were comfortable couches and lots of books, and the smells of baking bread and furniture polish. Young women chatted over pots of tea in the parlor, while somewhere in the building a violinist tried mightily to find her proper tune.

In coming to New York alone, McCardell had joined an unprecedented number of single women who were leaving home in search of autonomy and adventure. They were postponing marriage and children to pursue education and careers. New York, however, was wholly unprepared for them. American cities had been planned by men for a social structure in which single women weren't considered. Hotels often refused to accept unmarried women, worrying that they were of ill repute. Women were forced to rent closet-sized rooms in unregulated boardinghouses where the running water was cold and safety an afterthought. And since many public establishments refused entry to unchaperoned women, newcomers had few places to socialize and meet friends.

Women began flocking to city churches seeking advice and shelter. Jane Harriss Hall, a deaconess at St. Mark's Church, stopped counting the number of women who arrived on her doorstep. They came shaken, with tales of lecherous landlords or of strict matrons who locked the doors and refused them entry past a perversely early hour. All the rules made living difficult. There were "so many restrictions upon the inmates that they destroy the spirit of real home life and freedom, which the girls long for and have a right to expect," Hall told a reporter. The modern woman was no longer content with the old domestic drudgery, as Hall explained, and she yearned for something more. She believed she might find it in New York.

In 1902, Hall founded the Three Arts Club to house this "army of brave women who are self-supporting." For a modest rent, a woman under the age of thirty pursuing an education or a career in the arts got a clean, furnished room, a shared bath with hot water, and no curfew. Only a handful of women-centric residential spaces existed in 1925, and the Three Arts Club was one of the reasons McCardell's parents had allowed her to come to New York. That the accommodations were available primarily to white women of means was an unwritten but tacit rule.

McCardell's roommate that year was a fellow costume design student. Mildred Orrick (née Boykin) wore her jet-black hair brushed off her face in a loose bun. Her pale, smooth complexion and large blue eyes gave her the look of a silent movie star. Orrick had a Southern accent, but it wasn't like any McCardell had heard, even among her mother's relatives in Mississippi. Orrick dropped her final *r*'s when she spoke, and it made McCardell smile to hear her pronounce words such as "Never" as "Nevah."

McCardell had a lot in common with Orrick. They were both from middle-class families with Southern roots. Each had a rebellious streak.

When McCardell was getting into trouble ditching her swim stockings, Orrick had been donning flapper dresses in Florida, where the all-male state legislature had passed a law declaring such dress to be against the decency of the state. Only, Orrick's life had been touched by tragedy in ways that McCardell's had not. Orrick's older sister, Martha, had died of food poisoning a few years earlier. And shortly before arriving at school, she had lost her father to a sudden stroke.

Like McCardell, Orrick had attended an all-women's college in Florida prior to enrolling in Parsons. She, too, was ready to shed traditional academics for a full-throttle entry into the urbane, sophisticated world of costume design. They were in for a disappointment.

◆

It took less than ten minutes to walk from the club to their school's headquarters on Broadway and 88th Street. The gray brick Broadway Studio Building commanded the corner of a long city block. Over the street-level shops, large, high-ceilinged rooms flooded with natural light housed the students' art studios.

McCardell believed she'd be drawing the newest fashions that semester. It was the golden age of fashion illustration, with every magazine, department store, and catalogue company using artists to detail garments. Photography was still a new and expensive art form, and illustration was the dominant medium of communicating the look of clothes.

Now her professor explained that the three-year costume design program began with a study of art techniques and European art history. The primary objective was to help students develop a sense of quality and style. In her excitement to get to New York, McCardell hadn't appreciated that her first year would largely be a fine arts course.

The school had been founded in 1896 to bring a European sensibility to education in the United States. The current president, Frank Alvah Parsons, was a visionary when it came to professionalizing the arts. He saw the future markets for advertising and graphic and industrial design, and he created, among other things, one of the first courses of study for interior design in the United States. Art, he believed, was not meant for the few; anyone could become a working artist if given the proper training.

The faculty placed a heavy emphasis on European design because it was believed that the United States was still in a cultural vacuum. Shortly before McCardell began at the school, Frank Alvah Parsons had served as a delegate for the US government at the International Exhibition of Modern Decorative and Industrial Arts in Paris. The global showcase highlighted the latest fashion, art, architecture, and design, but the US Department of State declined to send any American designers, claiming that they had nothing to contribute. "As a nation we now live artistically largely on warmed-over dishes," one source said of the American absence. "We copy, modify and adapt the older styles with few suggestions of a new idea." Frank Alvah Parsons had gone only to take notes, and he returned alarmed by the encroaching modernism he saw in Europe.

In 1925, McCardell's curriculum remained firmly rooted in Old World European aesthetics and classical Greek symmetry. McCardell would take a series of drawing courses and study perspective, color, and proportion. She would learn pencil and pen-and-ink techniques.

It wouldn't be until her sophomore year that the study of costume design began in earnest. Costume illustration focused on drawing clothes for magazines, department stores, and advertising. Recent graduates with that degree worked for women's magazines, drawing the illustrations that accompanied articles. Or they worked for department stores such as Lord & Taylor, rendering the merchandise for store advertisements and catalogues. Others found jobs sketching for American clothing manufacturers. And if they excelled at sketching, they just might parlay that into a job as a designer.

But first, McCardell had to spend hours each day in the Broadway Studio Building taking life drawing classes. Models stood on a wood box in the center of the room, frozen in stilted postures. Charcoal and graphite blackened McCardell's fingers and stained her clothes. Her rapid mind became bored by the repetition of so many limbs and poses.

She and Orrick sometimes stayed late after classes to spend time with the men majoring in fine art and architecture. Sculptors, painters, writers, and musicians not attending the school also flowed through the Studio Building. The Studio Boys, as McCardell and Orrick called them, came in trailing cigarette smoke and with flasks tucked into their jacket pockets. Prohibition, despite what the law said, was a mere suggestion on the island of Manhattan. Temperance advocates routinely begged the city to eliminate the "wet element" once and for all, but alcohol flowed as surely as the Hudson River. Fiorello La Guardia, New York's future mayor, had recently summarized the city's sentiment about Prohibition when he'd said that it couldn't be enforced for the simple reason that most New Yorkers wanted to drink.

After class, they talked about art and politics as the flasks were passed around. McCardell's slight Southern drawl and initial shyness led some of the men to make assumptions about her intelligence. But then she'd level them with a quick comeback or a distinctive take on the politics of the day. "It's funny how all northern people think the one southern girl they know is exactly like all the rest," she later recounted to her mother. "Southern girls must have no individuality in their minds."

McCardell grew close with an art student named Chester Slack. He asked if she would model for one of his assignments and in return promised to give her the portrait after it had been graded. "Mildred and the other girls already have their portraits done by the other boys, but Chet says I'm harder to draw," McCardell wrote home. "He says I'll need to come back again."

That autumn, one of Slack's friends, an aspiring writer, fell hard for McCardell. He courted her with florid phrases, but when he decamped to a cabin in the woods of New Jersey to write, Slack broke the news: "He's plopped for three girls since you."

That stung. But she soon had a date to go swimming in a fancy new indoor pool at a midtown hotel. Another boy took her for supper and dancing at Park Avenue's Ambassador Grill, where the orchestra played dance standards until 1:00 a.m. Some of the women in McCardell's class seemed intent on using their time at Parsons to meet a husband, but she was far more seduced by the city's cultural life. Her letters home brimmed with stories of Broadway plays and jazz clubs where "the horns really can sing." New York was a city unleashed. The spigot had been turned on at the New York Stock Exchange, and money flowed as never before. No more steady work was necessary just to scrape into the middle class; great gulps of money were ready and waiting to be swallowed as soon as the brass bell rang the traders to life on Wall Street. Capitalism boomed aboveground as speakeasies fueled the madcap energy from below.

The flappers of F. Scott Fitzgerald's new novel, *The Great Gatsby*, were depicted as hard-drinking, coquettish creatures full of mystery and drama. But really, the term *flapper* had become a catch-all for any woman who dared to participate in public life while wearing slimmer, more revealing clothes. A moral panic had spread across the United States as a result. If a woman could dress that easily and with so few layers of undergarments, one argument went, she could certainly *undress* just as quickly. Women's fashion was being blamed for divorce, domestic abuse, and even homicide. Black and white women alike wore the flapper style, as did the wealthy and those who worked for a living. Suddenly, you couldn't easily identify class differences based on apparel. In New York and New Jersey, some workplaces and public establishments began enforcing stricter dress codes. Skirt hems couldn't rise more than twelve inches from the ground; sleeves had to cover elbows.

McCardell was a flapper for her ideals of independent womanhood, if not for the full adoption of the signature look. She disliked the tube-shaped dresses, a silhouette that one writer compared to wet asparagus stalks. Instead she developed her own New York style. She wore fitted jersey knit sweaters and tweed skirts that rose to her calf over gunmetal gray stockings and kitten-heeled Mary Janes. As women cut their hair into bobs, McCardell kept hers long, well past her shoulders. Dramatic makeup became another signature of the flapper, and it was influenced by technological advancements. Compact, portable tubes now replaced heavy jars and pots. Helena Rubinstein's Cupidsbow red lipstick came in a black tube as sleek as an Art Deco sculpture, and it fit in a purse.

McCardell, once described as having radiant skin, kept her face makeup free at a time when powder and rouge were considered as essential as underwear. An elderly friend of the McCardell family, after bumping into her on the street, reported back to her parents that their daughter looked half dressed and pale. "I think that's the funniest thing. Guess it's because I don't use three or four layers of powder," McCardell told her mother.

The flapper trend that she did embrace was the felt cloche hat. She had an affinity for hats, and she scoured the dime stores of New York for bargains. On a weekend trip home to Frederick that semester, she emerged in her New York outfit for a Sunday morning at church. "She came downstairs in a fancy hat," her brother Adrian recalled, and their father "sent her back upstairs to put on a more dignified one." Still, she turned heads in church because "the local women were always interested in seeing what she would be wearing."

◆

McCardell's favorite classes that year were the ones spent in the city's museums, especially the Metropolitan Museum of Art on Fifth Avenue. Her professors took the students into galleries and lectured about color and tonality and the *chiaroscuro* technique of the Florentine Renaissance painters. The students were instructed to absorb the historic fashions depicted in the art and replicate them in their sketchbooks.

McCardell homed in on a woman wearing a wine-dark cape, lined with ermine. The fur's bright white flecked with black intrigued her— such a crisp contrast to the otherwise muddied browns and reds in the painting. Ermine fur was a symbol of purity and royalty, she learned, and it featured prominently in European portraiture. A person's character and station were reflected in the material of their clothing. As McCardell painstakingly copied several historical outfits from the European paintings that day, she may have wondered how this exercise would translate into her working in the present world of fashion.

After class one day, their professor led them across Fifth Avenue to the penthouse apartment of one of the Met's patrons, a friend of Frank Alvah Parsons. He used his vast social and professional connections to bring students elbow to elbow with New York high society: the businessmen who might later employ their graphic design or architecture skills; the wives who might buy their art or hire them to decorate penthouses like that one.

Her classmates eagerly helped themselves to finger sandwiches and tea. McCardell went to the window and looked out over Central Park and the museum she'd just visited. She looked down onto the building's courtyard below, a well-manicured yard with marble statues and giant urns of colorful flowers. "This is the loveliest house I have ever seen," McCardell told Orrick that day. "She has a garden and everything. It's just like a real house." She was still getting used to the idea of people living in grand urban apartment buildings. More than her schoolwork, more than copying European art at the Met, it would be the society ladies of New York who would give McCardell her first real education in clothes that year.

◆

The benefactors of the Three Arts Club were a who's who of storied New York names, including Mrs. Frederick Vanderbilt and Mrs. Peter Cooper Hewitt. Once a year, the women and their wealthy friends opened their closets and donated last season's looks for a fundraiser for the club and to give the students and job-seeking artists access to French clothes at a deep discount. This was how, one afternoon, McCardell found herself sifting through clothes carrying the labels of distinguished French designers. She had never seen such fine silks and wools, such beautiful construction.

"The ladies of the board sent their discarded Paris clothes to be sold to us girls for a small sum, like $5!" McCardell later wrote to her parents, partly to explain how she'd spent that month's modest allowance from her father in record time.

It floored her, too, that fine clothes were being shed like so much snakeskin in preparation for the next season's offerings. What a waste to spend the equivalent of a year's worth of rent on a dress, only to toss it away as soon as the French designers rewrote the styles.

Back in their room, McCardell and Orrick examined their haul.

"We got a wonderful windfall," McCardell said.

"People are going to think that Mr. McCardell of Frederick keeps his daughter quite well with all these secondhand Paris outfits," Orrick joked. "We're going to be the best dressed women on the subway."

In addition to the clothes, the board members passed along tickets to their boxes at the opera and invitations to art openings. The patrons of the Three Arts Club were among a group of New York women helping to lay the groundwork for modern art museums. Women would establish the Museum of Modern Art in 1928, among others, and it was in the many small galleries of New York that McCardell witnessed exciting, contemporary art. Cubists were defying perspective. Surrealists were swapping realism for the unsettling images pulled from the unconscious mind. Fashion reflected and embraced that modernist shift, at least in France. *Vogue* showcased Cubism-inspired fabrics coming out of Paris. McCardell was drawn, as well, to the form-meets-function pragmatism of a new breed of modern French architects, such as Le Corbusier. Their streamlined approach reflected the way she felt about clothes: no ruffles or gadgets, as she called unnecessary embellishments, just high-quality fabric, well cut and constructed.

McCardell made a series of watercolors using a palette of black, red, and gray. Her illustrated women wore capes, slim dresses, and cloche hats, and they fitted together in their poses like puzzle pieces. Her work had the movement of an Alexander Calder mobile, the abstraction of a Picasso.

"I love modern art, furniture, and accessories," she confessed to her parents. "Am crazy about it. Lots of people can't understand it and don't think much of it [but] I am just cracked on the subject now."

Orrick was, too. "I think we're the only modernists in our class," she said.

That was a potentially dangerous shift for McCardell. She had to stay in the good graces of her professors and maintain the grades that were a parental condition of her enrollment. And modernism was not on the syllabus.

"Suppose you've gotten my report by now," she wrote her father in the winter of 1926. "Write me what the mark is—they won't tell us at school it's so dumb." Her grades, she learned, were passable but not stellar. "I promise. I will do better," she told her father. And with the start of the spring semester, she determined to buckle down.

But soon she found herself clashing with her father over her social life. On Sundays, she usually sat in the library at the club and wrote letters home. Increasingly, she went away on weekends to visit friends at colleges in New Jersey and upstate New York, or she slept in late after taking in a Broadway show the night before. Roy McCardell worried. "From your letter, Daddy, you'd think I had a house all alone in the back woods somewhere," McCardell wrote. She reminded him that "if we're not at breakfast they come up to our rooms to see where we are." Besides, she added, Orrick "always knows where I am going and when I expect to return."

Not long after, her father gifted her a new Bible. "I hope you will read this book daily," he inscribed it. "It will give you comfort when other things fail."

The girl with the perfect Sunday school attendance in Frederick now rarely went to church in New York. So much was changing for her that year, and she wasn't quite sure where religion ranked in her life, something she could never admit to her devout parents. Still, she felt the umbilical tug of familial duty.

A friend recommended that she attend service at St. Bartholomew's Church in Midtown. On her first visit, McCardell had to stand behind the pews because the church was full. Everyone was there to hear the young rector, Reverend Robert Norwood, a poet turned pastor who subscribed to a progressive view of theology. He believed that the traditional ways of interpreting faith couldn't keep pace with twentieth-century realities: the Great War and its ferocious, efficient destruction of human life; the industrialization of work; the rapid urbanization of America. Yes, illegal booze flowed through the speakeasies, but the city itself was an intoxication. New York was like "a brown bowl that contains a strong and heady drink," Reverend Norwood once said, and it "takes a sturdy man to drink from it and keep clear of delirium tremens." He routinely talked of the sacredness of nature and of art and beauty, which spoke to McCardell's sensibilities. His sermons weren't like any McCardell had heard in her childhood church. Norwood reinterpreted God for a contemporary audience. He was proof to her that even religion was modernizing.

◆

That spring, the women living at the Three Arts Club concocted a plan to host an exhibition for the wealthy board members. They wrote invitations, baked cookies, brewed hot tea, and turned the parlor of the club into a makeshift gallery. On an April afternoon in 1926, Manhattan's well-heeled society ladies wove between easels of oil paintings and watercolor still lifes.

McCardell felt desperate to sell some of her artwork. It seemed she was always asking her father to increase her $14 monthly allowance. It was hard to keep to the budget, even with the free theater tickets and the discounted clothes. "I've had to walk so much more than I thought and now I need to re-sole my shoes," she wrote. "I'm sorry as a deuce to be asking, but I have all of these art supplies for school, and the cost of stockings has gone up." She feared that if her needs outpaced her father's willingness to fund her art school in New York, he might yank her back home.

Selling even one of her illustrations would mean far more than a few extra dollars of spending money; it would mean she was helping to support herself through her own creative efforts. The women walked right past her sketches of dresses and hats, preferring the still lifes and landscapes. "They take much more interest in the girls studying fine arts than commercial ones," McCardell said to Orrick.

"It does seem like they'll buy a few of their oils just to help them along."

"They think commercial artists like us don't need it." They watched a wealthy woman chatting with other board members. "She seems more interested in showing off the Paris dress she's wearing to all the old girls than anything else. I've heard she is awfully nice to poor struggling art students who are from the south and starving in garrets, but I guess she doesn't think that applies to us."

How one made a living as a commercial artist was the question at the top of McCardell's mind. That semester, an answer came from one of her professors who'd recently taught costume illustration in Paris. She encouraged McCardell to spend her sophomore year at Parsons' Paris atelier. "She knows her business," McCardell assured her parents.

In the 1920s, with the end of the Great War, a new path to Europe had opened for American students. For the cost of tuition plus a bit more for spending money, anyone who could afford college could travel abroad. Frank Alvah Parsons had seen the market potential, and his had become the first American design school to open a campus in Paris. McCardell had barely persuaded her parents to allow her to come to New York. Now, less than a year later, she needed to convince them to let her go more than 3,600 miles across the Atlantic Ocean. To better understand the world of fashion—to even stand a chance of working in it one day—she would have to go to its center.

CHAPTER THREE

This Clothes Business Certainly Is a Gamble

1926–27

On the morning of August 19, 1926, SS *Leviathan* made a distinctive sight docked in New York harbor, her three white-and-red smokestacks as tall as city skyscrapers. McCardell stood on the dock in the shadow of the largest passenger steamship in the world—950 feet from stem to stern. It would speed her to France in a little over a week, inspiring its captain to liken it to an ocean greyhound.

McCardell boarded with Mildred Orrick and Orrick's mother, Angé Boykin, who agreed to chaperone the girls on their transatlantic voyage. They entered a two-story lobby with Grecian columns and a domed ceiling bathed in electric light. It was a luxury hotel floating on water, where, the ship's brochure boasted, "the absence of expensive lousy taste is notable." Their cabins were modest, though, situated on the lower decks in the budget Tourist Class III. McCardell thought it cruel to tour them through the ship in the name of an orientation, allowing them glimpses into the luxury-class accommodations before shuffling them down below. "First impressions aren't so good, especially after you've just been through the Presidential Suite," she wrote in a letter home, but after a few days at sea, she was "crazy about it."

The ship steamed into Cherbourg, France, on August 27. McCardell took in the quaint northern harbor town edged with white houses topped by red-tiled roofs. She was twenty-one years old and setting foot on foreign soil for the first time. She thought Cherbourg to be the loveliest place she had ever seen.

A train rumbled them south to Paris, and by evening, a taxi deposited them at a small hotel near the Musée du Louvre. McCardell would live for the next nine months on a strict allowance from her father, and relief flooded her when she learned the exchange rate. The taxi ride cost pennies.

The next morning, McCardell and Orrick left for orientation at their school headquarters, located on the Place des Vosges in the historic Marais district. Frank Alvah Parsons understood the value of a prestigious location, and he'd courted wealthy American expats, such as the famed interior designer Elsie de Wolfe and the writer Edith Wharton, to help him secure a former palace. The seventeenth-century school building at 9 Place des Vosges sat off a manicured square and had once housed French nobles. The luxe interior outfitted with French antiques "has the New York school beat by miles," McCardell wrote her parents.

The curriculum that year would focus on two priorities: studying French art, architecture, and design; and learning the French fashion system of haute couture. But first, they had to find housing, which wasn't provided by the school. They left that day with a list of suggested neighborhoods and booked rooms in a hotel on rue Bonaparte in the Saint-Germain-des-Prés quarter. The hotel had steep, narrow stairs that creaked underfoot and funny doors without knobs that opened using elaborate, ancient-looking keys. McCardell took a room on the second floor, with a window overlooking the street. Orrick bunked next door with her mother, who planned on sightseeing for a few weeks before returning to America.

Their neighborhood teemed with Americans, including students like themselves on study abroad programs. They crowded into rooms rented by the French, who were grateful for the influx of money even as they chafed at the young students with their "jazz manners and modern ways" who seemed to study nothing but life, as an article in *The New York Times* described them. They joined the numerous expat American artists, musicians, and writers who'd already flocked to Paris after the Great War: Gertrude Stein and Alice B. Toklas; F. Scott Fitzgerald and his wife, Zelda; Ernest Hemingway. "The scum of Greenwich Village, New York, has been skimmed off and deposited in large ladles on that section of Paris adjacent to the Cafe Rotonde," Hemingway wrote.

McCardell remained one step behind Hemingway in the coming months, as he was rumored to have just been drinking a whiskey at Harry's Bar near the Opera before she walked in or having just finished a plate of oysters at Le Pré aux Clercs near her hotel. She never saw the author in person, but she read of Hemingway's Parisian life, at least his fictional one, when his novel *The Sun Also Rises* was published that fall. Hemingway's description of the character Lady Brett Ashley particularly resonated with her. Ashley "wore a slipover jersey sweater and a tweed skirt, and her hair was brushed back like a boy's," McCardell wrote. "She started all that."

Where she wore her signature fashion was what interested McCardell. Lady Brett Ashley dressed in her "sports" clothes to go to a Paris bar. Sportswear was finding its way onto the streets of Paris and into Hemingway's breakout novel. And like the clothes, Hemingway's book was stripped of embellishment, earning its meaning through direct, muscular prose. The novel, like clothing, was being reinvented.

◆

McCardell got her first fashion assignment in late September. The professor instructed the class to visit the city's preeminent fashion houses and select a fall wardrobe; not to buy, of course—they could hardly afford French clothes—but to showcase their taste. The students would have to remember each garment and later sketch it from memory. They would be graded on their choices and on the accuracy of their illustrations.

McCardell began by visiting the House of Worth, whose founder had helped create the modern system of French fashion. Interestingly, he was an Englishman. Charles Frederick Worth had arrived in Paris in 1845 and revolutionized the country's sartorial traditions. Back then, women of means had taken their fashion cues from French royalty and nobility, mimicking their style. They had bought their own materials and had clothes made by anonymous dressmakers. Worth, who possessed a deep knowledge of textiles and clothing construction, began designing collections of seasonal outfits. He invited affluent women into his atelier to see these sample clothes worn on models. His couture house quickly became a favorite among the French elite. He began embroidering his name inside the bodice of his clothes, effectively signing his work as an artist would. He usurped the royals as the arbiters of taste. Now it was the fashion designer who set the trends.

Worth laid the foundation of haute couture. Translating as "high dressmaking," haute couture represented the finest quality of custom-made clothes. The designer, along with a highly trained assistant known as a *première* and a team of skilled seamstresses known as the *midinettes*, made garments from scratch, laboring over every stitch.

The French, ever expert at legally codifying their culture, created in 1868 what would become known as the Chambre Syndicale de la Haute Couture. Its purpose was to protect their burgeoning fashion industry. In order to be called haute couture, an item had to adhere to strict dictates, including being handmade to fit an individual, using expert construction. In the same way that any sparkling wine produced outside the Champagne region could not legally be called "champagne," any garment not created under the strict mandates of the Chambre Syndicale could not be called haute couture. It took more than money to afford couture; it also required a wealth of time. Strict rules dictated how many fittings a woman was required to have for each article of clothing. In 1926, as McCardell entered the House of Worth, French haute couture carried prestige and dictated fashion trends the world over.

At the House of Worth, McCardell saw an exquisite blue evening gown that she couldn't stop thinking about. "I'm crazy to buy it," she wrote home, and not just to sketch it. She agonized over the cost for days. It was so lovely, but ultimately, she wondered where she would wear it. She wasn't a socialite attending galas; she was a student on a budget. She let the fantasy go. "I need plain, common ordinary clothes much more."

The outspoken Coco Chanel was a favorite among the flapper set, but McCardell preferred the work of Chanel's rival Madeleine Vionnet. She next went to the House of Vionnet with Orrick. A doorman welcomed them into the atelier, the place where the queens of Spain, Belgium, and Romania had recently bought dresses. Vionnet, like most couturiers, required new customers to present a card of introduction, ensuring that only the worthy (and the wealthy) made it to the inner sanctum. McCardell and Orrick didn't have one. It didn't help McCardell's nerves that her outfit was hopelessly wrinkled. She'd packed an iron, which she'd updated to fit the European sockets, but she'd blown a fuse at the hotel as soon as she'd plugged it in. Now, she felt every inch the small-town girl.

That day, the world economy conspired to help. The French franc had started to climb against the dollar, and sales to visiting Americans were suddenly sluggish. The *vendeuses*, or saleswomen, "came at us with open arms not knowing we had only about 20 francs in our pocketbooks," McCardell later wrote.

They were led up a grand staircase to a salon decorated in the Art Deco style. Wall frescoes of contemporary women wearing Vionnet's popular designs mingled with images of classic Greek goddesses. That season, Vionnet took her inspiration from the simple lines of the ancient Greeks. McCardell and Orrick sat in modern bentwood chairs clad in sumptuous velvet. Models emerged from behind a screen. They wore long, sleek dresses that looked nothing like the boxy flapper garb. Gowns hugged their hip bones and dipped at their backs. The fabric danced against their bodies. A day dress in sapphire velvet tied with a simple bow at the back of the neck managed to look both smart and seductive, without tipping into being overtly sexy. McCardell was suddenly surrounded by the clothes she usually saw only in the pages of *Vogue* and *Harper's Bazaar*, and she was entranced. Vionnet's dresses seemed to shape themselves magically to the women's bodies, clinging in all the right places.

The effortless elegance was the result of a technique unique to Vionnet. She'd mastered the art of the bias cut. By cutting her fabric on the bias—diagonally at a 45-degree angle against the grain—she enabled the material to flow more fluidly. She believed that a couturier's job was to provide "the best manner of draping a given fabric over a given woman, so that each shall show off the other to the best possible advantage," Vionnet wrote. She never used the whalebone or cane that other couturiers did to shape a dress. All that armor-plating, as she called it, was antifeminine. "Until recently people seemed to consider a woman's body a shameful object, the shape of which had to be dissembled as far as possible," she once explained. Vionnet preferred to celebrate a woman's natural body.

Vionnet was revolutionary in other ways, too. She owned her business, and she supported her employees with essential services. The women who bustled around McCardell and Orrick that day received benefits many professional women didn't yet enjoy, such as paid holidays, maternity leave, a cafeteria with discounted food, and a dentist and doctor on site.

After they left, McCardell and Orrick did their best to re-create the dresses in their sketchpads. Orrick took her time, thoughtfully rendering each line and working with meticulous attention to detail. McCardell rushed, making quick, evocative strokes full of movement and with far less polish than her friend's. Her mind had already leapt to the next thought: *How do I make clothes like this?* Only, her education at Parsons Paris focused on drawing and copying, not creating.

◆

That fall, McCardell reveled in exploring the city and its fashion houses. But dusk sometimes made her homesick. One evening, she walked the Boulevard Saint-Germain after an early dinner alone. The sun set behind the buildings, and the electric and gas lamps fizzed to life. Her college French was improving daily, but she had a long way to go in speaking and understanding the language. Parisians clustered at sidewalk cafés, chattering. The smell of cassoulet, warm and garlicky, infused the crisp fall air, and votive candles illuminated jewel-toned carafes of wine. Funny how a person could feel lonely amid so much activity.

Suddenly a familiar face emerged from the crowd. There, at a busy café, was Billy Quinn, the son of a Frederick family friend. Quinn waved her over. He was on a brief sojourn to Europe and staying at a hotel in the Latin Quarter not so far from hers. He insisted that they go for a drink.

They headed for the Métro, where Quinn showed her how to use the subway. They ascended in Montparnasse and walked to La Rotonde. Expats and artists crowded the corner brasserie, their creative energy reflected in their wild fashions. At her hotel later that night, McCardell reported to Orrick what she had seen of Paris's café society: "You never saw so many queer-looking people in your life. The men have long curls and beards and wear broad-brimmed felt hats. The young American boys wear school coats and carry canes and gloves." She felt as though she'd been let in on some of the city's secrets.

A Parsons classmate, Joset Walker (née Josette Georgette Legouy), further introduced McCardell and Orrick to French social life. Walker was vivacious and fashionable, with jet-black hair and amused, dark eyes. She lived in New York but had been born in France. She had the self-confidence of someone who'd already resided in a number of countries, and a desire to do far more in Paris than study. Her uncle lived in town and gave them cheap theater tickets. They sat in the second row of the Théâtre de l'Odéon at a performance featuring the famed Russian actress Ida Rubinstein. "They say she's Sarah Bernhardt's only rival," McCardell wrote her parents. "Ida was so good that she even made us cry in French." At the Folies Bergère they watched the expat American Josephine Baker perform in a skirt of artificial bananas and little else.

Other nights, they attended street dances and public balls at the Opera. They frequented nightclubs, such as the Parapluie (French for umbrella), where professional male dancers worked the floor. "All the night clubs have them and you can dance with them as much as you want to, and then the men you're with are supposed to tip them," McCardell explained to her parents. "Mildred and I had the best time dancing."

They often ended their nights at a café. At Le Dôme, a young artist introduced her to Pernod. He showed her how to pour water into the clear liqueur, which then turned a cloudy white. It tasted just like licorice, and she loved licorice. The next morning, she woke with a stomachache and a throbbing head. She fished a bottle of castor oil out of her trunk, pinched her nose, and downed a shot, hoping it would cure her.

McCardell's mother supported temperance, and her letters warned McCardell to stay away from alcohol. "For goodness' sakes, don't get excited about the wine. Wish you could come to France and get cured of your distorted idea of drinking," she wrote to Eleanor. "Drinking may have been a terrible thing in the United States, but it certainly isn't over here. I'm all for the United States getting rid of its Prohibition laws if they could learn to treat drinking the way these people do," adding that the French "don't run around tight as fools all the time and they don't drink the stuff by the gallons either."

By November, McCardell had grown wise to the tourist traps designed for Americans like her. She avoided establishments with signs reading "We speak English" because she knew the prices would be higher. One night, she went dancing with a date at a bar in Montmartre and quickly understood it to be one of the places meant to draw in tourists. "It's called Heaven & Hell," she wrote in a letter. "We went in Hell and it was so tacky and amateur and drunk we didn't go to Heaven."

The trio of McCardell, Orrick, and Walker earned a reputation at school as "a kicky bunch of girls, very popular with the French," as one male professor described them, "but quite a handful for me, a timid young man just a few years older than they." For one assignment, the professor toured them through the medieval objects inside Paris's Cluny Museum. He challenged them to go out into the neighborhood and find an object that matched the ochre color in an ancient tapestry. He was amazed when the three of them returned with a little pile of yellowish dust they'd collected from a poultry market. It matched the color exactly and showcased their penchant for applying surprising materials and techniques to solving creative problems.

With all the walking and dancing that semester, McCardell wore through the soles of her shoes. She broke down and used some of her precious funds to buy a pair of suede oxfords. She found that the Parisians, who were brilliant with clothes, were abysmal cobblers. The shoes gave her blisters, and she stopped wearing them. Not long after, she read an article about a former Three Arts Club resident who'd begun manufacturing American-quality shoes for women in Paris. Her enterprise had earned an article in *Harper's Bazaar*. "She certainly was a smart girl. She's the only woman shoe manufacturer in the world," McCardell believed.

McCardell was beginning to understand the power of a market gap met with a bold vision—and a woman smart enough to harness the American fashion press to publicize her story. It was a combination she wouldn't forget.

◆

On Thursday, November 25, McCardell woke to a cold, clear day in Paris. She tried to not think of her family sitting around the table in Frederick, eating turkey and her mother's angel food cake. That year, American Thanksgiving fell on the same date as St. Catherine's Day, a French holiday. St. Catherine was the patron saint of the unwed, and the tradition was for French seamstresses who were not yet married to parade the streets in oversized lace hats. She and Orrick dressed up to meet their dates for the day, two American art students they'd gotten to know at a school-sponsored dance.

Revelers crowded the streets of Paris and brass bands played on sidewalks. The foursome snagged a table outside the crowded Café de la Paix. The couture houses had already treated their *midinettes*, or seamstresses, to champagne and cake in their ateliers, and the celebration had spilled outside, where "they run around in crowds and kiss all the men and the men take advantage of it and grab all the girls," McCardell wrote home. "It's quite an affair."

The midinettes, pursued by the pursed lips and clutching hands of strange men, were being symbolically chased into marriage. Yet the women helming Paris's most famous couture houses—Chanel, Vionnet—were known the world over by their maiden names. The twice-divorced Vionnet had feted her midinettes that morning, even as she acknowledged that no man could keep her because she preferred her own counsel.

McCardell's girlfriends from home were settling into engagements and marriage. In all her correspondence that year, she never once mentioned a desire to join them. Instead, she wrote of food and her favorite sculpture in the Louvre—the *Winged Victory of Samothrace*— and of theaters and clothes. She would go on many dates during her time in France. "The boys," as she called them, whisked her off to masquerade balls, plays, and intimate suppers at corner bistros. Each week she wrote detailed letters about her adventures, but none of the boys ever merited the recording of his name.

◆

The New Year in Paris meant one thing for the fashion focused: the debut of the next couture season. Icy winds blew across the Seine, but the couturiers were thinking ahead to warmer months as they prepared to show their 1927 summer lines. To make room for the new, the houses sold the winter season's floor samples at bargain prices. McCardell, Orrick, and Walker were lucky to be the same size as the dresses on sale. They pooled their money and began buying discounted clothes to share. That was how McCardell finally got her hands on a real Vionnet dress.

One afternoon, she took the prized acquisition back to her room. A dusting of snow covered the city, and she fed bits of thin wood from a bundle she'd purchased into her hearth, stoking the fire to life and warming the drafty room. The French, she noticed, were quite frugal when it came to turning on the central heat.

She spread the dress across the carpeted wood floor. She turned it over, turned it inside out, ran her hands along its edges. She made mental notes on what she saw. And then she took a seam ripper to it. She meticulously disassembled the gown "like a little boy with alarm clocks," as one writer would later describe the moment.

She no longer heard the crackling of the fire or the steam heat finally kicking to life inside the radiators. She was lost in a trance, the only thing before her that dress. In school, she sketched clothes or read about French sewing techniques in a textbook. But she was curious about the mechanics of the clothes themselves. What made them tick?

She gleaned all she could from the Vionnet before carefully stitching it back together. On the floor of that chilly rented room, she was "learning important things—the way clothes worked, the way they felt, where they fastened," she later said. She took her education into her own hands and taught herself the skills she would need to be a designer.

A few weeks later, McCardell and Orrick huddled near the fireplace in their classroom, watching the clock tick down to dismissal time. School ended earlier in February, at 3:30, because it got too dark to see properly in the classroom. The professors believed that electric light distorted colors and the ability to make art.

On their way out, a young woman approached them. She introduced herself as an alumna of Parsons and a buyer for an American department store. She'd just arrived from the United States along with the hundreds of New York manufacturers, magazine editors, and retailers who'd sailed to the city for the fashion openings. The woman had seen their student work and wanted to hire them to help sketch the new collections after school. The pay was paltry. But McCardell and Orrick jumped at the opportunity.

The next day, they left school and went to the Ritz Hotel on Place Vendôme. The former mansion was now home to the most fashionable hotel in the city, where artists, writers, and fashion designers such as Coco Chanel took suites and drank champagne at the bar. For the next ten days, as Paris couturiers showed their collections, the Ritz was home to the United States' most prestigious fashion journalists and store buyers.

McCardell and Orrick entered a lobby filled with hothouse flowers and Louis XVI reproduction furniture. It was a far cry from the tiny rooms where they'd been living. That night, they shadowed their boss to welcome parties all over town. By the end of the evening, McCardell's aspiration had shifted from illustrating clothes to selling them. "The height of my ambition now is to be a buyer," she informed her parents. "They come over four times a year to the openings and stay at the Ritz and The Claridge and spend their time running to Costume Houses [that] have regular parties for them." She had never seen so much iced champagne or so many exquisitely dressed women. "They serve ice cream and cake and just have a big time. And the nicest part is that it's part of your business to wear good-looking clothes."

The Paris couturiers entertained buyers with a dizzying array of parties, fashion shows, and private dinners. As her job progressed, McCardell's feelings once again shifted. That Americans copied Parisians was an open secret, but exactly *how* that happened was becoming clearer to her.

The legitimate way to bring Paris fashion to the United States was to pay a licensing fee to a house for the rights to their designs. But it was far cheaper to steal. The American woman's insistent demand for all things Parisian had "brought about a swindle that today permeates almost the entire dressmaking and millinery business in the United States," according to a reporter for *Ladies' Home Journal*.

One swindle involved procuring a designer's label, forging copies of it, and sewing it into clothes back home. The people McCardell and Orrick worked with aimed to steal the designs directly from the Paris showings. American buyers secured invitations to the openings for their young assistants, who pretended to be engaged in legitimate work. But really, their job was memorizing designs to sketch later.

The couture houses knew that spies were in their midst. They kept an eye out for those who wrote a little too fervently in their programs. The houses were on the alert for familiar customers who never purchased clothes. There were lists of those no longer allowed inside, and the seasoned spies had to pass their business on to younger American newbies. McCardell and Orrick were perfect for the job: neophytes with artistic skills who were not yet recognized by the couturiers, and who'd been trained by Parsons to memorize and sketch clothes.

At the same time McCardell was in Paris, another aspiring American fashion designer named Elizabeth Hawes was illegally copying French clothes. Hawes, a Vassar graduate, had attended a summer course at Parsons a few years before McCardell. Hawes would launch her own fashion house in New York in 1928 and become an outspoken critic of the rampant grift in fashion. But for now, she was, like McCardell, impressionable and young and learning the ropes.

Hawes spent months working as a spy for American buyers, and she and McCardell may well have attended some of the same showings. Hawes relied on her memory to avoid attracting the suspicion of the salespeople. She developed a mental shorthand. "Bl. 4 bts sq nk" meant "black dress with four buttons down one side of a square neck." After the shows, she quickly sketched. Her business was lucrative. Hawes could sell every drawing she made for $1.50 each. These drawings usually went back to skilled tailors in the US, who made copies.

Even more lucrative than a drawing, though, was a forgery of the dress itself. Hawes also worked inside a Parisian copy house. Those enterprises had a legitimate dress shop in front and a forgery business hidden in the back. They conspired to get their hands on original dresses in order to make detailed patterns. Wealthy clients sometimes gave their real haute couture items to the copyists in return for counterfeits of other styles. Mistresses of famous designers who were gifted clothes increased their windfall by lending them to forgers for a fee. One day, Hawes was instructed to retrieve several Chanel dresses destined for the United States from a port-side shipping office and stuff them inside her fur coat. She delivered them to the seamstresses at the copy house, who made detailed replicas before Hawes rushed them back to the shipping office just in time for the ship's departure. "Copying, a fancy name for stealing, is also interesting as an example of what a curious and rather degraded business dressmaking may be," Hawes later wrote in her book *Fashion Is Spinach*, joking that "the passion which has been created for being chic leads to almost anything, probably including murder."

McCardell understood that she could get into serious trouble. People caught copying were fined—or worse, arrested. One apocryphal tale recounted an American buyer who'd nicked valuable sketches off the desk of a Parisian target, rolled the papers tight, and stashed them inside a hollow walking cane. The gendarmes had cuffs on the spy's wrists before he hit the cobblestone street outside.

McCardell vacillated between feeling excited about being temporarily employed in fashion and deeply troubled by what she understood to be grift. "I've learned more about the Costume business in the last week than I ever have before," she wrote home. "This clothes business certainly is a gamble. . . . The person who can remember the models and sketch them for wholesale houses in the United States can make a fortune. The buyers try to get as many sketches as possible without paying the house for them." If she had any hope of getting into the fashion business, though, she believed she had to play that dangerous game. It was how the American fashion industry worked.

◆

A warm spring washed over Paris in a welcome reprieve from the months of bitter cold. On the evening of May 21, 1927, the rose geraniums and apple blossoms were in bloom in the Tuileries Gardens, and McCardell and Orrick sipped café crèmes on the patio outside Le Dôme. McCardell's birthday would be in three days, and they chatted about how best to celebrate. A night at the opera? Dancing at Parapluie?

The streets of Paris seemed charged that evening, as if the entire city were waking up to the excitement of McCardell's impending celebration.

Just then, the nasal honk of a car horn startled them. A taxi idled at the curb. One of "the boys" they knew—a young reporter from *The New York Herald*—frantically waved out a window.

"He's almost here!" he shouted over the traffic.

"Who?" Orrick shouted back.

"Lindy!"

The papers had been tracking the news for weeks. Charles A. Lindbergh, a military officer turned aviator, had entered the international competition to become the first person to fly solo between New York and Paris. His monoplane, the *Spirit of St. Louis*, had lifted off the ground in New York the day before, on Friday, May 20, and his success was far from assured. In April, two pilots had died while testing their plane at Langley Field in Virginia. A pair of French pilots had recently vanished over the Atlantic trying to fly from France to New York. It didn't help that Lindbergh had refused radio equipment, fearing it would weigh him down, so he navigated the 3,600 miles to France using visual landmarks and his instincts while sitting in a wicker chair.

Lindbergh's plane had recently been spotted flying over England. McCardell suddenly understood the heightened thrill on the Parisian streets: the cacophony as people ran for cabs, the shouts of excited bystanders. Everyone was heading to Le Bourget airfield where Lindbergh, with any luck, would soon land.

"Well, are you coming?" the reporter shouted.

They threw a few francs onto the table and piled into the cab already crowded with the reporter and two young men from the US Embassy.

The taxi crawled the seven miles toward Le Bourget on a road clogged with more cars than McCardell had ever seen. Lindbergh would later say that the traffic jam had created a kind of airstrip, all those headlights guiding him in.

More than 150,000 people crowded the field at Le Bourget. McCardell and Orrick clasped hands to stay together as they were pushed about by the frenzied mob. The reporter had VIP tickets that allowed them access to a special area close to the field. They found a spot behind an iron fence. Ahead of them, a line of police cordoned off the grass runway, as everyone craned their necks upward. They waited.

Suddenly a shout went up. Someone yelled that they'd spotted the plane. The crowd crushed through the line of police. McCardell and Orrick joined the race to reach the edge of the runway, where the international press had trained camera lenses at the sky. And there, from out of the murky soup of the evening sky, McCardell saw the *Spirit of St. Louis* emerge. The engine's roar grew louder, and when Lindbergh's plane touched terra firma, it was "the prettiest landing you ever saw," she said.

She again clasped Orrick's hand as they sprinted the length of the field, a half mile at least, and she feared that the crowd might tear Lindbergh to pieces. An American man reached the plane and practically pulled Lindbergh from the cockpit, hugging him and screaming "Hello, St. Louis!" before collapsing from the effort. A feeling sparked through McCardell's body then, a physical impulse that had her moving before her thought became clear: *I have to touch that plane.* Orrick felt it, too.

Fights broke out as people vied and pushed. McCardell and Orrick clutched each other as they fought the feral crowd. They placed their palms against the cotton-covered steel fuselage before being subsumed by a mass of bodies. The police rushed Lindbergh away. The friends they'd come with were nowhere to be found, and the multitude only grew in its madness. "I never have seen anything so wild before," she later described. It was time to retreat.

They retraced their steps toward the road. McCardell had lost the heel of one shoe. Orrick's hat was gone. They had no idea how they would get back to town until a cab emerged from the chaos. Inside was the bartender of Harry's Bar. He'd not only thought to pay a taxi to wait, but he'd also stocked it with bottles of whiskey for the slow ride back. McCardell and Orrick jumped in.

A few days later, Monday, May 23, McCardell's friends gifted her a bouquet of roses and toasted her birthday at a tiny café. In the ongoing excitement, even McCardell had confused the date. She wouldn't be turning twenty-two until the next day. The talk was still of Lindbergh. He had circled the Eiffel Tower on his way to Le Bourget. What a sight that must have been, the American in his homegrown plane swooping around the great symbol of France. While some pilots had been intent on building $100,000 trimotor planes with opulent interiors to win the race, Lindbergh had concluded that simplicity was best: a single-engine plane with one set of wings and one pilot. McCardell had spent the semester hearing her professors extol the superiority of the Europeans, but in Lindbergh's success, she saw an American alternative. It wasn't extravagance and expense that had won the day; it was thrifty inventiveness, savvy manufacturing, and sheer gumption.

McCardell and Orrick sailed home from Cherbourg a week later aboard the *Leviathan*. In her steamer trunk, McCardell didn't have that blue evening gown she'd craved, and the shared Vionnet would be hers to wear only sporadically. But she carried something she believed to be far more valuable. She had the phone numbers of a few women working in New York's Garment District. One of the buyers she'd met during her sketching job had given her a list of names to look up when it was time to job hunt. McCardell had one more year of school to complete in the United States, but in her heart and mind she'd already left academia. A single idea preoccupied her as the "ocean greyhound" sped her home: how to break into the New York fashion industry.

CHAPTER FOUR

This Town Doesn't Pity a Soul

1928–29

The chaos of New York's Garment District was a far cry from the refinement of Paris's couture houses—even if McCardell felt, as she walked Seventh Avenue, as if she'd been dropped into a European city. Shouts of Italian, German, Greek, Yiddish—the many languages of the immigrant men who worked the rag trade—competed to be heard over the persistent honking of cars stuck behind double-parked trucks. Delivery men hoisted bolts of fabric and boxes of materials onto the sidewalk. McCardell dodged their hand trucks while also keeping an eye out for the "push boys," the men who moved finished garments on wheeled metal racks. The push boys charged down the street, their heads bent with the effort and blinded by the sway of fabric, and if you weren't careful, you'd get clipped in the ankle. Models rushed by carrying hatboxes, seamstresses their lunch pails. Below, the screech and stench of the subway emanated from open grates.

It had been a year since McCardell had watched Lindbergh make history, and she'd recently achieved a milestone of her own: On May 23, 1928, the day before her twenty-third birthday, she'd sat through her final class at Parsons. Her father had only agreed to support her financially through art school, and now that she'd graduated, she had to make her own way. Her room at the Three Arts Club was paid through early July. She had cash to last a few weeks, but only if she walked to job interviews as she did today. She was on a deadline; she would have to find work or move home.

Breaking into the New York fashion world was proving to be more difficult than she'd imagined. The leads from the buyers she'd met in Paris hadn't panned out. The garment business, she learned, was a revolving door where people were forever changing jobs. And women frequently left when they married, never to return.

Most potential employers took one look at her anemic résumé and showed her the door. Others suggested that she accept lower pay in return for the experience. She'd been coached by the career girls living at the club never to let the men offer less than advertised. They might call it a "training salary," but really it was a tax on being a woman. And never answer an ad that stipulated "Only attractive girls need apply."

McCardell now subsisted on one meal a day—the afternoon tea that came with her room at the club—and she supplemented it with the Hershey bars and peanuts sent in care packages from her mother. After long days of job seeking, she and Orrick met in the parlor at the club and compared notes. "I don't know what there is about me," McCardell said one evening. "I must be so frivolous looking."

Orrick's luck hadn't been any better. They both missed the freedom of Paris. The dormlike atmosphere at the club, which had once felt so supportive, now rankled. They hatched a plan to get an apartment together as soon as they found jobs.

By mid-June, desperation sent McCardell to the classified ads for any work related to art. She interviewed to be an illustrator for a line of Christmas cards and the man doing the hiring stared, puzzled, at her portfolio of women in dresses. "You don't have any Christmas drawings?" She shook her head. The man paused to think. "Why don't you go home, work out some pencil sketches of cards and bring them back. No promises, but I'll see what I can do."

She debated drawing elves and snowcapped cottages. Instead, she diverted her energy to filling out her fashion portfolio. Freed from the rules of Parsons, she drew women in the kinds of clothes that she wanted to wear. The women slouched ever so slightly in their sleek modern dresses, and they had one hand tucked into a pocket, which was a fantasy since only men's clothes routinely included pockets.

Armed with her new sketches—and running out of money and time—she felt she had "the nerve to walk in any place now," she told Orrick. She set her sights on Fifth Avenue and its cluster of tony department stores.

◆

Until recently, the mansions of Gilded Age millionaires had dominated Fifth Avenue. But when Benjamin Altman had opened the first department store at the corner of 34th Street in 1906, the avenue had begun its transformation into a luxury retail destination. The modest, neighborhood-based general store that McCardell and the rest of America had grown up with exploded into block-long palaces of retail.

By the 1920s, the department store had blossomed into a space where women could linger and enjoy amenities in the same way men did at private city clubs. A woman could come to Fifth Avenue, drop her children at a store-provided nursery, and shop and stroll for hours. She could meet friends for lunch at the café, take in a concert, or attend a lecture. She could write letters on store stationery, mail her correspondence at the in-store postal desk, and arrange to have a concierge pick out items and deliver them to her home.

The stores provided phone booths, telegram service, shoe-shine stands, beauty parlors, even travel agencies. Uniformed attendants staffed ladies' lounges, passing out samples of perfume and lipstick. Those who needed extra refreshment could retreat to a private bath. The modern department store was, in the words of the Boston retailer Edward A. Filene, "an Adamless Eden." The stores were also among the rare places where women could find employment and, in some cases, ascend to the upper echelons of management. The male owners appreciated that women knew what other women wanted when it came to shopping.

Competition between stores was fierce, and art was the nectar that helped draw in swarms of shoppers. Fashion illustrations served as the primary method to advertise clothes. At Macy's, the man running the art department lauded McCardell's originality, but—and there was always a "but," she was learning—"your sketches are too advanced for our purpose," he said. "You should calm your aesthetic because customers won't understand your queer-looking ladies."

After being turned away from several more stores, McCardell wondered if she should stay the course and continue drawing clothes in the style she desired or compromise for the marketplace. She would grapple with that very question for the entirety of her career because it was the central concern of fashion. What she created would have to be purchased by customers.

She took her portfolio of "queer-looking" modern ladies to a place known for its fashion risk-taking: *Vogue*. A harried editor told her to come back in a few months and try again. "This job business is beginning to scare me," she admitted to her parents. "I've found out it takes most people almost three months to find one good enough to keep."

◆

Most evenings, McCardell returned to the club exhausted and too broke to go out. She closed the dark-green-and-rose-colored curtains in her room, shut out the city, and changed into pajamas. She propped herself up in bed and reached for something to read.

On her nightstand, McCardell kept copies of *The American Mercury*, the magazine edited by a fellow Marylander, H. L. Mencken. Mencken was a contrarian, and McCardell enjoyed contrarians. She'd recently met one of Mencken's contributors at a book event, the writer Herbert Asbury. He had the distinction of having a story banned by censors in Boston for its supposed wickedness. Asbury's latest book, *The Gangs of New York: An Informal History of the Underworld*, was in McCardell's pile of books to be read.

That night, though, she opened *A Mirror for Witches*, a new novel that was popular with the women at the club. The author, Esther Forbes, had set her story during the Salem witch trials, and the protagonist was a young woman accused of forsaking men because she "preferred a Demon to a Mortal Lover." Forbes captured the dark panic of seventeenth-century New England and how easily the fears of men had transmuted into laws and religious edicts meant to punish and control women. The fictional tale spoke to the very real witchcraft delusion that had ended the lives of thousands of women in America and Europe. It kept McCardell up most of the night. She thought so much of the book that she even recommended it to her very religious mother.

Around the same time, the novelist Virginia Woolf voiced her own theory about witches. She had been asked to discuss the growing number of women entering the profession of the arts, specifically, those writing contemporary fiction like hers. In Woolf's keen mind, that question blossomed into a more expansive one. Why, she wondered, was there no female Shakespeare? Why had men produced most of the literary works throughout history while women had primarily produced children?

The absence of women from professional artistic life, she said during two speeches given in England, should not be taken as a sign of inability or ignorance but of society's shackles on their potential. Anytime "one reads of a witch being ducked, of a woman possessed by devils, of a wise woman selling herbs, or even of a very remarkable man who had a mother, then I think we are on the track of a lost novelist, a suppressed poet, of some mute and inglorious Jane Austen, some Emily Brontë who dashed her brains out on the moor or mopped and mowed about the highways crazed with the torture that her gift had put to her," she said. Witches had come to symbolize the many women who possessed an intellectual gift they were never allowed to employ. Woolf could have been talking about any career, not just one in writing, when she concluded that "a woman must have money and a room of her own" to succeed. Those speeches were later expanded and published in a 1929 book titled *A Room of One's Own*.

McCardell had been thinking about those very ideas as she looked for work. "What I need now is money," she wrote to a friend, and "a place to live."

She instinctively understood that the room she required was more than a rental at the Three Arts Club; it was a place where she could have the freedom to choose her path without being fiscally beholden to a man. Most unmarried women continued to reside with their parents and were required to live under their rules. Carmel Snow, the firebrand fashion editor at *Vogue*, had left her family home only after she had married, scandalously late, at the age of thirty-nine. How might McCardell live on her own, free of a man's patronage, be it that of her father or some future husband? She resided in a city, in a country, that did not support a single woman like her. She couldn't open a bank account without her father's signature; she couldn't work at night in New York because employment laws refused women the night shift, except for entertainers. City codes for public buildings had only recently required women's bathrooms. "This town," she wrote, "doesn't pity a soul."

By the end of June, she'd developed a bad cold, and her teeth ached. She was afraid to see a dentist because of the cost, but one morning in the shared bathroom at the club, she felt a lightning flash of pain spark through an incisor and squinted at her mouth in the mirror. A small hole had formed in her front tooth.

The dentist delivered the news after a painful exam. She had fourteen cavities. It would cost two months' rent to fix them all. Ever mindful of her financial conundrum, McCardell told the dentist that she didn't think her father would approve of having all her teeth fixed for that cost, but if she got a job she could come back. The granddaughter of a candy maker with a penchant for developing cavities probably seemed a wise investment. The dentist said that he could help her find a job. McCardell was learning to network, even while in agonizing pain in the dentist's chair.

◆

A few days before McCardell would have to vacate her room, she answered a want ad and got a job painting parchment lampshades. Her salary was $20 a week, just enough to keep her afloat if she budgeted. She believed she'd be able to look for a fashion job on her lunch breaks, but after a few weeks she still hadn't found the time. "This boss we have doesn't think women are worth anything and I don't think much of him. I'm sick and tired of lampshades now," McCardell wrote home.

Soon after, Orrick came back to the club with exciting news. She'd just been hired by the famed costume designer Natacha Rambova. Rambova was setting up an exclusive clothing boutique in New York after years of designing for directors such as Cecil B. DeMille in Los Angeles. Orrick would be her assistant designer.

McCardell tried to be excited for her friend. "I can't imagine anyone with a better name to start out working for," McCardell told her parents. But she was deeply envious. Orrick had a job as a real designer, and with a celebrity no less, while she was painting roses on lampshades.

The upside was that they both had jobs and could afford to leave the club. With the help of Orrick's mother, they signed a lease on an apartment in a new five-story building on East 30th Street near Fifth Avenue. For $65 a month, they got three large rooms with closets, a kitchenette with a newfangled Frigidaire, and a bathroom with a shower. McCardell could walk to her job.

To afford the rent, Orrick's mother would take the third room. After her husband had died in 1925, Mrs. Boykin had lost the church housing provided to her spouse as the resident pastor. She had been living with family in Virginia ever since. Orrick had complicated feelings about her mother joining them in the city. She loved her, but she also felt responsible for her mother's happiness after the deaths of her sister and father.

Mrs. Boykin, on the other hand, was "thrilled to death about moving in because she hasn't had a home for so long," McCardell wrote to her parents. "We may have to sleep on the floor and struggle until we get settled but everyone has to go through this stage so I think we can stand it."

McCardell signed a year's lease without consulting her parents, and they wrote to say how deeply concerned they were that she'd taken that pivotal step. "You all evidently don't agree on the apartment subject," she replied. "The disagreement came too late, though, we already signed the lease." McCardell did what she had done since childhood: She acted first and worried about any fallout later.

They moved in on an oppressively hot July day, just as McCardell secured an interview for a magazine job. The publication, called *Park Avenue Social Review*, needed someone to design layouts, create the lettering for the magazine, write articles and headlines, and help with promotion. The editor told her that he worked like the devil until eight o'clock most nights and would expect the same of her. The pay was $25 a week. "It sounds like four jobs rolled into one," she told him, "and it sounds like a lot for $25 a week."

"I suppose we should consider each other overnight and talk in the morning," the editor said.

Back at the lampshade warehouse, McCardell confided in a coworker about the job offer. "Don't do it!" her coworker replied.

The woman knew of the magazine's previous owner, Gordon Duval. Just a week prior, he'd died in the middle of the night after plummeting down the elevator shaft of his Park Avenue penthouse. The police concluded that he'd mistaken the elevator door for the bathroom in the dark because the doors looked identical. They had found him in the morning, still in his pajamas. "You're taking a big risk because the business is on the verge of sinking," the woman told McCardell. "Duval ran it all, and this new man will work you to death." The beauty of the career girls in New York was that they always had the inside scoop.

McCardell stayed up much of the night mulling over the offer. Maybe it was Orrick's big new position that influenced her. By morning she'd convinced herself that she should take the job. She called the editor prepared to say yes, only to learn that he'd soured on her.

"He didn't think I could work like a dog during this hot weather," she told her mother. "He wanted someone to look like Park Avenue and work like Mott Street for nothing." The cold she'd been nursing for weeks took hold in her chest with a searing pain. "The rosebuds are making me sick," she wrote. Eleanor said it was time to come home.

◆

Walking into the house on Rockwell Terrace, McCardell looked a fright: thin, pale, and feverish. Her mother sent her upstairs to bed.

That evening, her father knocked on her bedroom door. Roy McCardell was never one for small talk, and he launched right in. He told her how surprised he'd been when she'd signed a year's lease on an apartment. "We thought you wanted to come home," he said.

"I never said I didn't want to stay in New York. The only thing that can draw me away is a job that will pay very, very well, and I won't get an offer like that until I've had at least a year's New York training."

How, he wanted to know, was she going to afford New York on $20 a week painting lampshades?

"I don't want to do lampshades forever. I'm going to keep looking for costume work. I want to be a designer, and if you knew anything about the dress business, you'd know that most firms pay their designers at least a hundred dollars a week and often two and three hundred," she said, in her desperation inflating the salaries.

Roy did know something of the dress business, and he was worried for his daughter's safety. For decades the dismal work conditions of New York's clothing trade had made national headlines. The garment business, at the turn of the century, was New York's largest industry, supplying customers all over the country. The work of making clothes occurred in dark, overcrowded tenements on the Lower East Side where immigrants, trained in sewing and tailoring techniques in their home countries, suffered in squalor while working for demanding bosses.

Mass production and ready-to-wear manufacturing exploded in the early twentieth century, and soon nearly one-third of working adults in New York were employed by the garment industry. Journalists wrote of the unchecked greed of owners, the corruption of Tammany Hall politics, and the young seamstresses left bloodied and beaten on the sidewalks after they dared to form a union and strike for better pay and hours.

New loft warehouses were being cobbled together about as fast as the clothes destined to be made inside them. The open floor plan buildings were factories in miniature, designed for long rows of sewing machines and tables for fabric cutting. There was a major flaw: Their height had outpaced the length of fire department ladders. In March 1911, fire consumed the ten-story Triangle Shirtwaist Factory in Greenwich Village. Firemen couldn't reach those trapped on the upper floors. The interior doors had been locked to keep workers from sneaking into the stairwells for smoke breaks or gossip and the fire escapes had never been completed. Seamstresses leapt from windows rather than wait to be incinerated inside. "I learned a new sound," the reporter William Gunn Shepherd wrote, "a more horrible sound than description can picture. It was the thud of a speeding, living body on a stone sidewalk." The Triangle Shirtwaist Factory fire, the deadliest workplace disaster in New York history at the time, left 146 people dead, 123 of them women.

So it was understandable that Roy fretted over his daughter's physical safety in an industry known for its deadly work conditions and an indifference to women's welfare. Fire, specifically, was a persistent fear not just for him but for many in his generation. They'd lived through entire cities burning to ash. Nearby Baltimore had burned in the Great Fire of 1904, one year before McCardell had been born. Closer to home, a fire had destroyed her grandfather's candy warehouse in 1915, nearly killing the family members living above it.

Roy was equally confounded by the career his only daughter aspired to: What was a fashion designer? He looked at her, huddled under blankets, wan from illness. Her jealousy over her best friend's job with the famous Rambova emanated off her like the fever. New York was doing that to her. He told her it was time to return to Frederick and take a sensible position, maybe as a local schoolteacher.

McCardell promised to think about it, and over the next several days, she did. Her friends were marrying and settling into life there. New York and its harsh realities were a distant 250 miles to the north. She was afraid of disappointing her family. But she was equally afraid of leading an inauthentic life.

New York called to her, as it did for so many women like her. Dorothy Parker, a regular at the Algonquin Round Table, had just published an essay about that very topic. "It occurs to me that there are other towns," she wrote. "It occurs to me so violently that I say, at intervals, 'Very well, if New York is going to be like this, I'm going to live somewhere else.'" Quieter towns offered a soothing sameness, but New York provided a sense that anything could happen. "London is satisfied, Paris is resigned, but New York is always hopeful," Parker wrote. And McCardell still had hope.

After a few weeks of rest, she recovered her health and her confidence. She went to her parents and assured them that she would be OK in New York. "I am sure I am going to make some real money if I stick long enough. It's so much better than worrying about a job at a schoolhouse in Middletown."

Eleanor believed in her daughter's resourcefulness and thought she should go back. McCardell's father remained fearful. But he took one of the greatest risks of love a parent could and respected his daughter's decision, even though it scared him. He set aside his protectiveness and put his faith in his feisty Kick. He lent McCardell enough money to get through the next month, or two, if she budgeted. It was an investment in her future, he said, and he expected repayment in full. If she couldn't support herself after those funds ran out, she would have to come home for good.

McCardell hugged him. "I hope I can pay you back soon," she said.

◆

Within days of returning to New York, McCardell's luck began to change. She got a job modeling sportswear at B. Altman and Company's palatial store on Fifth Avenue and 34th Street. For $25 a week, she walked the third floor, wearing the latest sports clothes. McCardell joked to Orrick that she was a "bum model," but the saleswomen at B. Altman didn't think so. McCardell had a unique way of carrying herself, with a slouching, casual walk. McCardell had noticed in Paris how European models held themselves with a rigid posture, their shoulders back, their necks long as swans. They wore clothes with a regal, patrician stance. Stateside, models copied that posture, even though American women walked with more of a hurried jauntiness, their bodies casual and confident and leaning back a bit at the shoulders. An American woman looked as if she had "first learned to walk upon golf courses on clean, crisp mornings," as F. Scott Fitzgerald wrote.

Customers loved her, and clothes sold when she wore them. The manager of the French Salon at B. Altman soon poached her from the sportswear department. She was now modeling Parisian imports in private showings to wealthy clients. She clocked in at 8:45 a.m. and left well after 6:00 p.m. She returned to the apartment so tired that she could hardly walk. It was "too much physical effort and not enough mental," she felt.

In October, she landed a sketching job in the very place that Roy McCardell feared, a twenty-one-story skyscraper in the Garment District. On October 15, 1928, as she toiled at her desk high above Manhattan, she heard a seamstress gasp. A giant balloon-shaped vessel, like an alien spaceship, floated in front of the loft's wide bank of windows. The Germans had developed a new dirigible called *Graf Zeppelin*, and it sailed right by them on the sixteenth floor. The zeppelin achieved something never before seen in the Garment District. It brought work to a halt. Models and push boys stopped in their tracks and crowded the busiest streets, undeterred by the usual traffic because cars had also stopped. The drivers stood next to their open car doors gaping skyward. The city watched as the airship moved across an aquamarine sky on its way to an airfield in New Jersey. It was almost as thrilling as Lindbergh's feat, McCardell thought.

◆

That fall, McCardell and Orrick's apartment on 30th Street became a hub for friends and out-of-town visitors. McCardell furnished her room with a free bookshelf from her Parsons friend Chester Slack, who'd moved to Paris, and with hand-me-downs shipped from home. "I feel like a bride or something," she wrote her mother after receiving a care package of towels and linens.

In early November, McCardell and Orrick hosted a dinner party for six of their friends. Over many bottles of wine, they discussed the upcoming presidential election. McCardell had been exchanging letters about politics with her father. Roy McCardell had entered politics the year prior, and he'd upset the favored candidate in an election for the Maryland State Senate. Roy, a Democrat, had bested his rival by more than two thousand votes in a district that traditionally went Republican. McCardell wrote to him about her excitement over voting in her first presidential election.

On Tuesday, November 6, 1928, Herbert Hoover beat Al Smith in a landslide to become the thirty-first president of the United States. McCardell walked to Times Square, expecting to find throngs of revelers basking in the successful execution of democracy. Women had earned the right to vote only eight years prior, and McCardell couldn't quite believe the laissez-faire attitude. "Wasn't nearly as gay as it might have been," she told her father.

Among the regulars at the apartment that fall was a woman McCardell had befriended at the Three Arts Club. Gay Roddy was a few years older than McCardell, and she worked as a ready-to-wear designer. "I know what a struggle it is starting out," Roddy said one night at dinner. "I lived on rice and milk one whole summer trying to be a designer."

Roddy was determined to help McCardell. She recommended her to a wholesale manufacturer of women's clothes named Sol Pollack. Pollack specialized in knitwear—sweaters, dresses, and casual suits—and he needed an assistant designer. Roddy had convinced him that McCardell held an important position in a New York garment firm.

"But it's not true," McCardell said. "I only just started."

McCardell wasn't comfortable lying about her abilities. She knew little about the real business of design, and she had no experience working in mass production. Roddy assured her that fibbing was par for the course. A woman couldn't get a good job without experience, and she couldn't get experience without fudging a little. Women had to stick together, after all, and look out for one another. Men had the advantage of being, well, male.

Pollack took an instant liking to McCardell when they met a few days later. "If my clothes suit you, they'll suit my customers," he enthused.

As Pollack's assistant, McCardell would be responsible for finding and sketching new ideas based on the Paris trends and helping to put together a line of seventy or so garments to present to buyers each season.

He offered her $45 a week. "No person can be a success without a certain salary because when your energy goes to worry about food and clothes you can't be a designer," he told her. "The only way to make a good designer is to feed her." Of course, he didn't add that he was getting her for a steal; most assistant designers earned twice that amount.

"I can't see why Gay has such confidence in me," McCardell confided to her mother after being offered the position. "I've been turned down at so many jobs that I can't believe this will actually be as good as it sounds. It's a gamble but it's worth taking. Gay says when I get started, I'll be all right."

McCardell set out to learn the ropes. In Paris, designers were at the top of the garment industry's hierarchy. In New York's ready-to-wear business, it was the owner of the dress house, like Pollack, who had all the power. And it was his firm's name that would go onto the labels inside the clothes.

She began making sketches for clothes, with Pollack's input. From there, the sketches went to the sample room. At many New York dress houses, manufacturers didn't bother with a designer at all; they simply relied on the skilled sample room staff and the pattern makers to copy garments bought (or stolen) from Paris.

Next came the cutters. They unfurled bolts of fabric across long expanses of tables and made thick piles of them. They pieced the finished patterns on top like a puzzle to get the most out of each yard. Wielding a sharp, motor-driven blade, they sliced through multiple layers at a time. A small error at the cutting phase that didn't use every square inch of material was costly. The precision and strength required for the work made cutters among the best paid on the factory floor. Any leftover scraps were carefully disposed of. It was believed that the Triangle Shirtwaist Factory had caught fire after an errant cigarette butt or match had ignited a basket of scraps.

The cut pieces then went to the finishers, gifted sewers each of whom focused on one element of construction. Some specialized in sleeves, carefully setting them into armholes. Others worked the massive buttonhole machine or sewed on collars. Their industrial sewing machines could do three thousand stitches a minute. Occasionally piecework was sent to independent contractors off-site, but for the most part, the clothes were sketched, draped, patterned, cut, sewn, finished, pressed, and boxed on-site in an assembly line of clothes making.

McCardell's instinct for clothes and her fast mind helped disguise her inexperience at first, but those working under Pollack soon realized how green she was. She'd underestimated the complexity of the job, and even Gay Roddy couldn't help her at the pace and regularity that she needed to do it. Pollack was not a man to abide questions, let alone errors. Since McCardell had lied to get the job, she lived in fear of making a mistake. Her insecurity showed. Pollack later remembered McCardell being "so shy, so gangly, and she walked sort of hunched over, like she thought she was too tall."

As out of her depth as she felt, though, she also felt a twin feeling: excitement. The propulsion and potential of mass production and the way a successful design could find its way readily and efficiently into hundreds of closets all over the country thrilled her.

In March 1929, a set of knit dresses came off the cutting tables in a dilapidated condition owing to McCardell's faulty design and they had to be remade. Pollock couldn't tolerate that kind of waste. He began to see what his other employees already knew: that she was out of her depth. By April, he'd had enough. He called McCardell into the showroom and assailed her with a speech about her incompetence in front of the staff. He needed an experienced designer, "not just a bright youngster with more ideas than knowledge," as one account of that afternoon related. He fired her with a parting shot: "You will never be a designer."

McCardell stepped out onto the bustling streets of the Garment District. The push boys kept pushing, the languages continued to swirl. She couldn't stand still to mope, not here, not with people pushing her like the currents of a mighty river. She walked, unsure of where she was going. She would later describe the feeling that day as a nightmare of frustration—not because she was ashamed of getting fired but because she understood, after a year on the job market, what it was that she truly desired. She'd had a taste of Seventh Avenue mass production, and she wanted more. If someone would give her another chance, she promised herself, she wouldn't blow it.

PART II

Some Damned Weird Stuff

(1929–40)

CHAPTER FIVE

Let the Girl Do It

1929-33

McCardell slipped into the phone booth at Bergdorf Goodman, closed the door, and prayed that no one had seen her enter. She pulled a small pad of paper and a pencil from her purse and began to draw. Her Paris training came back to her as she worked from memory, capturing the details of a dress she'd just seen on the sales floor.

It was June 1929. Outside the booth, perfumed and powdered women clacked through the spacious high-ceilinged rooms in summer silks. Bergdorf had opened the year before at Fifth Avenue and 58th Street, where the Vanderbilt mansion had once loomed large. The new white marble and bronze building quickly became the city's most exclusive department store with its opulent Louis XV–style interiors and attentive staff. Now, instead of dancing in the Vanderbilts' two-story ballroom, the scions of society shopped.

McCardell had a new job on Seventh Avenue, thanks again to Gay Roddy. She'd connected McCardell with a manufacturer and designer named Robert Turk, who'd just opened his own firm. This time, McCardell had been honest about her experience—or rather, her lack of it. She was no longer an assistant designer; Turk gave her the role of helper, a lower-rung entry-level position.

Turk was a patient mentor. He encouraged her to learn how ready-to-wear clothes were designed, manufactured, and sold. He sent her on errands to Garment District purveyors who supplied the belts, ribbons, trimmings, and buttons to finish outfits. He had her model the sample clothes for buyers, and tabulate orders. "I didn't sweep the floors," McCardell said. "I don't remember why. I did practically everything else."

Everything, that is, except designing.

Turk had called her into his office that June morning. "It's time to shop the stores," he'd said. He needed fresh ideas for his fall collection, and he didn't suggest that they might come from her.

Turk wasn't a particularly talented designer himself, according to some in the business, but he didn't have to be. He was a skilled copier of expensive French styles, and he could translate them into ready-to-wear sportswear, including a new category known as spectator sportswear. Sportswear had evolved from clothing made for golf and tennis into outfits meant to be worn while *watching* golf and tennis.

At twenty-six, Turk was only two years older than McCardell, but he was light-years ahead of her in the garment world. Handsome and gregarious, with black hair and gray eyes, he'd been running the design department of a busy wholesale dress manufacturer and making the biannual trips to Paris. He had launched Robert Turk Inc. that May thanks to a $30,000 investment by two partners with stock market money. He was young and hungry and ready to make a name for himself on Seventh Avenue.

Turk had learned the business from his father, Abraham, who was an accomplished tailor. Abraham was one of the thousands of Jewish immigrants who'd arrived from Eastern Europe already skilled in clothes making. In 1898, Abraham and his wife, Fannie, had settled into the predominantly Jewish Brooklyn neighborhood of Midwood, where the buoyant and expressive Yiddish that they spoke rang out amid Victorian houses and tree-lined streets. In the early 1900s, an expanded subway system and the new Brooklyn Rapid Transit Company line meant that Abraham could easily travel into Manhattan and work in its growing garment trade. Abraham toiled in the dress business for years, saving the money to open his own tailoring shop near Washington Square in

Greenwich Village. Now Abraham owned their house, a 2,400-square-foot brick duplex in Midwood, and Robert, still single, lived there with his parents and brothers. Turk was the second-oldest of seven siblings, and family was as important to him as it was to McCardell. The two came from vastly different backgrounds, but they had both been raised in tight-knit families. McCardell still spent every holiday and birthday in Frederick when possible, and she returned to celebrate milestones for her brothers, as when Adrian Jr. had recently graduated from college.

Turk had the acumen, at a young age, to barter legal licensing agreements with French designers, allowing for an easy France-to-America pipeline. He had the chutzpah to also illegally copy designs, as many in the industry did. But it wasn't just Americans spying on the French; Americans spied on one another, too. It was common practice to send design helpers such as McCardell to department stores as fake shoppers. McCardell had once been offered a job as a "comparative shopper" for Macy's, a position largely designed to steal ideas from other stores, but she hadn't had the stomach for it. Now there she was, thrown right in the middle of the subterfuge.

McCardell had tried not to look anxious inside Bergdorf as she nonchalantly walked by that French dress on a mannequin, pretending to be a customer. The benefit of having a woman like her "shop the stores" was that she was well camouflaged inside the Adamless Eden and she better understood women's clothes. Men overlooked important details. McCardell knew one Seventh Avenue manufacturer who'd tried to imitate a Parisian gown he'd seen only in passing. The original had had large real buttons closing the dress down the back to the waist. In his haste, he hadn't memorized where the buttons ended. The dress he had "designed" had had huge fake buttons all the way down the back and onto the skirt, making it uncomfortable for a woman to sit down.

The problem, as McCardell was beginning to see, was that the system of copying expensive French frocks in no way served working women like her. Ready-to-wear clothes couldn't replicate the refinement of hand stitching and made-to-measure fit. Mass production, for all its promise, relied on tricks to mimic finer-quality clothes. Buttons were sewn on as decorations, not as functional closures. Ready-tied bows were stitched into place to hide a subpar neckline. Gaudy baubles tried to make up for flimsy fabrics.

Only the wealthiest and most connected shoppers received the concierge services of a place such as Bergdorf. Its custom department included sixty tailors, eighty-five dressmakers, seventy-five alteration experts, eleven pressers, and three hemstitchers tailoring French clothes for customers. Even fewer could afford to shop at the New York specialty stores, such as the one owned by Hattie Carnegie on East 49th Street. Carnegie's boutique was as close as a woman in New York City could get to the experience of being in a French haute couture house.

Where, McCardell wondered, were the well-made, chic ready-to-wear garments? There was a market for such sophisticated clothes. *She* was that market. Instead, she'd bought a dress form and resorted to making clothes for herself at her apartment. The reliance on French derivatives discouraged inventiveness. The United States was a mass production country "where any of us, all of us, deserve the right to good fashion," McCardell believed.

She'd had enough for one day. She left the phone booth at Bergdorf, walked out onto 58th Street and turned north into nearby Central Park. She found a bench and continued to sketch. She knew enough to fake the French designs for that season, which continued in the tubular flapper style, so she drew dresses from her imagination. She returned to Turk and handed him her sketches. She never admitted that she'd invented the clothes. Not long after that, Turk stopped sending McCardell to the stores; he put her in charge of the sample room instead. Whether he saw her discomfort over "shopping" or he knew that she wasn't bringing him the real goods, he never did say.

♦

On Seventh Avenue, McCardell perennially lived in the future, a few months ahead of the actual weather. In June, the showrooms presented their fall lines. In November, they released Palm Springs and resort collections, beachy concoctions meant for those who could afford to winter in warmer climates. In February, they released their spring and summer collections.

The Seventh Avenue manufacturers released each collection in a hodgepodge of showings spread out over weeks. The editors of *Vogue* and *Harper's Bazaar* rarely deigned to attend those shows in their Paris gowns and fine suede gloves. Besides, they were rarely invited. Manufacturers feared being copied, and if fashion editors did arrive, they were told to embargo stories until the clothes reached stores weeks later.

Trade publications, such as *Women's Wear Daily*, were the exceptions. On June 18, 1929, Turk announced his first collection preview with an ad in the paper. "You are cordially invited to view our first showing of Paris imports and original creations in Sportswear," it read. His slogan: "The frock of the hour for every hour of the day."

In wholesale, manufacturers like Turk lived and died by the needs and opinions of American store buyers. Some of the buyers came directly from individual department stores. Others were employed by a buying syndicate, one of the cooperatives set up by America's most powerful national chain stores. If the buyers didn't care for your line, you were done for.

Each piece of apparel carried a corresponding number on an order form, accompanied by a short description. The day of the preview, folding chairs were set up in the showroom of the garment loft. McCardell and other models dressed in Turk's sample outfits in a tiny, dingy space walled off from the showroom by a curtain. Turk dashed about and frantically pinned the clothes into place, as the samples rarely fit the models perfectly. When it was McCardell's turn, she walked into the hushed showroom, where fifty-odd people scrutinized her outfit. She held a card with the item's number in front of her as she carefully wove between the seated buyers.

Creating and selling sportswear was its own kind of competitive sport. To win, a firm needed at least two dozen "good numbers" that would sell to buyers and make the season a success. Buyers wielded the power in the industry, and some grew imperious as a result. Previews could curdle into critiques. Buyers sometimes stopped a model as she walked the showroom to instruct the manufacturer on how to overhaul the garment.

Traditionally, the buyers had been male, but increasingly, women were joining their ranks. This created tension with the male manufacturers. "If the resident buyers don't like you or your sister or your brother for any real or imagined reason, you'll have tough going," one male journalist wrote in *Fortune* magazine. "So you treat them nice and call them 'Dear' or 'Darling' or 'Sweet' or 'Sweetheart' or 'Lovely'; you listen respectfully to their criticisms and you agree that the neckline is bad and that the print is lousy. . . . You have enough money in that one line to buy and sell the whole lot of the little bitches but they have you neatly in the palms of their well-manicured hands."

Lucky for Turk, his 1929 fall season was deemed a success. The buyers praised his discerning eye in bringing back the goods from Paris, and for clever little tricks, such as putting novelty buttons etched with a woman playing tennis onto a tennis dress. On October 8, 1929, McCardell helped model Turk's second collection for buyers and reporters from *Women's Wear Daily*. The trade magazine suggested that the dress house of Robert Turk was very much on the rise.

Twenty days later, on October 28, 1929, the world's economy came crashing down. The brokers of Wall Street did not, as the lore would soon claim, hurl themselves from windows when the bottom fell out of the stock market. But the apocryphal anecdotes about Black Monday and the weeks of panic selling that followed underscored the brutal reality. The economic boom of the 1920s was over. The country—and the world—plummeted into the Great Depression.

◆

Turk held tight to his company as long as he could, but by April 1931, he was struggling. His financial partners pulled out of the business, and he had to sell. Robert Turk Inc. was subsumed by Townley Frocks, a midmarket competing manufacturer of women's sportswear. His new role would be head designer. He was no longer a partner in his own firm. He agreed to the merger on several conditions, including bringing McCardell with him. McCardell was soon promoted from helper to design assistant.

Turk and McCardell moved a few blocks away, to 1412 Broadway, where Townley Frocks had its headquarters. Townley had been founded in September 1929 by four wizened rag trade businessmen. The man in charge of day-to-day operations was Henry Geiss, known around town as a harassed veteran of the garment world. Geiss couldn't be bothered, but also he was *always* bothered. A bluster of a man, he was a bottom-line thinker whose solution to women's clothes was to put a bow on it. What he lacked in design vision, he made up for in cheap tricks of frivolity that he hoped might distract a customer long enough to convince her that a Townley frock was worth it.

Turk knew how to handle a guy like Geiss through a mix of charm and budgeting, and they got on well. But to Geiss and the Townley staff, McCardell seemed far younger than her twenty-six years. An employee named Bessie Sustersic mistook Turk's assistant for a teenager at first, even though she was a few years younger than McCardell. McCardell still wore her long hair braided or topped by a man's untrimmed Panama hat. She preferred low-heeled shoes to the high heels most women wore. She sometimes removed her shoes altogether and went barefoot in the sample room. She continued to go makeup free, save for a swipe of silvery eye shadow. She didn't "spend all morning getting herself coiffed and ready" like a European, she said. It exasperated her when the women she passed on Fifth Avenue looked dressed for the Champs-Élysées.

McCardell had grown braver under Turk's tutelage, and she now asked questions of the men working the factory floor. She agreed to help sew collars onto black satin dresses, but when she couldn't manage the industrial machinery, she didn't get flustered. Instead, she acknowledged her inexperience and expressed respect for those capable of the detailed, manual work. Townley's production manager, Harry Friedman, instantly liked her. McCardell set a good example. Thoughtful, organized, and always on time, she kept the communication between Robert Turk and the staff smooth.

Still, there was much of the business that McCardell, as a woman, was not privy to. Seventh Avenue remained deeply gendered. The manufacturers and owners were predominantly male, while many designers, and most seamstresses and models, were women. The women were left out of the mentorship, ownership opportunities, and wealth accumulation that came with being a part of the boys' network.

The same bias held true for the industries that supported New York fashion. Wealthy, powerful men such as Condé Nast and William Randolph Hearst owned the magazines, even though many of their editors and writers were women. Men owned the department stores as well.

In 1928, Edna Woolman Chase, the longtime editor of *Vogue*, had gathered seventeen women, all significant in their positions, for a clandestine meeting at Mary Elizabeth's tea room in Midtown. They discussed how women might better codify and solidify their roles in fashion. Great gains had been made for working women through the founding of the International Ladies' Garment Workers' Union in 1900. But there was no group to advocate for the women working in the other positions that fed the fashion machinery. If suffragism and unionizing had taught them anything, it was that power came in numbers.

By 1930, the seeds of that meeting had blossomed into the Fashion Group (later the Fashion Group International, or FGI). The membership organization had the goal of advancing professional women in the fashion industry. The Fashion Group was notable for enrolling women at all levels of their careers. McCardell became one of the first dues-paying members, and it put her in company with established women such as makeup tycoon Helena Rubinstein and Eleanor Roosevelt, whose husband, Franklin D. Roosevelt, was governor of New York and soon to be president of the United States. McCardell knew the value of women looking out for one another.

Once a month, McCardell left work at noon for a lunchtime meeting of the Fashion Group. The women filled the ballrooms of the city's biggest hotels. Guest speakers from varying backgrounds—politics, psychiatry, manufacturing, business, the arts—offered their insights and helped frame fashion within the broader social, cultural, and economic realities of America.

Few men of industry had ever stood before a sold-out room of well-dressed businesswomen. Paul Mazur of Lehman Brothers took to the podium at the Hotel Roosevelt in April 1931 to proffer a banker's point of view on fashion and the Great Depression, and he, like many of the men invited to speak, went in straight for the jokes. "I have been completely confused as to why I am here. Certainly there is nothing fashionable about Wall Street at the present time. And it doesn't seem to me that fashion is a particularly virile subject, and if there is one thing we pride ourselves on—it is the only thing we have left as a matter of fact . . . it is that we belong to a virile group of males," he said. "For a mid-Victorian like myself to be plunked down into a group of modern women, well, I just can't describe the effect upon myself."

To help the male lecturers, a member of the Fashion Group reviewed speeches in advance. One of the more common suggestions was a steady slash through the word "girls," and a note that the speaker should refer to those gathered as "women." The speeches were then reproduced in bulletins and disseminated to members, who in the coming years, hailed from chapters all over the United States and abroad. Each month, McCardell attended the meetings, where she took notes and networked.

♦

By the winter of 1932, McCardell and Turk had settled into a good routine at Townley. Turk sailed for Paris on January 22 for a three-week trip, and McCardell was left in charge. There wasn't much to do until Turk returned with the goods from Paris. He called Townley using a transatlantic phone line in early February—newsworthy enough to make the pages of *Women's Wear Daily*—and dictated important notes, which she began to interpret in sketches for the new line.

Turk had been back in New York only a few weeks when McCardell received another phone call, this time with distressing news from home. Her grandfather Adrian C. McCardell had died at the age of eighty-six.

The funeral took place on Saturday, April 2, 1932, at the church in Frederick where McCardell had spent so many Sundays growing up. Her grandfather was buried in a family plot near those of other prominent Frederick citizens, including Francis Scott Key, the lawyer turned poet who'd penned "The Star-Spangled Banner." McCardell stayed in Frederick a few extra days to be with her parents and her brothers. Turk had encouraged her to take all the time off she needed. But she was eager to get back.

She returned to New York and discovered the great coping tactic of distracting oneself from grief with busyness. In May, she and Turk were in a tailspin trying to get the fall collection ready for buyers to see by June. McCardell skipped going home for her birthday so that she could keep working.

On May 23, during their chaotic preparations, it was announced that Turk had bought a stake in Townley after one of the original founders had retired. He was now a full partner. Turk decided to celebrate. The first week of June, he planned a long weekend away with his family. He would enjoy a well-deserved respite in the country and an early celebration of his twenty-ninth birthday, which fell on Wednesday, June 8. He left word that he would be back late on Monday, June 6, refreshed and ready to wrap up the autumn line.

McCardell arrived at work that Monday and immediately knew that something was wrong. The factory was unusually still.

She learned that the day before, Turk had taken his brother, Bernard, age eleven, to a popular swimming spot near New Hackensack, New York. Bernard had begun to struggle almost as soon as he'd entered the river. He may have gotten caught in a current. Several bathers noticed his plight, and Turk rushed in to help. In the excitement of Bernard's getting back to shore, Turk's absence wasn't immediately noticed. *The Brooklyn Times-Union* reported that fellow swimmers later found him in about ten feet of water. He was pulled to shore, but attempts to revive him had failed. The article ran that morning under the headline "Robert Turk Dies as Young Boy Is Saved." Turk had drowned rescuing his brother.

McCardell couldn't make sense of the news. Her grandfather's death at eighty-six had been difficult, but his funeral had been a celebration of a long, full life. There was no comprehending the death of a man on the eve of his twenty-ninth birthday, on the cusp of a promising new phase in his career. She couldn't believe that her boss—her mentor and her friend—was gone. On Tuesday, June 7, Geiss closed Townley so the employees could attend Turk's funeral.

The following day, the machines stood idle on the factory floor as the still shocked staff awaited instructions. The collection had to be presented to buyers in a few weeks. Geiss and his partner argued about how to proceed. How could they finish the Townley line? Could they poach a designer from another firm at the eleventh hour?

On the factory floor, a male voice piped up from the back of the crowded room. It could have been that of Harry Friedman, the production manager, who admired the work McCardell did on behalf of Turk and Townley. "Let the girl do it," the voice said.

Geiss didn't have much of a choice. He turned to McCardell and told her that she would be the one to finish the collection. McCardell panicked. "I don't know that I'm big enough for the job," she admitted. Geiss assured her that if he didn't think she could do it, he wouldn't have given her the task.

McCardell arrived at work each morning and spent her day collaborating with a ghost. She tried to interpret what Turk had started, tried to hear his voice in her head, all the while refusing to speak about his death or her grief. By the necessities of the situation and her own temperament, she walled off the emotions swirling inside her. She wrapped herself in the work to the exclusion of all else. It was a habit that would continue throughout her life.

Bringing a collection to completion was a frenzied and temperamental endeavor at the best of times. The silhouettes and materials had already been approved for the sample outfits before Turk had died, but the clothes still needed to be carefully fitted on models. Factory samples of belts, buttons, and trimmings had to be ordered. Hats and bags and shoes and costume jewelry had to be selected and procured to finish each look. There never seemed to be enough time. The Townley staff rallied to McCardell's side.

McCardell marshaled all that she'd learned from Turk, all that she'd taught herself, and all that she'd gleaned from the lunchtime lectures of the Fashion Group. Before the buyer's preview, she taught the models how to walk using the slouching, casual manner she'd developed at B. Altman. In the coming years, that walk would become the norm. According to one source, the way models would walk down runways in the United States had its origins in Townley's Seventh Avenue loft. Claire McCardell invented it.

The day of the showing, McCardell was both boss and assistant. The crowd of buyers and media had come to see how Townley would manage after Turk's death as much as to see the clothes on offer.

The audience may have gotten a glimpse of the busy young woman behind the curtain that separated her from the showroom. She dashed about with pins stuck to a red cushion on her wrist. She adjusted the garments on the models, her face pure concentration. She had no time to wonder whether buyers liked what they saw, or if, as one account described it, they might be "whispering to each other behind their smartly gloved hands" that a mere girl had had to take the collection over and it was a failure.

Henry Geiss tried to keep calm. Tens of thousands of dollars had gone into making the seventy-five garment samples that were now traipsing, no, make that *slouching*, through his showroom. He needed buyers to find at least twenty of the numbers viable so that he could make his investment back, with interest, over the eight-to-ten-week fall selling season.

The show ended, and McCardell finally had time to look up. She watched from the back as buyers began to write orders on their forms and hand them to Geiss. The clothes were selling. As one fashion journalist later wrote, "The whole fashion world knew that the understudy had proved herself."

Geiss came to her after the buyers had left. He would no longer advertise to replace Turk as he'd planned; he was giving her the job of head designer at Townley.

At twenty-seven years old, McCardell ascended to the role she'd long desired. She now oversaw the design department of a major sportswear manufacturer. It was harrowing to be given that opportunity only because her mentor had died. Later, when the words finally came, McCardell described those weeks as "very black." She'd matured a decade, it seemed, and she felt ready to show Seventh Avenue what she was capable of. With the next collection, she'd be the one making the decisions. Or so she believed.

CHAPTER SIX

Everyone Deserves Pockets

1933-34

The arguments with Henry Geiss began almost immediately. By 1933, McCardell had been at the helm of the design department for a year, and she did what every Seventh Avenue designer was required to do: She went to Paris. Still, she irritated her boss by refusing to make precise replicas. "I began to experiment, following basic trends instead of copying which was the usual dress-business procedure," she later explained. She designed her collections to be "a little more casual, a little less self-conscious, and a little more American."

Key to that effort, she believed, was pockets. She wanted every Townley dress and skirt to include them. Pockets were useful, obviously, but they also had the psychological benefit of giving a woman a place to put her hands. This was especially helpful to a young career woman "standing in front of your boss's desk trying to look casual and composed," she observed.

Geiss, like most male manufacturers, thought pockets had no place in womenswear. It was an assumption so widespread and ingrained in the industry as to seem right and decided in his mind. First, he believed that pockets were too expensive to make. Mass production techniques involved cutting clothes into an assembly line of pieces, and pockets complicated matters. Second, women didn't need them; they had purses. And most important, women didn't want them because carrying things about their hips made them look fat.

As Geiss made his arguments, he unwittingly carried centuries of bias into the Townley workroom. Pockets had been around since the 1600s at least. Originally, they had gone into men's breeches and had only slowly found their way into some women's apparel. Women predominantly used an exterior pouch called a reticule, the forerunner of the purse, and they affixed it to a skirt or hung it from a wrist. Pockets had initially been seen as dangerous, given their ability to conceal items such as a new technological wonder, the pistol. Guns had shrunk to fit inside clothing, and while the fear of men concealing weapons eventually abated, the idea that a woman might hide something "dangerous" on her body persisted. Even mundane items—private letters, keys, money—were seen as threatening. The more a woman could stash on her person, the more freedom she had to act. Men's clothing evolved to include many useful, sewn-in pockets, but women's garments did not.

When McCardell was a child, suffragists and dress reformers fought for pocket parity. They were "dragging the pocket into the female emancipation problem," a reporter for the *San Francisco Chronicle* wrote in 1913. Cartoons caricatured haggard-looking women stuffing their hands into "Suffragist skirt" pockets like a man. By 1915, the author and social reformer Charlotte Perkins Gilman noted that American ready-to-wear ignored the practical needs of women and even kept pockets out of the calico housedresses worn in privacy to clean. (Gilman had already depicted the systemic oppression of women through her fiction, most notably in her short story "The Yellow Wallpaper.")

McCardell didn't care about precedent. A man never had to think twice about forgetting a purse in a New York taxi. She wanted pockets and believed that other women did, too. She felt sure that if she could go straight to her customers, she'd win her case. As a wholesale designer, however, she first had to get her design ideas by Geiss and his Seventh Avenue salesmen. Those men liked to prop themselves against the Savoy-Plaza bar after work, knock back old-fashioneds, and predict what the French were thinking and what the American market might bear. They guessed at "the gossamer whim of the female mind," as one male journalist described it. They rarely asked the opinion of actual women, even the ones who worked for them.

McCardell went to her trusted sample room manager, Bessie Sustersic, for help. The two had grown close in the years since Turk had first merged with Townley, and their bond had tightened after Turk had died. Now they had a shorthand for working together. Sustersic could read McCardell's "stick figure drawings," as she called her boss's fast sketches.

They worked together on inserting pockets into the side seams of the sample skirts and dresses for one seasonal collection. McCardell then showed Geiss how economical and stylish they could be. Eventually, he relented. But then McCardell had to repeat the whole song and dance the next time she wanted to put pockets into Townley clothes.

In the 1930s, a lack of pockets wasn't the only wardrobe inconvenience for a woman. Closures often went onto the backs of their clothes, making it difficult for a woman to reach them and to get dressed without help. Around that time, McCardell began using a metal fastener in some of her garments. First invented in 1851, the "Automatic Continuous Clothing Closure," as it was originally called, would be refined and, in 1917, become the modern zipper. McCardell moved the closures to the side. A woman may live alone and thrive, as McCardell now did, "but you may regret it if you wrench your arm trying to zip a back zipper into place," she explained.

Simplicity in clothes was equally important to McCardell. Men had a practical uniform: the suit. Women, conversely, had housedresses, day dresses, tea dresses, evening gowns. A woman's wardrobe still largely followed the dictates of her mother's generation. The 1930s had also ushered in a renewed conservatism in dress. The casual, easy look of the freewheeling flapper was out. As *Fortune* magazine explained, "Many speculative persons believe that a return to dignity and formalism in attire presages an accompanying return to statelier morals and manners," and that required "a greater variety of costumes, each adapted to its particular social purpose."

McCardell's schedule didn't leave her time to pop home and change for different times of day or social events. She walked long blocks to work; she took the subway. She went from the grimy factory floor at Townley to a luncheon at the fancy Pierre Hotel. After work, she rushed to meet a friend for a movie or a date for drinks. She needed outfits that could move from one place to another, that looked fresh all day and could navigate city life. "Men are free of the clothes problem—why shouldn't I follow their example?" she asked.

She felt that her calling as a designer was to solve the clothes problem for herself and her customers. Clothes should "follow the instinctive demand of the woman who wears them," she said. "Clothes should fit the individual and the occasion. They are made to be worn, to be lived in." It was why she liked to put a dolman sleeve into many of her dresses. The dolman was cut wider at the shoulder, earning it the nickname of the batwing sleeve, and it provided a woman with ample room in her armpit. She could raise her arm above her head to hold a strap on the subway or hail a taxi without worrying about ripping a seam.

It came down to style versus fashion. Style was what best suited a woman's body, her personality, her circumstances. Fashion was what Paris unleashed every few months to keep a woman agitated and hungry and buying new clothes. "As we all know," McCardell said, "fashion is a very fickle girl."

In April 1933, McCardell's newest disagreement with Geiss came over shoulder pads. *Vogue* captured the precise moment the new shoulder silhouette debuted. "People who were at the openings in Paris, this spring, will tell you that, when the models walked in, there was a general gasp," the editors wrote. The models appeared with "wide, beautiful, Amazonian shoulders" that were, to mix their metaphors, architectural like the newest skyscrapers. "Instead of draping bits of cloth over what God gave you for a figure," *Vogue* proclaimed, shoulder pads could "build you out."

A woman's clavicle no longer swept into the graceful, shapely beauty of her naturally rounded shoulder. Fashion was done with naturalness, as exemplified by the immense shoulders on dresses made by the Italian-born, Paris-based designer Elsa Schiaparelli.

"We have gotten away from women's natural beauty," McCardell said. "A woman has hips—they are a part of her. She naturally has curves, too. A woman does not normally have football shoulders." Townley clothes, she argued, should have the easy unpadded shoulders of a man's shirt. Not because she wanted women to dress like men; rather, it was the simplicity of men's tailoring she was after, in service of a woman's comfort.

So what did Geiss do? He put shoulder pads into all the dresses. After the fact. Without consulting her. Geiss wanted shoulder pads because the Townley salesmen wanted them to appease the buyers at the department stores, who listened only to the French. It was a vicious cycle.

The seamstresses could barely look her in the eye, knowing how upset she'd be. Geiss said that a dress needed "hanger appeal," meaning it had to look good on a hanger in a department store in order to sell. But shoulder pads added to McCardell's simple, natural shoulders made it look as though a woman had forgotten to take the hanger out. *Vogue* claimed that that wasn't such a bad thing: "A short year ago, to say 'You look like a clothes-hanger" to a lady would have been a remark in the worst possible taste. To-day it is high praise."

Geiss further challenged McCardell over her novel use of fabrics. In McCardell's closet she had a pair of pants and a double-breasted jacket made of tweed. The menswear-inspired suit was considered radical at a time when women were prohibited from wearing pants in most public spaces, but, like Coco Chanel and the German actress Marlene Dietrich, McCardell ignored the dress code. The boat trips to Europe were cold and damp, so she made herself a long tweed evening coat, too. She suggested that it be included in the Townley collection, but Geiss balked. Tweed on a woman at night was considered far too informal.

McCardell didn't stop at tweed. She used cotton calico for formal day dresses, even though cottons were typically relegated by the industry to informal housedresses and shirtwaist blouses. She made evening wear out of wool, even though it was usually reserved for daytime suits, coats, jackets, and outerwear. But "if houses are cold, warm clothes are important," she believed. "There should be comfort in the snow, comfort in the rain, comfort in the sun, comfort for active sports, comfort for sitting still and looking pretty." While on a ski trip to New Hampshire, she had seen a woman wearing an ice blue satin evening gown, and the poor woman had frozen because she was following fashion's dictates, even in the snowcapped mountains. "This awful anachronism sent me home to make my blue wool evening dress," she recounted.

Women, she said, should have "clothes that are easy to put on and take off, and with buttons that button, sashes that tie, real pockets. In other words, common sense in clothes." She aimed to make "independent clothes for independent working gals."

The fabric salesmen of Seventh Avenue came to love McCardell. They knew that when they stopped in at Townley, she would consider all manner of fabric samples, even those usually reserved for menswear and even work wear. "I wondered why women's clothes had to be delicate to be feminine, why they couldn't be practical and sturdy as well as feminine," she said.

McCardell never hesitated to wear her own creations, but her fashion taste didn't translate into sales at Townley. On the rare occasions when Geiss allowed her to include her original ideas in the collection, they didn't always take. "The buyers very often are afraid of them," she said of her designs, "and the clothes have to be taken off the line." Geiss repeatedly said that McCardell's clothes were too crazy for Seventh Avenue. McCardell happily appropriated his term. She began calling her original creations "my crazies."

◆

In 1934, McCardell had her craziest idea yet. She'd been contemplating a specific clothing problem since 1926, during her first trip to Paris.

When traveling, a woman often had to use a steamer trunk to store the many components of her wardrobe. Empty, the trunks could weigh as much as a hundred pounds. The fanciest of them hinged open to reveal a puzzle of intricate drawers and miniature closets capable of corralling every wardrobe item for the often jarring journey across the Atlantic. Special compartments cradled hats; others held shoes. Gloves, scarves, and jewelry went into silk pouches and drawers and dresses had to be padded with tissue paper to prevent them from wrinkling. A panoply of straps and snaps kept everything secured inside.

For McCardell, hauling steamer trunks from her apartment on East 38th Street in the Murray Hill neighborhood to the docks of the Hudson River, then onto the ocean liner and off again, became an endurance sport she loathed, even with the help of well-tipped porters at each stage. In 1934, the growth of domestic commercial air travel brought additional challenges. A woman's wardrobe had to further shrink into a suitcase even though the rules of conventional fashion remained. Fitting housedresses, day dresses, tea dresses, and evening gowns into a suitcase proved to be difficult. Men carried far less baggage. They only had to contend with suits, and one suit could last a whole trip with the right change of shirts and ties. "The comfort and ease of men's clothes always attracted me," McCardell later explained, and she thought now of how a set of matching elements, like a suit, might offer a solution for women.

McCardell began to wonder: How many dresses can I get into one suitcase? How will they look when they come out? It was like the geometry problems she had loved solving in high school.

McCardell envisioned a system of five different garments that could work together and be combined to create different outfits: a jacket, a halter top, a pair of culottes, a skirt, and slacks. They could be made from the same material, so that they easily mixed. She decided on black ribbed jersey. The fabric didn't wrinkle, and it could be folded into nothing. Wouldn't it be wonderful, she thought, to unpack crease-free wool jersey and thumb your nose at an iron?

McCardell showed Geiss her sketches: five interchangeable pieces, each cut along simple lines, with no ornamentation or trimming—in other words, nothing to constrain their flexibility. "Clothes without glitter, only fabric cut and constructed," as she later described them.

It would be great for travel, as well as a boon to women living on strict budgets and busy women like herself who worked in the city. Women could dress the clothes up or down with their own jewelry and accessories, taking, for instance, the halter top and culottes from work to the theater simply by adding the jacket and a necklace or an armful of bangles.

McCardell was describing a system of separates that would, in fifty years, become the foundation of American fashion. In 1934, however, it was not how merchandising worked. Stores did not sell five pieces all in one color, and they did not offer distinct items that could be mixed and matched. The buyers were absolutely baffled by McCardell's separates. Novel concepts, particularly those that hadn't originated in Paris, were a difficult sell. The separates were removed from the collection.

♦

Change was in the air, though, even if many buyers and the men of Seventh Avenue couldn't yet see it. American designers and their original ideas were beginning to make inroads at some major department stores.

Two years earlier, in the spring of 1932, window shoppers strolling along Fifth Avenue near 38th Street had come upon a surprising window display. Prominent behind the polished plate glass of Lord & Taylor was a sign that read "American Designers" along with mannequins wearing new dresses. One of the country's largest retailers had given prime real estate to the work of unknown, homegrown creators.

Newspaper headline writers had a field day with the development. The *New York Evening Post* called it a "Revolt from Paris." Another newspaper declared, "Store Executive Predicts Eclipse of Paris."

The store executive in question was Dorothy Shaver, a founding member of the Fashion Group. Shaver had begun working at Lord & Taylor in 1921, and by 1931, her merchandising acumen earned her the position of vice president. She believed in the potential of American fashion. She plucked three independent designers—Elizabeth Hawes, Adele Simpson, and Edith Marie Reuss—from relative obscurity and commissioned them to make originals for the store. She chose women because "who but women are best able to judge the evanescent wants and needs of their own sex?"

Shaver launched a national media blitz to promote the idea. "Long entrenched and highly organized French couturiers have been accustomed to dominating the fashion news," she told reporters. "But in the meantime, brilliant young American women have been quietly studying the needs of their countrywomen and have created designs typifying the swing and freshness that is uniquely American."

"Swing" was a well-chosen word. In the 1930s, the big-band horns and raucous joy of Count Basie and Duke Ellington had replaced the jazz quartets of the 1920s. Ellington had recently released the hit "It Don't Mean a Thing (If It Ain't Got That Swing)." The dresses in the Lord & Taylor window were precisely the kind of active, appealing casualwear that could shine on the dance floor. Shaver assured the public that there were plenty of American designers who were not yet household names but who represented a great wealth of hidden talent in the industry and the country.

Henry Geiss didn't appreciate that just such a bright young talent was hidden in his midst. The name Claire McCardell was nowhere associated with the clothes that Townley made, beyond the occasional article in trade publications such as *Women's Wear Daily*. And unlike the women Shaver had selected for her American Designers promotion, who worked for themselves, McCardell toiled inside the machinery of Seventh Avenue. Shaver's innovative idea to promote American designers had yet to trickle down to the manufacturers, who continued to keep their designers anonymous.

That spring of 1934, the retailer Best & Co. prominently featured several Francophile outfits from Townley Frocks in its window on Fifth Avenue. "Five dresses from one creator in a Best & Company window," the ad copy read, calling it a "stunning group of dresses." McCardell was thrilled to see her clothes pictured in the newspapers. She cut out the photos and glued them into a scrapbook. Still, she felt deeply aggravated that her name wasn't mentioned.

It may have been on the advice of Mildred Orrick that McCardell sought the counsel of an astrologer that year. Orrick's interest in the mystical had blossomed when she had worked with Natacha Rambova, who was a devout occultist. In 1930, a fortune teller had predicted that Orrick would find her husband and shortly afterward, she'd met and married Jesse Orrick.

Fortune-telling thrived in postcrash America. The biggest calamity since the Great War had struck largely undetected, and divining the future was alluring. In New York, untold numbers of clairvoyants squinted into glass balls and palmists scrutinized hands. Tasseography, the reading of tea leaves, became popular. One man assured *The New York Times* that "the leavings of ground spinach on a dinner-plate are full of auguries for the future." Prophecy by spinach never caught on, but astrology soared. Horoscopes began to be published in respectable newspapers alongside the weather forecast.

McCardell received a six-page typed report from an astrologer. As a Gemini, the analysis began, she was influenced by peculiar vibrations that gave her a "deep, resourceful and sensitive type of character." She had a devotion to beauty and an intense aesthetic strain in her nature. "You do not care for drudgery at all and are prone to ignore authority and convention."

At twenty-nine, McCardell was still single, but according to the stars, a man would soon come into her life. McCardell should proceed with caution. "Though you may have pleasant associations with him, the final result will eventually be of no advantage to you," the astrologer warned. Before closing the report, the astrologer ventured another obvious prophecy: "Your chart further signifies that you are destined to travel twice to Europe in 1935." McCardell hardly needed the planets to tell her that.

CHAPTER SEVEN

Abdication

1934-37

In the mid-1930s, Geiss dispatched McCardell to Europe with such frequency that she wore a medal of St. Christopher, the patron saint of travelers. Each year, she lived a few months in her Murray Hill apartment, a few months in Europe, and several weeks on an ocean liner crossing the Atlantic.

Luckily, McCardell had an iron stomach. She rarely fell seasick, even during rough crossings. During a stormy trip aboard the *Queen Mary*, the ocean had whipped up to a frothy white, the boat rolled wildly, and everything on board went damp from the sea spray. "The furniture in the grand salon smashed into a group of people last night and some of them were knocked out," she wrote in a letter home. Her steamer trunk, winnowed to just one thanks to the space-saving separates she'd made for herself, "was thrown on the floor so many times some of its hinges are in a bad way."

Whenever possible, McCardell booked passage with her college friend Joset Walker. Walker was now designing for a Seventh Avenue manufacturer, after a stint working for the film industry. In 1931, she had been the head of costume design at RKO Pictures, where she'd designed gowns for Katharine Hepburn in her film debut, *A Bill of Divorcement*. Ironically, Walker's personal life mirrored the plot of the film. She, too, was heading for a divorce. She'd wed Edward De Lima, a Frenchman of Cuban heritage, in 1929, and their marriage was crumbling. Divorce wasn't unheard of in the New York circles that Walker and McCardell ran in, but the social stigma it carried, especially for women, kept it an anomaly. Right after Walker left RKO, the film industry adopted a new set of morality guidelines called the Hays Code. It prohibited, among other things, revealing clothes on women, suggestive dancing, and positive portrayals of divorce. A woman could no longer rid herself of a cheating husband or celebrate her sexuality on film.

In the mid-1930s, Walker gave her New York address as McCardell's apartment building in Murray Hill, and by 1938, she listed her status as "single" for the ship's manifest. She was unfettered and ready for some fun.

Once a steamship left dock, debauched revelry and excess rippled across the decks. McCardell and Walker enjoyed first-class travel, their passage paid for by their bosses. Liquor flowed in the cocktail lounges, tuxedo-clad waiters delivered seven-course meals, and orchestras kept the passengers dancing well into the night. Gentlemen were told to be "very cautious about playing cards, or other games, with strangers," as one ship's pamphlet warned, "as professional gamblers are constantly crossing the Atlantic, looking out for the unwary."

There were other games afloat on the high seas, as well. McCardell enjoyed wonderful flirtations during her crossings. On one voyage, she danced each night in the ample arms of a beefy Italian boxer. She didn't know he was Enzo Fiermonte, the man at the center of a tawdry, and ongoing, affair with Madeleine Astor Dick. The captain pulled Walker aside and spoke to her in urgent, whispered French. "I danced with Enzo all the way over and the Captain got worried," McCardell recorded in a letter.

On the Italian ship *Conte di Savoia*, a famous baritone on his way to the Paris Opera hummed into McCardell's ear as the orchestra played. On the *Queen Mary*, she swam laps with Johnny Weissmuller, the star of the Tarzan movies. "He's a wonderful swimmer but every once in awhile he yells," she wrote home. "Thinks he's still playing Tarzan, I guess."

Boat trips were full of champagne and clandestine intimacies until McCardell reached the dock, where the intoxication stopped right along with the boat's engine. Only rarely did a shipboard dalliance continue, as it did briefly with one handsome Italian. He opened his love letters to McCardell with the salutation "Beautiful!" In one, he enclosed a photo of himself—his rakish smile aimed right at the camera lens—to "remind you of a good friend [who is] very sincere about your funny, laughing face."

In November 1934, McCardell sailed out of England for New York on the SS *Paris*. She was alone that time, without Walker for company. There's no record of how McCardell and Irving Drought Harris first met on the ship. But the dashing American architect with the chestnut brown eyes and chiseled jaw would have been hard to miss. Harris towered over others at six feet, four inches tall. Clad in well-tailored suits, he walked with a confident swagger, often with a chilled martini in hand. From certain angles, he resembled the handsome Prince Edward, who was in line to become the next king of England. McCardell was twenty-nine and single. He was eight years her senior and married. He was traveling alone, though, and his marriage was on the rocks.

◆

Irving Drought Harris was born in San Antonio, Texas, in September 1897. His father died when he was a child, and his mother supported the family as a dressmaker before remarrying. By the time Harris graduated from high school in 1915, he had an intense desire to be more than a fatherless boy from a small-town working-class family. He aimed to leave the South. In November 1917, he got his wish, albeit not in the way that he'd hoped: The US Army deployed him to the western front of the Great War, where he fought for two years.

By 1920, at age twenty-two, he was back living in Texas and had already divorced his first wife. He moved to Houston, where he apprenticed for several architecture firms, but he had his sights set on a posher life in New York.

Harris finally arrived in Manhattan in 1925. He rented a suite at the Shelton Hotel on Lexington Avenue in Midtown. At thirty-one stories, the Shelton was among the first residential skyscraper hotels in the world. The painter Georgia O'Keeffe and her husband, the photographer Alfred Stieglitz, lived on the thirtieth floor. Harris's choice of building was strategic as its respectable address transferred its dignity to those who lived there. Harris was singularly obsessed with entering New York high society. He was, as several of McCardell's friends would later describe him, a great snob.

During the Gilded Age, Caroline Astor's list of the Four Hundred had dictated who could enter the upper crust of Manhattan society. In the new New York of the 1920s, wealth could buy a man social standing. Harris aimed to make his fortune in the city, and in the summer of 1929, it danced right into his arms.

Her name was Jean Ferris. Her grandfather, the late sugar magnate Claus Spreckels, had been one of the wealthiest men in the world, worth a reported $50 million when he died in 1908. The Spreckels family was to sugar what Andrew Carnegie was to steel and the Rockefellers were to oil. In his lifetime, Spreckels had amassed a vast fortune and a portfolio of real estate along the California coast. He also had a history of lawsuits and family scandals that played out in newspapers around the world, among them the sensational criminal trial of Jean's uncle Adolph Spreckels, who'd walked into the offices of the *San Francisco Chronicle* in 1884 and attempted to kill the newspaper's owner with a pistol.

Jean's mother, Emma Spreckels Hutton, had also made her share of headlines. Emma had been doted on by her protective father. When he'd built the family's mansion in the Pacific Heights neighborhood of San Francisco, the teenage Emma had a bathroom where water flowed from solid gold faucets. But at twenty-six, she eloped with a man twice her age, whom Claus believed to be an elderly fortune hunter. Claus disowned her.

Emma fled to England, where her daughter, Jean, was born in 1910. Emma was back in Claus's good graces before he died, and she inherited a significant portion of his estate. Emma died in 1924, leaving Jean to be raised in Surrey, England, by a stepfather. Jean had never met her wealthy

Spreckels relatives. She was away at boarding school in 1926 when the news arrived that she'd just inherited millions of dollars. Reporters described her as slender, blue-eyed, and infatuated with riding horses. "I understand public interest in the news of big fortunes," her stepfather told reporters. "Interest in Jean herself will come later, especially from young men."

In the summer of 1929, Jean visited her uncle Rudolph Spreckels at the Ritz-Carlton in New York. When Harris met Jean at the Ritz-Carlton during one of Rudolph's infamous parties, it could have been true love. But it was likely her wealth that lowered him to bended knee shortly after their whirlwind courtship began. In August 1929, Rudolph announced the couple's engagement at a dinner at the hotel. Jean was nineteen years old; Harris was thirty-one. Her wealth far outpaced her maturity, and it's hard to imagine that the Texas war veteran saw an equal partner in a teenager raised in the cloistered environment of European boarding schools.

They married in October. That Harris had managed to win the international battle for Jean Ferris's hand was a testament to his ample charms. Newspapers on both sides of the Atlantic covered the wedding, noting the famous guests from Jean's wealthy family in attendance. Irving's modest past was now largely scrubbed.

Their son, John Wakefield Harris, was born less than a year later, in September 1930, and the marriage was already in decline. Harris had "a Vesuvian temper" as John would later describe his father. Jean was said to be obstinate and entitled, inspiring one woman who worked for her to declare, "Woe betide anyone who crossed her!"

Harris and Jean fought, broke up, and reconciled in a cycle of public spats that was catnip to gossip columnists. After one epic argument in November 1931, Jean packed her things and took infant John to Rudolph's apartment at the Ritz-Carlton. She refused to see Harris, so he sued Jean for abandonment. They reconciled in January 1932. They may have hoped that a change of scenery would repair the marriage, or perhaps they were desperate to escape the tabloid news of their litigious love life. Whatever the case, they left most of their possessions in their rented apartment and fled to Europe on the steamship *Olympic*, surprising even their closest family and friends. Jean's fortune bought them a château in the south of France. It was there, in 1933, that they welcomed a second child, their daughter, Elizabeth, who would later go by Liz.

Fourteen months after Liz's birth, in November 1934, Irving Harris and Claire McCardell traveled together aboard the SS *Paris*.

Did Harris admit straightaway to being married? Did he tell McCardell that his wealthy wife was back in their château, along with their son and infant daughter? Or did he, like the Italian boxer Enzo Fiermonte, let the no-rules, hothouse atmosphere of the ocean voyage carry them along in cocooned intimacy, so that his charms had already won her by the time they docked in New York? Chances are good that he didn't explain his precise circumstances to McCardell, at least not initially. As his daughter, Liz, would later say: "Father was a great liar."

The *Paris* docked in New York Harbor on November 20, 1934. McCardell returned to her apartment in Murray Hill. Harris checked into a suite at the Waldorf Astoria, eleven blocks away. Six months later, Harris was back in France, packing up his things at the château. In October 1935, he petitioned for a divorce from Jean in the French courts. He took John, age four, to New York, along with his son's longtime nanny. Liz remained with Jean in France. The precise moment that the romance between McCardell and Harris began isn't known. But it wasn't long after first meeting on the *Paris* that the two quietly began dating.

◆

Three years later, in May 1937, McCardell was still dating Harris as she steamed toward the Paris openings, this time aboard the SS *Normandie*. New Yorkers had started referring to the ship as the "Seventh Avenue Shuttle" for the number of American clothiers booking passage. The boat traveled so swiftly that the yellow roses her parents always had waiting in her cabin at the beginning of the trip lasted for the entire voyage. Aside from "a few mistakes in color," McCardell thought the interior of the *Normandie* was brilliant, "like Radio City on water."

In Paris, the chestnut trees were in bloom, and the city glowed in the warmth of spring. Paris "certainly can be perfect when it tries," she wrote. She checked into her usual room at the Ritz on Place Vendôme and then headed downstairs to the bar, where guests imbibed gossip as much as strong drinks. Coco Chanel, who kept a suite at the hotel with her latest lover, was a regular, as were the many designers, buyers, and journalists McCardell had gotten to know over her last five years as Townley's head designer. "Paris is really like a small town," she wrote home. "You always see the same people."

That night, two bits of news preoccupied the crowd as they drank champagne cocktails and the Ritz's famed sidecar, a mix of cognac, orange liqueur, and lemon juice.

The most serious news came out of Spain, where, a week earlier, the Basque town of Guernica had been all but obliterated. The Nazi air force had joined the Fascist Italian regime to support Francisco Franco's overthrow of the Spanish government. The Spanish Civil War had been raging for months, already claiming thousands of lives, but the bombing of Guernica on a public market day, when so many civilians were out in the streets, portended a brutal shift in aggression and a dangerous alignment of Fascist dictators. The horrors of what happened on that day would be depicted in the mural-sized painting by Pablo Picasso titled *Guernica*. Millions of people, including many in the bar that night, would view the painting during the International Exposition of Art and Technology in Modern Life in Paris later that year. The warmth of the candlelit room and the copious amounts of alcohol did little to stave off the cold reality that Europe seemed headed for another war.

The crowd turned its chatter to the less harrowing and more salacious revolution happening to the north, where the coronation of the new king of England was set for the following week. Five months earlier, on December 10, 1936, Edward had shocked the world when he had abdicated his position as king in favor of his love for the twice-divorced American socialite Wallis Warfield Simpson. Edward's younger brother would now be crowned as King George VI.

Wallis Simpson and her exiled prince were staying at the Château de Candé, about 150 miles from where McCardell sat sipping her drink. (Decades earlier, the two women had been much closer in proximity, living just sixty miles apart in Maryland, where they had both been raised.) Simpson was photographed that week for *Vogue* wearing an Elsa Schiaparelli haute couture gown. The Surrealist artist Salvador Dalí had painted a giant steamed lobster on the front, its ample tail fins fanned out at Simpson's pelvis, the body and claws falling toward the hem. Delicate green flowers dappled the edges of the dress, but on closer inspection, they came into focus as sprigs of parsley. Dalí was rumored to have wanted to paint a jar of mayonnaise on the dress as well.

The lobster dress signified the kind of clothes-horse abundance that annoyed McCardell, as well as the others promoting a new American simplicity. The women central to New York's fashion world wanted to distinguish American sensibility and talent from European excess and extravagance, especially during a global depression. As Dorothy Shaver told a reporter that year, "a dress that is worn once and thrown away is not smart." And once you'd donned a crustacean-covered evening gown, chances were strong that it would go into mothballs afterward.

McCardell, meanwhile, moved about Paris wearing, and rewearing, a rotating cast of items from her personal collection of interchangeable clothes. Her separates idea still hadn't caught on with Seventh Avenue manufacturers, but the concept represented precisely the kind of thoughtful minimalism the tastemakers of New York, including Shaver, were espousing. "I don't want to look like a royal princess or a world-famous hostess," McCardell later wrote, and she could have been talking about the duchess of Windsor when she added, "I don't live in a palace and my dinner parties are for six, not sixty."

McCardell's own romantic entanglement with a divorcé wasn't yet public knowledge in 1937. The McCardells of Frederick weren't the British monarchy, and the stakes weren't nearly as high as those of the rule of the British Empire. Still, remaining unmarried at thirty-two and dating a divorced man represented its own kind of rebellion.

McCardell was more focused on her career than on marriage, and Harris fit her priorities. Harris was in no hurry to marry again. He was still untangling the complex financial fallout of an international divorce. McCardell was in no hurry, either. She didn't want to be tied down, and she didn't harbor maternal longings. She realized that she didn't want children of her own. The two shared interests in design, theater, and opera, though she had quickly learned that Harris found Seventh Avenue garment lofts distasteful. He didn't take any interest in her career.

McCardell had also seen the sacrifices her married friends had been forced to make. Mildred Orrick and her husband, Jesse, had had to leave New York in 1932, when they had struggled to find work during the Depression. They had moved to rural Virginia, where Mildred's mother had inherited land, a working grain mill, and a dilapidated miller's house. Jesse, an architect, renovated and modernized the house, paying the townspeople a welcome ten cents an hour to help, before returning to New York to continue job hunting. Mildred stayed behind to raise their two young children. She cobbled together freelance design work as best she could.

It was a particularly fraught time to be a married working woman in America. The Depression had ushered in a backlash against wives in the workplace. The public sentiment had been simmering during the boom years of the 1920s, but it boiled over when millions of men were suddenly jobless. Working women were seen as cruel for robbing jobs from more deserving men. Moreover, any household with a dual income was believed to be unpatriotic, as married women were thought to be working only for extra cash—so-called pin money—to spend on frivolities.

In truth, women supported their households as they took jobs men wouldn't. Low-wage "women's work," in the form of clerical jobs and domestic service, wasn't what men wanted, even as traditionally male jobs in heavy industries, such as steel production and manufacturing, evaporated. More than a quarter of women in the United States entered the workforce during the Depression, and many raised children at the same time. President Franklin D. Roosevelt's New Deal did little to address the concerns of women in that regard. Roosevelt's secretary of labor, Frances Perkins, made history as the first woman appointed to a presidential cabinet. But Perkins, herself a married woman in the workplace, denounced her own. "The woman 'pin-money worker' who competes with the necessity worker is a menace to society, a selfish, shortsighted creature, who ought to be ashamed of herself," she said.

In 1932, Congress passed the Federal Economy Act, stipulating that only one spouse in a married couple could work for the federal government if layoffs were necessary. The act didn't specifically prohibit the woman from keeping the government job, but it was implied that a wife would be the one to defer. Federal rules further discouraged couples from cheating the system by requiring any woman working in the federal government to take her husband's last name. Eleanor Roosevelt, who had remained a member of the Fashion Group even after she became first lady, openly condemned the rule. But polls showed that most of the country, including women, favored limiting the number of women in the workplace.

During the Depression, fashion was one of the few industries where women's work was sanctioned. McCardell did not have to contend with marriage laws, but she did experience a different form of prejudice as a single woman in her thirties. The average age of marriage for a woman was twenty-one years old. She often had to work around her womanhood, as when she needed her father's assistance to open a bank account because she wasn't allowed to do so without a male signatory; or when she was required to have a male chaperone to enter restaurants, clubs, and music venues in New York. As a single woman, she couldn't get a mortgage to buy a home. Chastity and vice laws, including the 1873 Comstock Act, controlled a woman's bodily autonomy from access to birth control and abortions to how she could dress.

McCardell wanted to have agency over her life, and she wasn't alone. Women were fighting for their rights to divorce, to determine when and whether they had children, to choose what they wore. Modern clothes represented a great unshackling of women, in McCardell's estimation. In

1937, she was forming ideas that she would later articulate in writing: "In the days of dependent women—fainting women—delicate flowers—laced to breathless beauty—a girl couldn't cross the street without help. Her mission in life was to look beautiful and seductive while the men took care of the world's problems. Today women can share the problems (and possibly help with them) partly because of their newfound freedom from clothes." Sports clothes, in McCardell's mind, were far more than fashion. They were a physical manifestation of women's increasing power.

◆

On May 11, 1937, McCardell left Paris for London. She would sail home out of Southampton in a few days. She had planned to avoid the pomp and crowds of the coronation of King George VI, but at the last minute she decided to go. The morning of May 12 dawned a perfectly British spring day—overcast and cold. McCardell bundled up and sat in bleachers erected outside the luxury Dorchester Hotel on Park Lane. Hotel staff, dressed in livery, served breakfast to the ticketed guests, and soon the procession of royalty and military passed in front of them.

McCardell looked over the program and made a game of trying to identify who she was seeing. She had no trouble recognizing King George and his new queen in a gold coach led by a team of majestic horses. It was then that the rain began, and a British man in the stands behind her laughed. "We're having the King's weather," he said.

This was originally meant to be Edward's coronation day, before he'd abdicated. Now the people in the stands joked that the displaced king had sent storm clouds from his exile in France to rain on his brother's parade.

In the taxi on the way out of town, McCardell's driver expressed regret over the loss of Edward and Wallis. "It was a pity Mrs. Simpson couldn't have been a maiden lady," he said. The societal rules around marriage, divorce, and a woman's reputation were stringent, especially among the royals.

McCardell sailed out of Southampton on the *Normandie* the next day. Ernest Hemingway was on board, returning to America after months spent fighting in Spain. He told stories of what he'd seen on the ground there. The world seemed to be turning, and quickly, away from the rush of "enormously important trifles," as Wallis Simpson once described her society life, to far darker matters.

Back in her apartment in Murray Hill, McCardell wrote in her notebook about the urgency she felt over the events of the world and the state of her career. She'd recently turned thirty-two, and she felt desperate to bring her original designs into the world. "You're too old to waste time waiting for the right time," she wrote.

She pulled out a sheet of linen stationery embossed with her address and wrote her parents about the trip. She signed off with love, but not before telling them, "It's good to be home again. I've had enough for a while."

CHAPTER EIGHT

Hanger Appeal

1938

The night of the Beaux-Arts Ball, March 24, 1938, an unseasonable heat settled over Manhattan. A warm, sticky breeze blew up from the East River to Murray Hill, where McCardell was getting ready for the party in her apartment on East 38th Street.

The annual Beaux-Arts Ball had long been among New York's most anticipated galas. The men who planned it were members of the prominent Society of Beaux-Arts Architects, and their guests spent months creating elaborate costumes to match the annual theme. A few years earlier, in 1931, the costume ball had taken place in the Hotel Astor, attracting more than three thousand people. Trumpets blared at midnight, announcing a parade of the city's preeminent architects, each dressed as the modern building he'd designed. William Van Alen wore a tubular replica of the Chrysler Building over his torso and a crystal-capped gold helmet. William F. Lamb went as the Empire State Building. Even as the Depression had sunk its teeth into the prosperity and prospects of most New Yorkers, the wealth and vision of a majestic midtown Manhattan continued. Within a year, construction would begin on Rockefeller Plaza.

By 1938, though, Manhattan's robust gala season had diminished. Lavish displays during the eighth year of the Depression were considered callous. The architects had canceled the gala the year before, but now they'd reimagined it as an intimate, scaled-back dance.

The 1938 theme, "Mi-Carême," was an inspired choice. Literally translating as "mid-Lent," the ancient tradition of Mi-Carême dated back hundreds of years to when religious authorities had conceded one night of reprieve halfway through the forty days of penance and dietary restrictions leading up to Easter. It was a time for masquerade balls and feasts and costume-clad revelers dancing in public squares. In 1938, the mid-Lent theme seemed apt, given the austerity and sobriety of many people's daily lives and the hope that economic resurrection might soon be on the horizon.

McCardell had attended a Mi-Carême ball once before, in the spring of 1927, when she and Mildred Orrick were students in Paris. They'd donned dresses and masks and ascended the broad steps of Paris's famed Opera House. Inside, orchestras played, candlelight glinted off endless glasses of champagne, and the whole night had felt golden and intoxicating. It's possible that remembering that ball—and a thwarted trip that she and Orrick had tried to take to Algeria over their winter break—inspired McCardell's outfit for the Beaux-Arts Mi-Carême ball in 1938.

The invitation stated no specific rules for a costume, only that one must be worn. McCardell had sewn colorful cotton fabric into a robe like those worn by Algerian women. Her dress was a simple tunic with a rounded neckline, no discernible front or back, and no zippers or buttons. She now slipped the tentlike dress over her head, and the cotton, soft against her skin, fell straight from her shoulders and nearly to the floor. She added her favorite detail, an "important" belt, as she jokingly called it. She'd taken a wide piece of brown leather to her cobbler to make up a belt studded with shiny brass nail heads. She bloused out the dress above the belt to give the fabric a bit of form, and the simple folds of the skirt fell beautifully.

◆

At the Beaux-Arts Institute of Design on East 44th Street, searchlights illuminated the building's striking Art Deco facade. Tonight, McCardell was a guest of Harris, who was a member of the Institute and helped organize the evening's festivities.

Inside, the exhibition hall had been made over to look like an Italian courtyard. A gallery of painted murals hung from the walls, and an electric blue fabric flecked with bits of silver draped the ceiling, an attempt to reproduce a starry Mediterranean sky. Giant hourglass-shaped paper lanterns cast a warm, diffuse light over the guests crowded inside. A woodsy camphor odor emanated from a copse of live cedar trees flanking the orchestra stage. The gourmet foods of caviar and terrapin soup, once served by tuxedoed waiters in the city's finest hotel ballrooms, were a distant memory, but a fully stocked bar had encouraged people to go out onto the dance floor.

McCardell loathed large events like this one. She had an innate discomfort around crowds of strangers and an allergy to small talk. Her boyfriend, on the other hand, loved to mingle. His seven-year-old son, John, who was at home with a nanny, would later attribute his father's frequent absences and late-night revelry to the fact that Harris was a social climber. John, even at his young age, saw that McCardell was the opposite of his father. That special friend who came around was "dead honest, amusing, thoughtful, down-to-earth, and with no pretense," John would later say, a set of traits that was a great relief to a young boy growing up without his mother and sister and with a father preoccupied with socializing.

Lately, McCardell had been escaping the city's social life altogether to spend her weekends in the quiet countryside of Frenchtown, New Jersey. The small town was an easy train ride away. She had felt a pang of familiarity when she first saw the historic mills and the Main Street shops organized around a creek. In the surrounding countryside, a scatter of farmhouses dotted undulating fields. It had felt a bit like going home to Frederick.

McCardell rented a small nineteenth-century stone farmhouse with primitive plumbing and no electricity but with views for miles and a kitchen fireplace large enough to stand inside. Her small kitchen garden produced herbs, and the horses and a donkey from a neighboring farm often wandered by, nosing her kitchen window for a carrot or a lump of sugar. She whitewashed the kitchen walls, bought proper French copper cookware from a store in Manhattan, and hung it over the mantel. She spent many happy hours cooking French-inspired stews that simmered inside a large pot suspended over the fire. She may not have wanted to copy French clothes, but the food and the wine she would keep. Sipping a glass of Bordeaux and reading a good book by the fire while the aromatic smells of simmering herbs and garlic filled the house was her idea of heaven. "It's lovely," she told her parents of country life, "only candlelight and no telephone."

A covered bridge crossed the nearby Delaware River connecting Frenchtown to Pennsylvania and to Bucks County, where the writers of the Algonquin Round Table had established their own rural retreats. The New Jersey side, though, was the haven of the fashion crowd, and her neighbors included a fellow designer, Vera Maxwell, and the fashion photographer Louise Dahl-Wolfe. The writer James Agee and his wife, Alma, lived in a rambling Victorian on Second Street, where Agee was working on his new book, *Let Us Now Praise Famous Men*. He hoped his manuscript would make vivid the lives of poor Southern sharecroppers who struggled to supply the raw cotton that became bolts of fabric lining the shelves of Seventh Avenue sample rooms.

Harris wasn't one to spend long, quiet weekends in the thrall of nature and one's own thoughts. He preferred skiing and chalets, yachting and yacht clubs. But he tolerated the occasional weekend at the farmhouse, and in turn, McCardell tolerated a few of his social events.

The society pages always covered the Beaux-Arts Ball. The next morning when *The New York Times* published its official list of guests at the Mi-Carême party, McCardell's name wasn't included among those who'd been invited by Harris. In 1938, they continued to keep their relationship a secret. The *Times* reporter might have been describing McCardell, though, when he wrote of a woman in an alluring Romanian peasant dress, possibly mistaking the geographic origin of her costume.

◆

McCardell's name may have been inconsequential to society page writers, but among New York fashion insiders, she was gaining a reputation for her unique style. That year, a writer from *Women's Wear Daily* spotted her on a train to New Hampshire for a ski trip. She was wearing a highly unusual ski coat: a hooded peasant's cape that she'd found at a rural market in France.

McCardell often found inspiration when she escaped the couture shows in Paris and traveled through Europe. In Budapest, she bought bags of cheap, colorful glass beads and had them strung as necklaces and bracelets. She once joked that an appraiser would deem her jewelry collection unworthy of insuring. "Money is not the determining factor in the kind of jewelry I like."

In Austria, she admired the practicality of the traditional dirndl skirt, which women wore on farms. It buttoned at the waist with a long, full skirt that allowed for easy movement. She had come home and made one for herself. It translated well to America, where it was perfect for work attire and for socializing afterward—not to mention cold weekends with friends in Frenchtown, where the skirt billowed out like a blanket around her legs as she warmed herself by the fire. She'd been working on convincing Geiss to let her adapt a dirndl skirt for the Townley collection.

She had an affinity for sturdy work clothes that could double for other uses, and the hood of her peasant's cape provided warmth in the mountains while skiing. In the 1930s, a woman was still expected to wear a hat when she left the house. A bare head was deemed indecent. McCardell loved hats—she would even go on to design a few—but like other modern women, she balked at dress codes that dictated what she had to wear. Municipal codes in many states included rules about hats, both when and how they should be worn and how they should look. After women began using their hatpins to defend against lecherous men, some cities banned any that were longer than nine inches. To which one Chicago woman retorted that if men "want to take the hatpins away from us, let them make the streets safe. No man has a right to tell me how I shall dress and what I shall wear."

Going without a hat in public was a transgressive act, and on that day,

McCardell further shocked with her pull-on hood. A newspaper sketch depicted McCardell, her back to the viewer, her head casually turned over her right shoulder. Her slim fingers clamped a cigarette. She looked like the heroine of a fairy tale in the dark, hooded cape. Her wardrobe "reflects her adventurous approach to new ideas," *Women's Wear Daily* reported. "McCardell leaps a year or so ahead of the design trend."

◆

After the Beaux-Arts Ball, McCardell couldn't stop thinking about her Algerian-inspired costume and how wonderful she'd felt wearing it. She made a second version, this time for work. She bias-cut red slubbed wool into a robelike dress that fell just below her knees. She sewed in ample pockets, like those found in men's trousers. Paired with a wide black leather belt, the dress looked magnificent.

It also solved one of McCardell's biggest design challenges. "Mass production, wonderful as it is, can't take care of fit," she once explained. "Even the fashion model, who seems to be perfectly fitted in a ready-to-wear dress, is likely to be pinned-in at one spot or another where it doesn't show."

She didn't have the luxury of sculpting a dress to an individual body, as a haute couturier could. Ready-to-wear creators "aren't temperamental creatures dreaming in an ivory tower over a drawing board or a length of material," the fashion writer Beryl Williams wrote about McCardell and her fellow designers. "They don't make *a dress*. They, together with the production lines of which they are units, make thousands of dresses."

However, standardized sizing didn't yet exist in women's clothing. In the United States, ready-to-wear garment making began modestly with the rise of textile mills in the early nineteenth century. Low-paid pieceworkers sewed undershirts and pantaloons for men and, by the mid-1800s, women's corsets. During the Civil War, hundreds of thousands of soldiers needed uniforms, requiring measurements to be taken. That resulted in the first ever standardized sizing for men.

After the war, the factories that had produced uniforms switched to making men's suits.

No such data had been collected for women, despite women's wear accounting for more than three-quarters of ready-to-wear manufacturing by the 1920s. The sizing system for women had been made up by manufacturers largely through trial and error. Garments labeled the same size varied widely between brands. Women had to add as much as 25 percent to the cost of their clothes for alterations at home or by a seamstress.

The burden of that added expense during the Depression caught the attention of the Roosevelt administration. In the 1930s, the federal Bureau of Home Economics conducted the first large-scale scientific measurement of women's bodies, which would later inform standardized sizing. The surveyors, it was later revealed, relied predominantly on white women as volunteers, and when their report was published in 1941, it failed to capture the true range of body types in America. Sizing for women would remain a tenacious problem.

McCardell had long considered how her customers might be able to adapt a dress to their body without the need of additional tailoring. With her Beaux-Arts costume, she had an answer. She'd draped material around her body the simplest way she could. The belt then did the work of shaping it. Her Beaux-Arts dress could be as snug or as loose as the wearer wanted, and it didn't have to fit perfectly at the waist.

McCardell added another feature that helped with the fit. She included inches of extra fabric along the hemstitch of her clothes, so that hems could easily be raised or lowered by the wearer. And since hemlines often changed from season to season, the extra fabric made it easier to keep up with the trends. McCardell disliked waste, something she had learned from her parsimonious parents, and that instinct only deepened with the Depression. She imagined clothes that could last for years with easy updates. Her design philosophy wasn't shared by Seventh Avenue. Manufacturers made money only when women bought new clothes. They created demand by outdating last year's styles. McCardell's loyalty, though, was always to her customers.

She took her red wool dress to Henry Geiss and made a pitch to include it in the next Townley collection. Geiss saw a tent of fabric, flat as a pancake off the body. Bessie Sustersic, in making McCardell's original ideas in the sample room, knew that what looked formless off the body would transform into something exquisite on a model. Geiss had no such vision. The dress, he felt, had zero hanger appeal, so it couldn't possibly be of interest to buyers. He said no. "Geiss," McCardell told her friends, "is such a dope."

◆

McCardell wasn't alone in her frustration at being stymied by a male boss. Many of the designers working anonymously in Seventh Avenue lofts were women. The questions of self-promotion and career advancement had become a popular subject among the members of the Fashion Group.

In March 1938, shortly after the Beaux-Arts Ball, Hortense Odlum hosted Dale Carnegie at a Fashion Group luncheon. Four years earlier, Odlum had become the first woman president of Fifth Avenue's Bonwit Teller department store. The business had been on the brink of financial ruin, but under her leadership, sales had tripled. Odlum had invited Carnegie, whose book *How to Win Friends and Influence People* was a bestseller, to tailor advice for women working in fashion. Before the event, she reminded Carnegie that the Fashion Group audience was smart, sophisticated, and cultured. He shouldn't, she said, dumb down his remarks because he was addressing a room of women.

Carnegie jokingly titled his speech "How to Keep a Man." His presentation offered ways for the women to persuade their male bosses to do what they wanted. "Do you realize that probably the most important question anybody in this room can ask himself or herself is this: What do I want out of life and what is the best way to get it? That is so simple and so obvious, you would think that everybody would do it, but unfortunately a lot of people blunder through a lifetime without ever intelligently asking themselves that question." He may have signaled his own answer when he'd changed the spelling of his last name from Carnagey to Carnegie, thus aligning himself with Andrew Carnegie, who'd been one of the wealthiest men in the world.

McCardell knew her answer: She wanted to leave copying behind and produce her own designs. More, she wanted credit for her work. And if she were really dreaming big, she wanted her name on the label. But unless a designer owned their own firm, as Turk had, no designer on Seventh Avenue had their name sewn into the clothes they created. Certainly not a woman.

McCardell left the lecture inspired nonetheless. Afterward, she signed up for courses with the Dale Carnegie Institute. She had no mentor at Townley to teach her how to manage her career advancement, and self-promotion didn't come as naturally as the design work itself. She would have to take her business education into her own hands.

One night a week, she left Townley and walked to the nearby Hotel Astor in Times Square. She joined a group of mostly professional men who were all looking to bolster their communication skills. Each session, she had to stand up and make a persuasive speech on a topic of her choosing, after which she was critiqued. The person who improved the most over the course would earn a symbolic red pencil from Dale Carnegie himself.

The first night, McCardell stood up from her chair to address the group and her stomach churned from nerves. A hot flush rouged her cheeks. Her mind went blank, and her voice disappeared. She eventually managed to stammer something but later had little recollection of what she'd said.

At the next meeting, McCardell pulled Carnegie aside. "I told him he'd have to hold me up, so he did, and he asked me questions and that helped," she reported home in a letter to her parents. By her third meeting, she managed to talk well enough, she thought, and by the last session she aced her speech. At the end of the evening, Carnegie presented her with the red pencil.

During their sessions, Carnegie warned that nagging never worked to achieve your goal. You had to be calculated. You had to be singularly focused and selfish. Carnegie called it *intelligent selfishness*. "Let's do it in a way that will get us what we want instead of the very antithesis of what we want," he said.

If McCardell couldn't talk Geiss into accepting her fully original designs, she realized, she'd just have to get clever about outmaneuvering him.

◆

Her moment came five months later, on August 3, 1938. McCardell learned that a buyer from Best & Co. would be at Townley to shop for the fall season. She hatched an intelligently selfish plan.

She put on the red dress she'd designed based on her Beaux-Arts Ball costume and went to work. What happened next at the Townley headquarters quickly took on the sheen of industry legend.

Geiss greeted the buyer from Best & Co. McCardell was consigned to the back of the warehouse while Geiss attempted to schmooze. He was in a constant state of alarm over his designer's crazy ideas. He didn't want her bringing any of her "damned weird stuff" as he called it, into the showroom and infecting the buyer's opinion of Townley's bread-and-butter numbers, the ones Geiss made her copy from Paris.

As one report later described it, the buyer was getting ready to leave after being less than enthused by Geiss's selections. McCardell hurried across the showroom floor with a carton of coffee in her hand, ostensibly restocking the refreshments. She nearly knocked down the buyer, who paused to take in her dress. "Wait a minute," the buyer said, turning to Geiss. "You didn't show me that one."

When the buyer left that day, Geiss had an order for a hundred dresses. Unlike McCardell's separates concept from 1934, the dress required no explanation. The buyer instantly recognized its style and refinement as McCardell wore it. A fully original Claire McCardell was headed to one of Fifth Avenue's most prestigious stores.

Yet no one would know that the design was hers. Geiss agreed to sell the dress to Best & Co. in a deal that completely anonymized the source. Not only would McCardell's name not appear on the label, neither would Townley's. The dress would become a branded item, part of Best & Co.'s exclusive in-store collection known as the Nada line. A popular way for a store to generate its own brand of clothing was to license designs from wholesale firms such as Townley. It was common practice for retailers to put their labels inside Seventh Avenue–made clothes to build loyalty for their store versus for a manufacturer. Best & Co. did it the legal way by licensing from Geiss, but some stores were known to simply snip manufacturers' labels out of clothes without permission and sew in their own.

McCardell's dress hit stores on September 20, 1938, priced at $29.95 and it sold out in twenty-four hours. Best & Co. immediately ordered 165 more. "I finally designed a dress that is a tremendous success. It will be in *The New Yorker* this week," McCardell wrote home.

On a crisp Saturday in early October, a writer from *Women's Wear Daily* stood at the corner of Fifth Avenue and 35th Street and watched shoppers stroll past Best & Co.'s display, where the dress was featured. "To stand by this window for a few minutes is to get a liberal education in customer reaction to this silhouette. Women of all ages and sizes like it."

"Not only is it becoming to tall and short figures but an exact fit through the waist is not necessary," the journalist Alice Hughes enthused in the *New York World-Telegram*.

McCardell's dress arrived in stores several months after *Vogue* published its annual "Americana Issue." The French-focused magazine, for that issue, turned its attention to the United States. The editors wrote that in America, everyone had the right to look good, not just those who could afford custom-made French finery. Most women craved well-designed, high-quality clothes, but such garments were hard to come by at a good price. That year, the least expensive custom-made dress by the American designer Elizabeth Hawes cost $135. McCardell's dress was, as one prominent designer later described it, a "luscious bargain." The industry soon dubbed it the "Monastic" because it was, according to press material, as simple as a monk's cassock.

With the Monastic, McCardell solved for fit and cost. She also offered a solution to what a woman might wear in office settings and public places. In 1938, dress codes still restricted women from wearing pants in many spaces. Around the same time that McCardell's Monastic dress came out, a kindergarten teacher in Los Angeles named Helen Hulick was being reprimanded for wearing pants. She was in a municipal court testifying against two men who'd robbed her, but the judge stopped the proceedings and told her to go home and change into a dress. She refused. "I like slacks. They're comfortable," she told the *Los Angeles Times*. She spent five days in jail.

The Monastic provided the comfort and ease of pants, including the convenience of pockets. American career women needed to "look businesslike in the office and unbusinesslike at lunch or tea all in the same costume, for you never have time to change," as the writer Margaretta Byers wrote that year in her popular book *Designing Women: The Art, Technique, and Cost of Being Beautiful*. A woman who wished to "move with ease and social security in a chosen sphere of society starts by dressing the part," Byers wrote. "Her costume, if advisedly chosen, conspires to help her relegate it to the subconscious. Therein lies the test for good clothes: the wearer must believe so wholeheartedly in the smartness and suitability of her costume that she can forget about it."

The plainness of the dress, far from being a liability as Geiss had originally presumed, was its strength. Women could use it as a blank canvas over which they could layer their own style in the form of accessories. Best & Co. created an advertising campaign highlighting the dress's versatility, saying it was "as appropriate above a typewriter as a tea table" and was "a dress that women envy, a dress that men admire." A Best & Co. executive marveled that "it takes a lot to foist a uniform on women," and McCardell had done just that. The Monastic, like a man's suit, became a uniform for America's working women.

American design had long been derided as ill equipped to compete with Parisian design, but McCardell upended that assumption nearly overnight. "It has long been the correct thing among fashion dictators to sneer at American ready-to-wear," one fashion journalist wrote. "With yards and yards of rough, exquisitely colored fabrics and an untarnished belief in the beauty of a woman's figure, Miss McCardell has created gowns to make Seventh Avenue sit up."

Suddenly the showroom at Townley was mobbed. Each time the elevator doors dinged open, buyers flooded in, desperate to request their own Monastic design. Geiss hadn't seen it coming and the success of the dress took him completely off guard. The workroom struggled to keep pace with the demand. He hadn't secured enough fabric or extra help to fill the orders. The women behind the counters at Best & Co. were told to presell the dress on deposit, a process that was usually reserved for expensive couture copies coming from Paris. Orders piled up, and Geiss struggled to make a dent in the backlog.

In the fall of 1938, Geiss was the only remaining partner at Townley. He'd never replaced Turk after he'd died, and his other partner had suddenly left in May, telling *Women's Wear Daily* that he planned to take a very long vacation after the chaos of working in the dress business. The Garment District had a way of churning through people. Geiss was now on his own to run things. "The thing that frightens me is that Geiss can't handle the production," McCardell confided to those close to her. Within weeks of the dress's release, McCardell became a victim of the very thing she loathed: copying. One agitated dress manufacturer was reported to have shouted at his staff, "There's a girl up the street making a dress with no back, no front, no waistline, and my God, no bust darts!"

Manufacturers didn't need to book passage on a steamship to France; they had only to walk as far as Fifth Avenue. An exposé in *Fortune* magazine described how design piracy was carried out. Manufacturers shopped Saks' display windows at night. Then they sent their wives or girlfriends in the next morning to buy what they saw, after which their pattern makers copied the dresses.

Then the good wives return the copied dresses for cash, getting more dresses at other stores until these [manufacturers] have their lines together. The stores try to spot the pirates, but it's nearly a hopeless task; for a wife, if too well known, can be changed for a sister or relative willing to give a helping hand. The people sketching a dress from a parked car or candid-camera enthusiasts getting shots of upper Fifth Avenue windows are usually pirates or in the pay of pirates.

Seventh Avenue began copying McCardell's design, meaning that they replicated the style with cheaper fabric and a poorer cut and sold it for $8.95. But it was also being copied "up" and selling for $125 wholesale.

Geiss appealed to the Fashion Originators' Guild of America, an organization that had, since the early 1930s, worked to stanch the production of unlicensed copies. A large percentage of manufacturers were so in the habit of copying Europe, and "were so lacking in originality and in facilities for doing their own designing that they turned their attention to copying the styles which were originated by the leaders in his country," as one article explained.

The guild had begun sending undercover shoppers into stores to spot knockoffs, and they'd had some success in compelling retail stores to remove them. Geiss hoped that the guild might deter stores from carrying fake Monastics. He bought ad space in the trade papers warning that "The Nada Frock, advertised and promoted by Best and Company . . . and manufactured by Townley, Inc. . . . is an original creation designed on August 3, 1938." He warned his competitors that Townley would present all offending copies before the guild's Impartial Retail Committee on Style Piracy and if the dresses were deemed to be copies, stores would be instructed to remove them.

Manufacturers shrugged off Geiss's warning, claiming that McCardell must have copied the dress from abroad. Didn't it look a bit like something that Madame Bruyère was doing that season, or Vionnet? It was difficult to take the high road and claim American originality when the entire industry was predicated on copying French products, and one another.

McCardell kept her parents up-to-date on the latest developments in letters home. "One manufacturer who copied the dress said it's just what the dress business needed, we'll all be busy through the end of October because of it," she wrote. "All the manufacturers on Seventh Avenue seem to have copied it and we spend our time proving that it's my original and not taken from an import. It's better training than I got at Dale Carnegie. I'll be a lawyer when I finish this."

Philip LeBoutillier, the president of Best & Co., gave McCardell the name of an actual patent attorney. The Monastic knockoffs were bad for his business, as well. In addition to the flagship store in Manhattan, Best & Co. had stores in Garden City, East Orange, and Mamaroneck, New Jersey, that were selling McCardell's design under the Nada label. The dress had been such a boon to autumn sales that the store had commissioned winter variations. McCardell designed a version in satin with a V-neck and a version in jersey with patch pockets and a jeweled belt.

The attorney explained that there wasn't much McCardell could do to combat the knockoffs. The horse was already out of the barn. "I seem to have proved to everyone that I did it first, but I should have [patented] the pattern," she told her parents.

At first McCardell was disappointed. As the weeks passed, though, she grew angry. She couldn't abide Geiss's disorganization. He loved to tell her how to design her clothes, but then he couldn't keep his own house in order. He focused his energy on fighting the copies, failing to see that his designer had plenty of other ideas ready to go. The Monastic was Geiss's "big number," and his myopic view excluded all else.

"The controversy about my dress is still going on," the exasperated McCardell wrote her parents later that fall. "It's been copied by every manufacturer in the country. A man who sells copy for *Women's Wear [Daily]* said he'd been in the business twenty-six years and has never seen anything like the way it's spread through the country."

The Monastic should have made Townley a mint and it should have been a springboard into future successes. But the dress that had revolutionized the dress industry, as Geiss would later describe it, was hobbling his company with legal fees instead. The design had become so prevalent that even the Fashion Originators' Guild couldn't help. The Monastic was legally deemed an open item, meaning that Geiss couldn't claim it as his own. Exhausted by production problems and fighting counterfeits, he muttered about closing the business altogether. Seventh Avenue had ground him down.

"Geiss has made such a mess of everything," McCardell wrote. The greatest success of her career threatened to tank Townley Frocks and with it her job.

CHAPTER NINE

Gushing Nitwits

1938–39

In the fall of 1938, as Henry Geiss floundered with production issues, McCardell took matters into her own hands. The success of the Monastic dress emboldened her. She wanted to get credit for her work and to ensure that more of her designs would find their way into stores. To that end, she engaged the help of a new breed of female professional, the fashion publicist.

The year before, she had struck up a professional relationship turned friendship with Peggy LeBoutillier, whose father, Philip, was the president of Best & Co. LeBoutillier was among a subset of Fashion Group members who worked to promote women designers. And like many in that burgeoning field, she took her cues from the indomitable Eleanor Lambert.

Lambert had been a publicist for modern artists such as Jackson Pollock and Isamu Noguchi before she focused on fashion. In the early 1930s, she'd been shocked by how poorly the press treated American designers. Lambert aimed to elevate their work and make them relevant to the average citizen. She was aided in that endeavor by the rapid growth of women entering journalism. Smart, ambitious women were often relegated to fashion coverage. Many expanded that seemingly narrow beat to include stories about the political, social, and economic impact of the garment industry. Lois Long of *The New Yorker*, Virginia Pope of *The New York Times*, and others began bringing intelligent fashion coverage to millions of readers. Still, the American press largely favored the French, and some writers were nothing more than elevated stenographers dutifully copying the haute couture press releases from Paris. Breaking in as an American designer remained difficult.

McCardell invited LeBoutillier to Townley to see her designs and to ask how she might promote them. LeBoutillier loved what she saw. "If I had dreamed of someone who would be good to sell my clothes, I couldn't do better than Peggy," McCardell believed. "She's clever and she's chic."

LeBoutillier understood the inner machinations of New York media and society in ways that McCardell did not. She'd been reared in its cutthroat debutante culture, where a girl's life was assiduously planned. She had attended the Brearley School on the Upper East Side, done a year at Princess Mestchersky's finishing school in Paris, and come out at a grand ball held in the Pierre Hotel in November 1930.

LeBoutillier always aspired to be more than a society bride. In 1933, she announced her professional aspirations by skewering the debutante system in an essay that she cowrote for *Collier's* magazine. She described, with the humor and eye for detail of an Edith Wharton novel, a world of parental striving and outdated Gilded Age rules. A person "rolls out of the debutante machinery as uniform as an engine from an automobile plant," she wrote. "The society girl is less of an individual than any other class member. She is, in miniature, a perfect reflection of American mass production."

McCardell hadn't been raised in the urbane wealth of the debutante class, but she recognized in LeBoutillier a rebellious independence. There were, at every socioeconomic level, rules for a woman's life, and the two quickly bonded over their shared desire to thwart them. Even after LeBoutillier married in 1936 and became known in the society pages as Mrs. N. Bronson Williams, she maintained her maiden name professionally.

LeBoutillier had a talent for generating news coverage about fashion. The year before she visited McCardell at Townley, she'd participated in a media stunt with Saks Fifth Avenue. She and others were photographed on the ski slopes at Sun Valley, Idaho, wearing Saks merchandise. The images arrived at *The New York Times* in fifteen minutes, becoming the first photos sent over a wire for commercial use. The story made news, and the photos were blown up and displayed in the windows at Saks.

Modern photography offered new ways to promote and sell fashion, and LeBoutillier encouraged McCardell to go in front of a camera wearing her own designs. McCardell chose a dress of white jersey fabric that wrapped behind her neck in a halter, with a hem that touched the floor. She donned her custom-made leather belt studded with the brass nail heads and added a matching leather-and-metal-studded wrist cuff.

They hired the Swiss-born photographer Herbert Matter, who posed McCardell against an all-white background with large metal triangles suspended from the ceiling. Matter often collaborated with his sculptor friend Alexander Calder, and the resulting photos looked as if McCardell was a modern goddess surrounded by Calder's mobiles. An American ready-to-wear designer modeling her own clothes in that way was a novelty. LeBoutillier circulated the photos to store buyers and magazine editors. "Peggy is telling everyone how wonderful my clothes are and how I've been hidden by bad selling, etc.," McCardell told her parents.

Next, LeBoutillier moved the Townley winter collection preview from Seventh Avenue to the posh Savoy-Plaza Hotel overlooking Central Park. Manufacturers still largely showed collections in their loft warehouses, but LeBoutillier modeled the event on the French system and included drinks, music, and glamorous décor. She sent printed invitations to the media, which was still uncommon in the Garment District.

At 5:00 p.m. on October 17, 1938, New York fashion media and store buyers crowded into the Lentheric Perfume Salon to see McCardell's latest collection for Townley. "Peggy did it!" McCardell reported afterward. "Carmel Snow, the editor of *Harper's Bazaar*, and Edna Chase, the editor of *Vogue*, and all the girls who write for the newspapers, and all the stylists in the stores were there."

McCardell's collection included several original designs. One novelty caught the eye of fashion writers. In the mid-1930s, hoods began to appear on work wear and athletic gear for men. McCardell often turned to work clothes and menswear for inspiration—as she had when she had appropriated the French farmer's cape as a ski coat. Now she designed a woman's suit jacket of gray flannel with an attached hood. Worn down, the hood folded into a graceful collar. Pulled up, it protected the head and ears. She jokingly called it striptease attire, ready to be pulled on or off depending on the temperature.

At a time when a woman still wasn't considered fully dressed in public without a hat, a hooded woman's jacket was a design risk. It paid off. Marian Young of the *New York World-Telegram* was among those who believed the collared jacket was "the designer's greatest gift to one whose budget is limited. Claire McCardell is outstanding among the American designers who are making really important little outfits that Mrs. Average Woman can afford."

Afterward, McCardell could "hardly get used to praises instead of complaints so quickly," she joked. "They even say I'm one of the only creators of fashions in America."

In the coming weeks, LeBoutillier further harnessed the free publicity of the city's society pages. She wore a McCardell evening gown to the opening of a Broadway play, knowing it would land her in the paper. Peggy "has done me more good than anyone since Turk," McCardell believed.

So had LeBoutillier's father, Philip. On the heels of the Monastic dress success, the president of Best & Co. commissioned her to design outfits for the Norwegian prima ballerina Vera Zorina, that he could then turn into a ready-to-wear collection sold in stores. Zorina was about to make her Broadway debut in the Rodgers and Hart musical *I Married an Angel*, and the glamorous ingenue was being written about in the press with the same breathless attention given Hollywood starlets. McCardell went to Zorina's apartment with a sample room helper to take the dancer's measurements. Her young assistant was "so excited, I was afraid she wouldn't live through it," McCardell later recounted.

McCardell managed to keep her composure, even though she was equally excited. The movement and grace of ballet inspired her. With the Zorina line, McCardell further crystallized her ideas of modern American clothes. She designed streamlined attire that could move with the body, and that didn't include anything overtly precious or extraneous. The life studies classes that she'd complained about to Orrick when they were students at Parsons now came in handy as they provided a foundation for understanding anatomy. McCardell considered the human form, how it moved, how clothes complemented that movement.

For Zorina, McCardell designed evening dresses as well as playsuits, which were active wear ensembles meant for exercising. McCardell made a one-piece romper topped by a whirling, wrap-around skirt inspired by the chiffon warm-up skirts worn by ballerinas.

That winter, Zorina was spotted wearing McCardell's dresses out on the town with the actor Douglas Fairbanks, Jr. She was photographed at the Rainbow Room, the pinnacle of New York dining with its revolving dance floor. One fashion writer described Zorina as "refreshing as strawberries in January," wearing the "fine wardrobe of clothes . . . designed by Claire McCardell, the youthful American who developed the 'Monastic silhouette.'" The exercise suit was so popular that it became the style "after which exercise suits have been cut ever since," Marian Young reported several months later.

McCardell was swiftly becoming the most talked about designer on Seventh Avenue. And it didn't take long for her name to reach the ear of Hattie Carnegie.

♦

McCardell ducked out of work one March afternoon in 1939 and walked up Seventh Avenue in the chill of a bright spring day. A few weeks earlier, a buyer from Hattie Carnegie's boutique had visited McCardell in the showroom at Townley and purchased several dresses. Now Hattie Carnegie had summoned McCardell to a meeting.

McCardell suspected that a job offer was coming. After the Monastic, she'd fielded calls from manufacturers looking to poach her from Townley. One "swell offer" had "money and everything as far as good management and selling goes, but I'd have to make their kind of clothes I'm afraid. I don't know whether I want to give up my kind," she confessed in a letter home.

She walked through Times Square and turned right at 49th Street, where the tall buildings of Rockefeller Center stood luminous in the sun. She passed Saks Fifth Avenue and crossed the noisy chaos of Madison Avenue before entering a prodigious shadow. A large canopy reading "Hattie Carnegie" blotted out the sun. A doorman in a double-breasted jacket and knife-pleated pants opened the door, and as it closed behind her, the beeping and bluster outside was hushed by the plush carpet and muted tones of Manhattan's finest retail establishment.

It's like Paris in here, she thought. And in fact, many pieces of the furniture were antiques imported from France. Hattie Carnegie's retail boutique at 42 East 49th Street was considered one of the premier shopping addresses in the country, and it was nearly as big as a department store in size and scope, running the length of the block. Prominent women milled amid the fox stoles and silk dresses, and McCardell tried not to stare as she recognized some of the famous Hollywood stars and models she saw pictured in magazines.

The first floor held jewelry, bags, and hats, and a ready-to-wear department where copies of Carnegie's Paris-adapted originals were made in standard sizes starting at $110, more than three times the cost of McCardell's Monastic dress. The second floor was where the most exclusive clients had personalized fittings, paying thousands of dollars for the privilege of a custom-made Carnegie wardrobe. The upper three floors held the workrooms where designers sketched and fabricated the clothes.

Hattie Carnegie had never learned to cut a dress or work a sewing machine, and she couldn't so much as hem a skirt, but she knew how to hire the best designers in the business. The clothes in her shop derived from Paris, and she knew how to rework them for the American market. At fifty-two, she wore her own clothes with an unerring confidence that made even young Hollywood stars stop and stare, and she had an intuitive sense of style that surpassed that of her peers. Carnegie liked to say that "taste is so much more important than fashion."

The way a once poor Jewish immigrant with no sewing or design skills had become the doyenne of American high fashion began, it was rumored, on a steamship in 1892. A precocious six-year-old named Henrietta Kanengeiser was traveling with her mother and six siblings from Vienna, Austria, to reunite with their father in the United States. Henrietta asked an adult on board to name the richest person in the country that would be her new home. "Why, Andrew Carnegie, of course" came the reply. That year, the steel tycoon had consolidated his vast holdings into the Carnegie Steel Company, and the size of his bank account rivaled those of the Rockefellers, the Vanderbilts, and the Astors. Henrietta later reinvented herself as Hattie Carnegie, joining the ranks of hopeful immigrants who assumed that surname.

Carnegie and her family crowded into a tenement on the Lower East Side, where her father worked as a tailor in the rag trade. He died when she was just thirteen, and Carnegie went to work. She became a messenger girl at Macy's before joining her friend Rose Roth in opening a small hat and dress shop in 1909. Roth had the tailoring skills; Carnegie was the cunning saleswoman. Carnegie bought out Roth after nearly a decade together and launched Hattie Carnegie Enterprises. It wasn't long before her entire family adopted the last name and went to work for her.

Carnegie knew that advertising her growing business would seem uncouth to the rich clientele she aimed to attract. She shrewdly worked the city's social network instead. She dressed in designs brought back from Paris, wearing them to the opera, the ballet, and luncheons in the finest establishments. Seeing a beautiful hat or dress over the white linen and cold Sancerre at Sherry's restaurant was far more powerful than anything Madison Avenue could generate. The blue bloods did not take their style cues from display ads.

Mrs. William Randolph Hearst, Mrs. W. K. Vanderbilt, and the future duchess of Windsor all went to her for their custom-made wardrobes. They could buy a real Chanel suit for $500 or a Hattie Carnegie interpretation of a Chanel for a bit less. Regardless, they paid. In return, they received impeccable service. Their measurements were kept on file, the saleswomen knew their every desire, and a woman could spend hours in the shop, her crystal tumbler of single-malt whiskey never empty, her ashtray never full, and the latest gossip served on a platter along with delicate canapés. The most dedicated clients spent annually what one wealthy husband estimated to be the cost of maintaining a stable of racehorses. At a time when a house in the United States cost around $4,000, the actress Gertrude Lawrence was known to drop $22,000 on Carnegie clothes in a year.

Carnegie's success came not only from her commitment to customer service but also from being three steps ahead in women's clothing trends. She'd seen, in 1928, that the future of American high design would move away from purely custom-made to include ready-to-wear. She had hired a talented young designer named Norman Norell to help run that new division. She set her prices high enough that common riffraff didn't darken her boutique door, but she also sold less expensive wholesale clothes through national department stores. She had two retail stores in New York and one in Palm Beach, Florida; she had a thriving wholesale business for buyers out of a showroom on Fifth Avenue; and another building that housed Spectator Sports, her division of upscale sportswear.

Designers hoping to break into fashion had long made pilgrimages to Carnegie's boutique, but only a lucky few were admitted. McCardell hadn't thought to apply there when looking for work after Parsons. Carnegie's want ads often cautioned that "only those with high-class experience need apply," and back then, McCardell didn't rank herself as high class. But now she was a world traveler who'd just designed the city's most popular dress. She'd landed Vera Zorina in the fashion pages. Now Hattie Carnegie had come looking for her.

McCardell was led to an office where a handsome figure sat behind a polished desk. At four feet, ten inches, Carnegie's small stature belied her outsize personality. She wore her bottle blond hair swept off her forehead in a deep side part. On her ring finger, an enormous pearl sat inside a setting of sparkling diamonds. Carnegie liked to wear more pearls at her neck, three short strands that usually sat above the bow of a fine silk shirt. A jacket with the cut of a Chanel was often draped on Carnegie's shoulders, ready to be shrugged off as soon as she began pacing the floor of her store. For now, she fixed her discerning blue eyes on McCardell.

Carnegie explained that she was launching a new department under her Spectator Sports division. She was going to call it Workroom Originals. It would supplement her ready-to-wear offerings, but this line would include more than just sportswear. It would have gowns, hats, jewelry, lounging pajamas. Carnegie wanted McCardell as the designer for Workroom Originals. McCardell would create exclusive looks for the Carnegie label in ready-to-wear sizes that would be sold in the 49th Street boutique and department stores around the country. And she would design custom, made-to-order numbers for private clients as needed.

McCardell couldn't help but feel excited as she listened to the most powerful woman in American fashion offer her a job. Working for Hattie Carnegie would mean that she'd officially arrived. Still, she understood the devil's bargain being offered her. "Of course, it is the height of designing," she later explained to her parents. "But I'd have to give up the Claire McCardell stuff and be Hattie Carnegie's designer." Everything created in that building carried the Hattie Carnegie label. McCardell asked if she might have time to think it over. Carnegie, not one for being put on hold, told her to be quick about it.

In the coming days, McCardell debated moving to 49th Street. It would be wonderful to leave Seventh Avenue behind for the prestigious address and the bigger budgets that would come with it. Yet even after all her struggles with Geiss, it wouldn't be easy to walk away from the place where she'd worked for seven years. She wished she could talk it over with Peggy LeBoutillier, but her trusted adviser and friend had recently decamped to her country house near Frenchtown after having a second baby. McCardell missed having her nearby.

After work one evening, McCardell went for cocktails at Joset Walker's new place, hoping to get her friend's counsel. Walker had moved uptown, where she had a lovely apartment and a new boyfriend. She was already talking about marriage. That night, Walker was absorbed by her romance. After so many months of close friendship and travel, McCardell may have felt the sting of her friend's preoccupation. "I'm a bit tired of hearing about how wonderful she is," McCardell admitted to her mother.

Mildred Orrick, meanwhile, had returned to Manhattan from Virginia with her husband and two children. They lived in a railroad flat on East 92nd Street. Orrick was designing dresses on commission, and she'd recently begun working on costume designs for a 1939 World's Fair exhibition called *Futurama*. In a triangle of friendship, one of the three is sometimes left out, and Walker and Orrick had been the closer of the friends lately. Walker frequented Orrick's home, where she doted on Orrick's children. Everyone McCardell's age seemed busy with marriage and family.

McCardell came to a decision without the guidance of her friends. She was going to work for Hattie Carnegie. With her mind finally made up, she allowed excitement to seep in. She would have the best of both worlds: the ability to design ready-to-wear plus the support of Carnegie's prestige and superior production system. She gave Geiss notice, and on March 21, 1939, the news of her departure from Townley made the pages of *Women's Wear Daily*. After the Monastic dress debacle, the new job seemed too good to be true.

◆

In her new position, McCardell believed, she would be able to make all the "crazies" she'd never been allowed to at Townley. She had, after all, been hired on the strength of her original Monastic. She quickly realized her error.

She had barely set up her new sample room when she discovered that Hattie Carnegie kept a vice grip on her designers. Carnegie likened her house style to that of a high-functioning orchestra, where a "well-groomed woman should be as perfectly coordinated as a well-turned-out piece of music."

Carnegie was a perfectionist. She stalked the workrooms, critiquing her designers, noting when a button was one-tenth of an inch off or a shoulder seam was a quarter inch too short. McCardell had spent the past few years deconstructing clothing to its simplest form, and now she was in an atelier known for its precision tailoring. Carnegie assured McCardell that she didn't have to make the Workroom Originals as flawlessly constructed as those in the hand-tailored department, but her new boss did warn that it was important to aspire to perfection, even in wholesale. McCardell's initial feeling that the job might be too good to be true seemed accurate.

McCardell had never worked with so many designers. In such a big organization, she found it hard to tell if she was doing well. Norman Norell became a fast friend and a valuable interpreter as McCardell tried to read Hattie Carnegie's moods and interpret her dictates. Norell had been on Carnegie's staff for a decade, and it was easy to see that Carnegie favored him, probably because he was infinitely patient with her. Before a buyers' preview, Carnegie had kept Norell up all night taking apart the sleeve of one jacket seven times until she decided he'd done it right.

Norell was soft-spoken and kind. With McCardell, he talked frankly and "cut through the crap," as he liked to say, a quality she admired. He explained that Carnegie had a knack for keeping everyone stirred up and for keeping her designers on their toes. Carnegie had a vicious temper. She could reduce even the strongest man to pulp in a matter of seconds and then just as quickly turn sweet again. She had once discovered two fitters chatting during a coffee break, and she had reduced the women to tears with an angry tirade about laziness. She'd stormed out and returned with two handkerchiefs to console them, simultaneously muttering "And furthermore, [you're] crying on my time!"

The best tactic, Norell said, would be for McCardell to keep her head down, keep quiet, and do the work. Oh, and never talk to the press. Carnegie disliked publicity for the designers who worked under her. McCardell had to shelve all the promotional work she'd done with LeBoutillier.

McCardell made a careful study of her boss. Carnegie brooked no fools, which could be frightening to an employee. But it was equally inspiring to see a woman in charge. Carnegie handled the buyers deftly, and "after those 7th Avenue salesmen I've been listening to for so long it's amazing," McCardell wrote. "She certainly makes them cry for it. Then she gives them the prices. She is wonderful."

McCardell acknowledged that Carnegie "can be mean when she wants to be. You can't blame her though. I'm sure I'd do the same thing." Being the rare woman at the helm of a business couldn't be easy.

McCardell embraced her inner boss, particularly as everyone in her private life had a sudden interest in her new employment. Over the years, she had become the fashion and cultural pipeline for her family in Frederick. She bought clothes and accessories for her mother and aunts. She was tasked with buying gifts for weddings and helping her brothers pick out presents for their girlfriends. In addition to hosting her friends and her brothers at her apartment, she was regularly called on to take her parents' friends to tea or a Broadway show. McCardell, ever the dutiful daughter, managed to juggle those engagements even as her work life got busier.

But now friends of the McCardell family began popping in at Carnegie's famous boutique and asking for her by name. "How many more times do I have to tell you to tell people to call me at home," she wrote her parents. "I am not running an amusement stand and I see no reason for having people come to see me only because I work for Hattie Carnegie. I'm not a salesgirl and I'm not standing at the door receiving. I see no reason for entertaining gushing nitwits while I'm supposed to be working."

Speaking of gushing nitwits, Geiss was still kicking. "He's in business one week and out the next. He'll never be able to give it up until he's lost his last cent, I guess," she told her parents. He'd dispatched his secretary to visit McCardell in her new workroom. "They wanted me to come back at any price. It seems they've found that their customers want my clothes." She had declined. Geiss held on for a bit longer, but in the fall of 1939, Townley would close.

◆

On Thursday, April 27, 1939, McCardell's first official design for Hattie Carnegie made its public premiere during a tea dance and fashion show on the Starlight Roof of the Waldorf Astoria. The event was a preview for the House of Jewels, one of the many exhibitions scheduled to open three days later at the 1939 World's Fair in Queens. The House of Jewels was one of the smallest structures built on the 1,200-acre fairground at Flushing Meadows, but it would arguably contain the largest value— over $7.5 million in diamonds and gems from De Beers, Tiffany, and other Fifth Avenue jewelers. To promote the exhibit, sixteen American designers had been asked to conceive outfits that would complement the rare gems. Hattie Carnegie put McCardell in charge of her company's contribution.

The fashion models that night were society women. Mrs. Alan Lehman, a devoted Carnegie customer, sashayed by hundreds of guests wearing McCardell's white summer wool dress cut in simple lines reminiscent of the Monastic dress. Its plunging neckline allowed Cartier's three-strand pearl necklace and gold-and-ruby choker to settle regally on Lehman's neck. Pins studded with rubies, diamond baguettes, and dark topazes shimmered from the lapel. McCardell chose a turquoise paisley for a wide belt and matching hat to complement the topaz.

The printed program credited the dress to Hattie Carnegie, but it was Claire McCardell's name that the judges called when the design earned first prize. They handed her a commemorative silver loving cup. Flashbulbs popped, and sketch artists got to work capturing the winning look.

The next day, the news of McCardell's win ran in several national papers. Carnegie's famous temper now turned on her. Carnegie did not abide publicity for those who worked under her. McCardell was deeply offended at being blamed for the media attention, but she took Norell's advice and kept quiet. Later, she unloaded to her friends and family. "I didn't know there was to be a prize, but I got it, and my name has been all over the place. It wasn't my fault."

The next day, Peggy LeBoutillier called her from New Jersey with gossip. She'd heard that a reporter from *The New York Times* had tried to interview McCardell about the win. Carnegie intercepted him. Instead of McCardell's picture, it was Hattie Carnegie's that ran in that Sunday's paper.

◆

On Sunday, April 30, thick clouds darkened the sky above Flushing Meadows as the 1939 World's Fair officially opened. The epicenter of New York fashion temporarily moved seven miles from Manhattan to Queens, where the Hall of Fashion stood amid two hundred other structures built for the event. The landscape that F. Scott Fitzgerald described as an ash heap in *The Great Gatsby* had been transformed, thanks to $170 million in investment, into "The World of Tomorrow." It was one of sleek, modern industrial design and new consumer products, including air-conditioning, Lucite, and, in the RCA Building, the first commercially available television. Franklin D. Roosevelt addressed a crowd of over 60,000 that overcast Sunday afternoon, and his black-and-white visage was shown on countless little screens around the fairgrounds. He was the first president to appear on television.

The Long Island Rail Road from Penn Station dropped fairgoers just outside the Hall of Fashion, where department stores and manufacturers staged regular fashion shows. One of the new developments displayed at the fair that season—nylon stockings—garnered the most discussion among the women who gossiped over aspic and iced tea inside the Hall of Fashion Café.

After the initial rush of excitement surrounding the fair's opening, McCardell settled into making her line of Workroom Originals. She continued to play with designs that allowed a woman to customize the fit of her clothes. She sketched dresses with belts, sashes, and thin ties at the waist, which she called spaghetti ties. One of the dresses, a brown-and-ivory rayon wraparound with a long sash, was featured prominently in *Vogue* and *Harper's Bazaar* as a Hattie Carnegie original.

That summer, McCardell kept being pulled away from her ready-to-wear collection by requests for custom outfits. Evalyn Walsh McLean, the mining heiress and socialite rumored to own the Hope Diamond, went home with two McCardell dinner dresses. Babe Paley, a *Vogue* editor and one of the best-dressed women in the country, bought a linen suit and a pair of lounging pajamas. A salesgirl sent two McCardell dresses to Hollywood star Joan Crawford.

After work, McCardell was further subsumed by a whirlwind of social events. Carnegie encouraged her to build relationships with potential clients. McCardell attended a party in honor of Anita Loos, the author of the popular novel *Gentlemen Prefer Blondes*. That night everyone wore a blond wig. At another fete, she met the actor John Barrymore and his young wife. The parties drew international guests owing to the World's Fair and because New York was fast becoming a haven for those escaping the growing fascism in Europe.

Irving Harris didn't join McCardell as her date to work events, even though the couple had finally gone public once she had started working for Carnegie. Harris's second wife, Jean, had remarried the year before. She'd landed herself a marquis, a dashing nobleman named Charles Louis d'Espinay-Durtal. They had wed in a historic chapel in Champeaux, France, and when they'd exited, ten huntsmen bleated horns to announce the marriage. Jean wanted everyone to know she'd become a marchioness.

Harris assiduously avoided anything to do with his girlfriend's fashion career. He preferred going dancing on the St. Regis Roof and attending black-tie benefits. McCardell was several years into her courtship with Harris now, and she'd experienced his moodiness and quick flashes of irritation. "He had a strong personality," as John Harris later described his father. "He could be kind and loving one day. The next he could be a son of a bitch." Unlike Jean, McCardell had grown up the only girl in a household of three outgoing brothers, with a strong, present mother and a supportive father. And she'd cut her teeth as a young professional working with the men of Seventh Avenue. She knew how to hold her own against the male ego, even one as outsize as that of Harris.

McCardell attended fashion events with her coworkers instead. She noticed that people perked up when they learned she worked for the famous Hattie Carnegie. One buyer for Bergdorf Goodman fell over himself chatting her up at a dinner party, completely forgetting that they'd met a number of times when she'd worked on Seventh Avenue. "I always thought he was an awful pain in the neck, but he seems to be very nice," McCardell reported afterward, "or maybe it's because I work for Hattie Carnegie now." Part of her job was to see and be seen—while, of course, never being so "seen" as to steal media attention from Hattie Carnegie.

One very influential member of the media did get to know McCardell, if only by accident. Diana Vreeland had recently been appointed the fashion editor at *Harper's Bazaar*, and she was a regular at Carnegie's boutique. Vreeland was an exclamation mark of a woman: tall, angular, lavishly dressed, and smitten with the world. She had grown up wealthy and connected, her address book a roster of European royalty. "I mean a new dress doesn't get you anywhere; it's the life you're living in the dress," she liked to say.

The story, as Vreeland would later tell it, was that she took in an expensive French jersey fabric in a light beige color to have a "little two-piece Chanel kind of uniform" made, but she got a simple one-piece McCardell instead. She loved it so much that she asked to meet the designer, sparking a lasting and fortuitous professional relationship.

The story was likely an embellished fib. Vreeland was a stickler about her clothes. She would never have entrusted yards of expensive French fabric to a designer without a firm understanding of the look she wanted, but she never let facts get in the way of an excellent anecdote. "Fake it!" she liked to say about storytelling. So when she later recounted first meeting McCardell, she gave it her signature panache. What the story expresses, though, is a truth about McCardell. She wanted simplicity in her designs, and she didn't want to be swallowed by the Carnegie aesthetic. She certainly wasn't about to make a Chanel "uniform."

The story also speaks to Vreeland's desire to be at the center of fashion history—in this case, the discovery of Claire McCardell. Before entering New York journalism, Vreeland had owned a custom lingerie shop in England. She claimed to have sold Wallis Simpson three negligees in the early days of her affair with Prince Edward, intimating that it was Vreeland's discriminating taste and quick turnaround time—the delicate lingerie was handmade in just three weeks, in time for the lovers' first trip together—that had sealed the deal. Whatever the actual story of that Carnegie outfit, Vreeland saw McCardell's brilliance. She thought her to be a "wonderfully independent, clear thinking and creative person." Vreeland decided to keep an eye on the young designer.

Not everyone was as impressed. The British actress Gertrude Lawrence, in New York to star on Broadway, was apoplectic over a very plain dress that McCardell had suggested for her. Norman Norell had come to McCardell's rescue by adding sparkly beads, and Lawrence had been appeased.

McCardell's sample room fit model, Connie Wald, had followed McCardell from Townley, and she had concerns about McCardell's longevity in the job. Hattie Carnegie customers wanted to be "poured and stitched right into their clothes," she said, and "they found Claire's things too plain for the money." McCardell struggled to suppress her own style in deference to that of her boss.

In August, McCardell did not pack her steamer trunk for Paris as she had for years at Townley. She was a cog in Carnegie's well-staffed enterprise and was no longer required to attend the seasonal shows. Carnegie went herself, usually taking just one employee along. Carnegie reveled in the busy chaos of the premieres. She took a suite at the Ritz, where the telephone rang every few seconds and her sitting room filled with Paris designers hoping to sell to the famous American. A milliner once presented a new collection of hats while Carnegie soaked in the bathtub.

Carnegie returned from France on August 28, 1939. American reporters greeted her as she stepped off the *Normandie* wearing, they noted, a pinstripe navy flannel suit and a cranberry pillbox hat. Paris designers, she said, had the craziest notion. They wanted to bring the full corset back. "I can't believe American women will suddenly wrap themselves up in corsets when the uncorseted waistline is so much more natural and much prettier," she said. Of course, she'd bought several of the torso prisons anyway. She dutifully followed Paris's lead.

The milliner Lilly Daché also returned on the *Normandie* that day, but she had a different interpretation of the shows. "The 1939 collections prove that [the French] are afraid of war," she said. And if war breaks out, "all the rich, elaborate and regal clothes women plan will be thrown away."

Four days later, on Friday, September 1, Adolf Hitler's army invaded Poland. On September 3, 1939, the United Kingdom and France declared war on Germany.

CHAPTER TEN

The Specter of War

1939-40

I n the fall of 1939, discussions in New York quickly turned to whether haute couture could continue with Europe embroiled in war. The November issue of *Harper's Bazaar* aimed to settle the question: "The French have decreed that fashion shall go on, even in the dark, anxious night."

The Paris designers assured American buyers and editors that the spring fashions would be presented in January as usual, even as Chanel and Vionnet shuttered their boutiques. The couture industry was a major component of France's economy, employing not only thousands of workers in Paris but many more across the country. Trade had already ceased in Europe owing to the war, so the neutral Americans remained Paris's primary hope. If the French could somehow keep designing and the Americans could somehow keep buying, there might be a way to save haute couture.

In December, Hattie Carnegie announced that she would join a small group of buyers and editors sailing to Paris. She asked McCardell to join her. The invitation could have signaled Carnegie's investment in her young designer's future; she could train McCardell's eye to see what she liked as they worked the couture shows together. But it could have also been McCardell's status as an unmarried and childless woman. Not every designer employed by Carnegie wanted to go shopping in a war zone.

McCardell waited until Tuesday, January 9, 1940, to break the news to her parents in a letter, even though she'd recently been in Frederick for the holidays. She hadn't wanted to ruin Christmas. She began her letter with the equivalent of nervous chatter, recounting a recent ski trip to Vermont with friends and complaining how cold it was in New York, before she finally got to it. "Can't decide whether I should tell you or not but I'm going to Europe Saturday with Miss Carnegie."

They would sail on the United States Lines' SS *Washington*, headed to Genoa, Italy, which remained a neutral port. From there, they would take a train to Paris. "It should be very exciting because only a few fashion people will be going. Please don't worry about it. It's a wonderful opportunity and I can break my neck skiing, too."

Even as McCardell downplayed the dangers of the trip, she felt anxious. She had been nine years old when the British ocean liner *Lusitania* had been torpedoed by a German U-boat in May 1915. The bomb had killed 128 Americans and helped pull the United States into the world war.

More immediately alarming was what had transpired on September 4, 1939. A British passenger ship, the *Athenia*, had been bombed by the Germans. More than 1,400 people were on board, including travelers from Baltimore. Over a hundred people died, 28 Americans among them. After, President Roosevelt reasserted the United States' neutrality while also limiting Americans' trips to Europe unless "imperative necessity" could be proven. The American fashion editors and buyers were able to make the case for their voyage given the country's millions of dollars in trade with France.

A few days before their departure, Hattie Carnegie pulled out of the trip. Her family had convinced her, after weeks of pleading, not to go. Carnegie may have changed her name, but she was famous and she was Jewish, and the idea of sailing toward the Nazis while Jewish refugees were scrambling to sail away seemed beyond reckless. Carnegie reluctantly agreed, but the rumor around the shop was that she was quite angry about it. Her decision to stay in the United States was so last minute that the "Ocean Travelers" report in *The New York Times* mistakenly placed her among the first-class passengers on the *Washington*. In fact, it was Carnegie's ready-to-wear buyer, Marjorie Franklin, who was on board with McCardell. "Miss Franklin is young and very gay and very nice but I'm a little sorry not to see Miss Carnegie operate in Paris," McCardell lamented. Carnegie's absence added a layer of pressure to an already harrowing journey. "She always complains about what she gets when she doesn't go to Europe herself."

McCardell filled a suitcase instead of a steamer trunk; her instinct told her that she should pack lightly for the trip. She woke on the morning of Saturday, January 13, 1940, to overcast skies and a chilly wind. She made her way to Pier 59, where the *Washington* loomed large in the harbor. Massive signs hung on the hull and clearly identified her as belonging to the neutral United States Lines—a stark reminder of the dangers that lurked in international waters.

She joined the 165 passengers who made their way aboard. They were the largest group of civilians to sail to Europe from the United States since war had been declared. The roster included fashion editors, buyers, retailers, and designers as well as reporters from *Collier's* magazine, employees of and ambassadors from the State Department, and men from Standard Oil. A *New York Times* journalist grabbed Carmel Snow, the editor of *Harper's Bazaar*, as she boarded. What did Snow think awaited her in Paris? Snow declared that the couturiers' spring collections would surely be as brilliant and elaborate as ever, war be damned. "I'd make a big guess that the styles will go in for femininity," she said. "They'll be very gay and will not show the influence of war. I'm sure there will be corsets." An attaché at the French Embassy, Count Gabriel de Gramont, also spoke to the reporter. He predicted that the war would be over in no time. "The Germans will attack this Spring and will be stopped. Then the Hitler machine will collapse."

◆

The seas churned and the wind whipped their first day out. The passengers rattled about a ship that had been designed to hold six times as many passengers. Everyone was on their best behavior. "I suppose it's because they all have pretty serious reasons for going to Europe," McCardell wrote. She and Franklin played bridge and read. They wore thick tweed suits to stay warm in the winter chill and reclined in lounge chairs on deck.

Those aboard reported a feeling of camaraderie with "all rivalries forgotten. Bendel loved Bergdorf. Bergdorf loved Saks. Even *Vogue* loved *Bazaar*," as *Harper's Bazaar* reported. The last was hard to believe, given the ongoing rift between *Vogue* editor Edna Woolman Chase and *Harper's Bazaar* editor Carmel Snow, who'd once been Chase's loyal protégée.

Some in the group had brought emergency rations such as sardines, tinned soup, and instant coffee. Wartime deprivation had not yet reached the luxury liner, though. The chefs outdid themselves, even serving caviar. Everyone seemed hell-bent on preserving normalcy. McCardell and Franklin joined their fellow passengers in dressing for dinner. Cocktail parties kicked off the evenings, with plenty of dancing after. Franklin was declared to be the best dancer and the belle of the boat. Romances flourished, as they always did on steamships, even as they churned toward war.

After several days at sea, the ship approached the southern coast of Spain. The *Washington* dropped anchor in the Port of Gibraltar. The British stronghold monitored ships as they maneuvered in the Atlantic and the Mediterranean, and the *Washington* had to sit off the coast for eleven hours as they waited for inspectors to search the cargo for anything nefarious.

The crew served McCardell and her fellow passengers tea on deck in the afternoon. Across the harbor, the Rock of Gibraltar rose in the distance, its dramatic peak soaring over 1,300 feet above sea level. McCardell couldn't know, as she sipped her hot tea and took in the view, that tunnels were being blasted within that limestone mountain to house a massive underground military city replete with barracks, offices, and an operating theater—or that in two years, America's own General Dwight D. Eisenhower would command European operations from within. Looking around, she saw no battleships and no excitement. In fact, the harbor seemed quiet and full of only "funny looking" freighter boats.

They continued on and finally disembarked at Genoa, Italy. Inches of snow, once glistening and white, had turned sooty and slippery from being trampled by so many feet. The Parisian couturiers had arranged for a train to ferry the Americans to Paris, but there was confusion over which one to board. Many trains had been co-opted for military purposes. McCardell felt sorry for the travelers burdened by too much luggage. Even so, she and Franklin scrambled to get onto the train with their suitcases. They were among the lucky ones. The train was so overcrowded that several of the buyers were forced to stay behind and find other means of transport.

McCardell rode for several hours perched on her luggage in the aisle along with Polish soldiers traveling from Hungary to join the French Army. At the French border, the train stopped, and they were ordered off. McCardell and Franklin retrieved their luggage and went back out into the frigid winter weather. They stood in line for over an hour waiting to have their passports stamped. The cold from the snow seeped through the soles of McCardell's shoes and chilled her. More than anything, she hated being cold. And with coal rationed, the trains had no heat.

Night fell, but their carriage remained dark so as not to become a moving target. McCardell marveled at Carmel Snow's energy and positive attitude throughout the long, arduous journey. Snow prided herself on being tough. Her native Irish blarney continued into the inky evening as she kept the people around her entertained.

After twenty-four long hours without water, food, or sleep, the train pulled into the Gare de Lyon. McCardell was exhausted, hungry, and in desperate need of a bathroom. She hadn't lost her suitcase, though, which she counted as a small miracle.

A light snow had dusted Paris, and they had difficulty finding transport to their hotel. Most buses, taxis, and even private cars had been requisitioned to transport troops. Towers of sandbags hid the monuments. Sausage balloons, meant to confuse enemy pilots, swayed above the Tuileries Gardens.

"I'd forgotten how gloomy Paris was in January and now the specter of war makes it awful," McCardell wrote in a letter. "Everyone is mobilized. Even the photographers for *Vogue* and *Harpers* wear uniforms."

It had been five months since Germany's invasion of Poland, and Parisians were on tenterhooks waiting for Hitler's next move. Aside from a few skirmishes, no significant fighting had occurred since war had been declared, spurring some to call this time the Phony War. Bettina Ballard, the Paris fashion editor of *Vogue*, later wrote in her memoirs that everyone in France "had been wound up like a clock and never allowed to strike." The city was "corroded with boredom, and the abnormal tension of waiting for something, you couldn't imagine what, had a numbing effect."

The arrival of the Americans lifted the spirits of the French. There was a "fever of Franco-American enthusiasm," according to Ballard. On February 2, McCardell attended an evening reception thrown by the French government as a show of gratitude. Their hosts gave impassioned speeches, saying that the Americans were saving France by saving haute couture. The act of buying was an act of rebellion and a dagger to the heart of fascism.

At night, darkness drenched the City of Light. Blackout curtains covered windows; street lamps were extinguished. Many restaurants closed early. The famed bistro Maxim's still bustled, though, and gas masks littered the coat check room. The restaurant became insular, smoky, and hot, the noise and chatter held in by the thick drapery. The French government arranged for a handful of nightclubs to stay open late for the visiting Americans, but the theaters that McCardell had frequented during her routine trips for Townley were closed. Some were now soup kitchens for out-of-work artists. After dark, Parisian women wore white gloves that would make them visible to vehicles.

McCardell and Franklin spent the next week visiting the couture houses that remained open. The realities of war couldn't help but creep into the 1940 spring couture collections. The color navy dominated that season, echoing the blue of the lampshades used to dim interior lightbulbs during blackouts.

Claire McCardell, age seven, wearing a dress she made with Anna Koogle. *Maryland Center for History and Culture, H. Furlong Baldwin Library, Claire McCardell Photograph Collection*

LEFT: McCardell around the time she studied home economics at Hood College in the 1920s. *Maryland Center for History and Culture*

BELOW: McCardell stands with her brothers (from left to right) Adrian, Max, and Bob in front of their family home, 1954. *Courtesy of the McCardell family*

Ink portrait by Parsons classmate Chester Slack, 1927. *Maryland Center for History and Culture*

McCardell on a steamship wearing a "menswear" tweed suit, circa 1930s. *Courtesy of the McCardell family*

Friend and fellow designer Mildred Orrick (far left) with McCardell in Paris, 1927. *Courtesy of Sarah Orrick*

McCardell kept scrapbooks of her successes, including this 1938 ad for her breakout design of the Monastic dress.
Maryland Center for History and Culture

ABOVE: The designer was her own best model. She wears a version of her Monastic dress, circa 1939.
Maryland Center for History and Culture

LEFT: McCardell believed women deserved pockets and she fought to include them in all her designs.
Maryland Center for History and Culture

McCardell, standing at left, presents clothes to buyers inside a Seventh Avenue garment loft in 1940. New York Fashion Week had yet to be invented.
Bettmann/Getty Images

McCardell with a model inside the Townley loft, 1953.
Maryland Center for History and Culture

Inside her Seventh Avenue office at Townley, 1953.
Maryland Center for History and Culture

McCardell spent weekends at a rustic farmhouse in Frenchtown, New Jersey, where she gardened, cooked, and hosted fashion industry friends. *Maryland Center for History and Culture*

McCardell in the kitchen at Frenchtown. *Hood College, Beneficial-Hodson Library, Archives and Special Collections/ McCardell Family*

Irving Drought Harris (left) with McCardell a[nd] a friend having cocktai[ls] in Frenchtown. Harris and McCardell met on [an] ocean liner in the 1930s when Harris was still married to the heiress [of] a sugar fortune.
Courtesy of the McCardell family

Harris and McCardell b[y] the fire in Frenchtown. The two dated for years living largely separate lives, until personal tragedy and a world wa[r] brought them closer.
Courtesy of the McCardell family

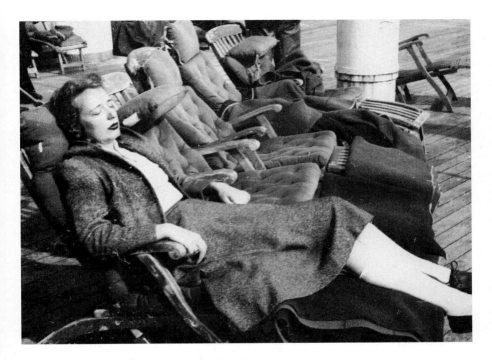

ABOVE: McCardell naps on the deck of a steamship, circa 1940, during one of her many trips to Paris for the fashion openings. World War II would end these trips.
Maryland Center for History and Culture

LEFT: A model wears McCardell's Office of Civilian Defense uniform, circa 1941.
Maryland Center for History and Culture

Portrait of McCardell taken by her friend, the photographer Louise Dahl-Wolfe.
Untitled, circa 1940s. Photograph by Louise Dahl-Wolfe.
© *Center for Creative Photography, Arizona Board of Regents*

FAR LEFT: An original 1942 Popover wrap dress with attached oven mitt. *Image copyright © The Metropolitan Museum of Art. Image source: Art Resource, NY*

LEFT: This evening gown worn by McCardell appears to be one piece, but it is actually a halter top and a skirt and represents the designer's concept of versatile mix and match separates. *Maryland Center for History and Culture, Gift of Mr. and Mrs. Adrian McCardell*

Louise Dahl-Wolfe juxtaposed McCardell's edgy plaid playsuit against the modernist house designed by architect Frank Lloyd Wright. *Untitled, circa 1942. Photograph by Louise Dahl-Wolfe. © Center for Creative Photography, Arizona Board of Regents*

McCardell's pastime of skiing inspired many of her fashion innovations, including the "Superman Hood" she wears at left to keep her ears warm, along with a pair of her patented SunSpecs sunglasses, which she designed in 1952 as a chic alternative to the "goggle-eyed owlishness that passes for sunglass fashion today," her publicist, Eleanor Lambert, wrote.
Maryland Center for History and Culture, circa 1950s

McCardell, wearing her Future Dress, became the face of the American Look, 1945. *Photograph by Erwin Blumenfeld. © The Estate of Erwin Blumenfeld 2024*

McCardell's love of swimming prompted the designs of her form-fitting (and scandalous) bathing suits. *Untitled, circa 1945. Photograph by Louise Dahl-Wolfe. © Center for Creative Photography, Arizona Board of Regents*

McCardell on the beach. *Maryland Center for History and Culture*

McCardell and Harris picnic at the beach. McCardell was known for her infectious laugh. *Maryland Center for History and Culture*

McCardell poses for a photo while sketching on a drawing board. By the 1940s, she'd become a household name and had begun designing everything from jewelry, ballet flats, and outerwear to paper dolls and a signature fragrance called White Sash.
Maryland Center for History and Culture

When years of fabric rationing finally ended, McCardell designed her 1947 spring line to include longer, fuller skirts and a fitted bodice.
Untitled, circa 1947. Photograph by Louise Dahl-Wolfe. © Center for Creative Photography, Arizona Board of Regents

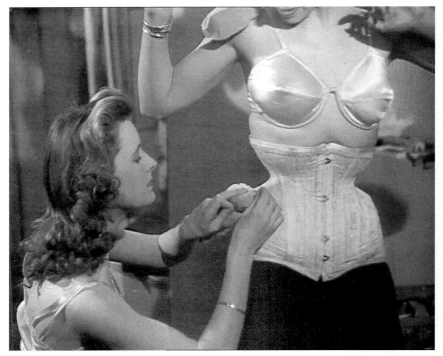

In 1947, Parisian designer Christian Dior unleashed his "New Look." A still from a British newsreel shows models donning the severe corset, padded bra, and shoulder and hip pads made for Dior's clothes. *Courtesy of British Pathé*

American women picket outside Christian Dior's hotel, protesting his designs. September 1947. *Bettmann/Getty Images*

In April 1950, McCardell, standing far right, traveled to Washington, DC, to receive a professional achievement award from the Women's National Press Club. President Harry Truman presented the certificate during a gala dinner. Fellow honorees included dancer Martha Graham, far left, and actress Olivia de Havilland, to the right of President Truman.
Bettmann/Getty Images

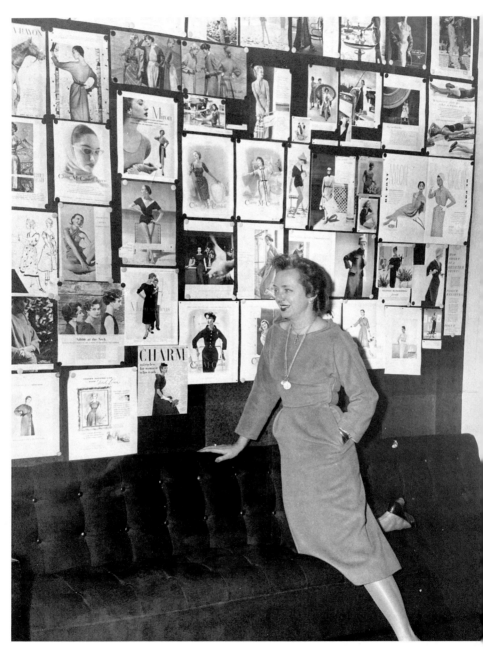

McCardell in the Townley showroom at 550 Seventh Avenue poses in front of a wall of press featuring her designs, circa 1950s. *Courtesy of the McCardell family*

It was difficult for McCardell to focus on clothes as the threat of violence and starvation hung in the frigid winter air. "There are no bombs and no actual fighting at the front but there is a sickness that is much worse than the war. It's the change, the end of something and not knowing what it will be after," she wrote home. "Starving and cold and not knowing what to do next is almost worse than dying."

She and Franklin purchased as many clothes and as much fabric as they could—they had money to spend, thanks to Carnegie—but it was difficult to find items to buy. Vendors told McCardell that there would likely be no more silk or wool after their current stocks were gone. McCardell saw the effects of leather rationing, too; the supply of new purses and shoes was limited.

McCardell and Franklin left Paris on February 8 and traveled south to Genoa. They spent three lonely days in port waiting to sail home on the SS *Manhattan*. Once on board, as the coast of Italy receded from view, McCardell realized that she'd been holding her breath for days. The voyage came as a relief, but it had none of the defiant optimism and revelry of the boat ride over. Refugees crowded the decks—the ship had been oversold by the hundreds—and somberness pervaded the journey. McCardell was heading home, but many of her fellow passengers were leaving everything they'd ever known.

Three months later, the Phony War ended. In May, Germany launched a brutal offensive on the western front. The French government fled Paris, and on June 14, 1940, Nazi soldiers goose-stepped down the Champs-Elysées.

◆

Four weeks after Paris fell, the Fashion Group convened at the Biltmore Hotel on Madison Avenue in Midtown. McCardell huddled with fellow members around tables set for a light lunch, and they considered their uncertain future. New York, home to a $1.5 billion garment industry, was clearly the heir apparent to global fashion, but how exactly was a commercial enterprise founded largely on Parisian influence to come into its own?

Mary Lewis kicked off the discussion. The former marketing executive at Best & Co. had helped promote McCardell's Monastic dress in 1938, and for the past year she'd been organizing the US fashion pavilion at the World's Fair. She acknowledged that New York had a steep hill to climb. Paris fashion edicts had reigned for centuries. In normal times, as many as five thousand new garments were shown during the ten-day couture openings, and they infiltrated every level of the US garment industry. The designers of even the most basic and inexpensive clothes took their style cues from Paris. Where would America get her ideas? Additionally, US textile mills made mostly humble cottons, not laces and silks. Luxury fabrics would no longer be coming from Europe.

Yet Lewis believed that being physically cut off from Paris offered a rare opportunity. "For haven't we always been somewhat in the position of the pampered wife or child who never had to face reality, but who faces it and shows her mettle, in adversity?" she asked. "We must now answer the question, 'Are we mice or designers?'"

It was time to abandon the long-standing tradition of keeping American designers' anonymity. "Let us highlight our designing personalities more—they have names—let us make them known to the public," Lewis said as she reached a fever pitch. "Nineteen-forty, perhaps, marks the end of an epoch—whether it also marks the beginning of a great one in American fashion history is for us to say."

PART III

Clairvoyant Claire

(1940–45)

CHAPTER ELEVEN

Shooting Craps

Fall 1940

Shortly after Paris fell, McCardell had a conversation with her oldest brother, Adrian. They spoke about the war in Europe. The loss of Paris had shocked the country, and they wondered if the United States could maintain its neutrality. Adrian, thirty-two, held a master's degree from Harvard now, and he'd followed their father into banking. Bob, twenty-seven, lived in Frederick and worked in the family candy business. Max would turn twenty-four that summer. All three fell within the draft age range, should it come to that.

The conversation turned to life in New York. McCardell admitted that she no longer wanted to work for Hattie Carnegie. The concern that had given her pause initially—that she would have to "give up the Claire McCardell stuff and be Hattie Carnegie's designer"—had proved to be a real issue. She didn't enjoy making $200 lounging pajamas for society ladies or sewing sequins on dresses for Gertrude Lawrence. She aspired to make clothes for women like herself. The eighteen months she'd spent away from Seventh Avenue confirmed what she truly desired, which was to design for the masses.

McCardell's ambition had grown during her time with Hattie Carnegie. She'd begun doodling garment labels in her notebook that read "Claire McCardell Clothes." She sketched a silhouette of her face from the side with the words "Claire McCardell" underneath. And as if in rebuke to the fussy formality of Hattie Carnegie's house style, she wrote

"Simplicity Can be Spectacular" and jotted down words such as "messy casual." She was dreaming of starting her own label. Mary Lewis had said in her July speech that it was high time American designers came into their own. McCardell determined to do just that.

She left Hattie Carnegie that summer. No public announcement explained her departure. Carnegie didn't court such publicity, of course. The rumor was that both women had agreed to the split and that it had been cordial.

McCardell returned to Seventh Avenue. A small manufacturing firm called Win-Sum scooped her up immediately with a job offer of head designer. The company wasn't nearly as large or reputable as Townley had once been, but its business was in a prestigious new loft building at 550 Seventh Avenue along with many of the best sportswear labels.

The country's retailers assured American women that they had enough French designs to last for months. Bergdorf ran ads letting customers know that its buyers had bought as many French clothes and hats as they could on their final trip to Paris. The designers on Seventh Avenue, however, admitted to feeling paralyzed. The fashion reporter Marian Young heard some lamenting about where they might "find inspiration for the hundreds of designs which will be ready for distribution in September."

McCardell had no such concern. She had a sketchbook—and a closet—full of ideas and clothes. Her new bosses at Win-Sum assured her that they wanted original designs. They believed that buyers would be eager to see novel American ideas now that Paris was cut off from the rest of the world. For the first time in her career, McCardell was being given the green light to produce without the influence of France.

◆

In August 1940, as McCardell readied her collection for Win-Sum, New York's mayor, Fiorello La Guardia, summoned twelve female fashion editors to his office. La Guardia had been New York's powerhouse leader since 1934, guiding the city through the Depression, tamping down corrupt Tammany Hall politicians, curbing the Italian mob's stranglehold on the city, and earning national attention for his willingness to work across party lines. He had also been an early and outspoken critic of Germany's rising antisemitism. He'd denounced Nazism as he worked to support American and immigrant Jews.

On that day, as the twelve journalists took seats around his conference table, the mayor's focus was set on making New York the clothing capital of the world. But first he needed someone to explain fashion to him. "I'm interviewing you today; you are not interviewing me. I want to learn something about the fashion business," he said.

The women in the room were uniquely positioned to advise the mayor. They'd been covering Paris fashion for years. La Guardia knew the nuts and bolts of American manufacturing— he had long supported the garment industry—but the anonymous designers toiling in its employ were unknown to him. And "fashion" was a mystery.

"What's all the conflict about in the dress designing field?" the mayor began.

Going around the table, the women explained that Parisian designers had long provided direction for the American market, to the diminishment of domestic talent. One editor explained how fashion was dictated by those at the top of the social set and that snobbery, and a bias for Parisian clothes, set the trends. The women explained what the American designer Elizabeth Hawes had dubbed the French Legend. The power of the French clothing business meant that "for decades nobody ever questioned its God-like quality," Hawes once wrote.

Still, the Americans were organized and enterprising. They'd built a national system for the manufacture, distribution, and advertising of clothes. Up until Paris fell, that system had largely been in service to French design. But imagine if American designers could be plugged into that existing infrastructure.

The mayor listened, rapt and mussing his hair as he did when deep in thought. "Snobbery can't be the controlling power any more; times are changing," he told the room. " . . . We boast of our progress, our enlightenment and wealth, yet there are hundreds of thousands of women who never have anything soft next to their skins, and have not got pretty dresses; we must see to it that they get them."

La Guardia now understood that he needed to boost the status of designers who, like novelists and composers, needed protection. The United States required an organization like the Chambre Syndicale de la Haute Couture. He vowed to help create one. "Then if France regains her soul and Paris comes back, we will have established a wholesome and stimulating rivalry."

La Guardia would approach the challenge, as one reporter later described, with the same explosive energy that he gave to four-alarm fires and the prosecution of New York mob boss Lucky Luciano. The result, in a few months' time, would be the creation of the New York Dress Institute. It would function much like France's Chambre Syndicale and work to both promote and protect the designs of American clothiers.

◆

The normally frenetic atmosphere on Seventh Avenue was especially heightened as fall collections were cobbled together without Parisian input. McCardell thrived under the deadline, reveling in the familiar breakneck pace of mass production. She marshaled the stored-up creative energy that had languished in her final stagnant weeks at Carnegie's boutique.

On Seventh Avenue, manufacturers tended to stick to a narrow lane. They made dresses and coats only. Or they made sportswear but not evening gowns. McCardell imagined a business as diverse as the one run by Carnegie. That season she branched out and designed jewelry, hairpins, and belts to accompany her dresses and suits.

With European trade cut off, McCardell went directly to American textile companies, including the textile producer Hope Skillman. Skillman was one of the first women in the country to own her own textile mill, and she warmly welcomed McCardell whenever she knocked on the factory door. Skillman was impressed that McCardell used fabrics such as cotton for fashionable evening clothes when few other designers had dared to do so. McCardell found the collaborative act of selecting and designing fabrics with manufacturers as creatively profound as designing the clothes themselves.

Options for synthetics had expanded in recent years, thanks in part to female scientists who'd studied home economics. They were developing and testing materials in textile labs at universities and conducting studies on materials such as hosiery thread to determine what best held up when worn by working women. The domestic textile companies were developing alternatives to Japanese silks and French laces, which were no longer available because of the war.

Once again, McCardell hired Peggy LeBoutillier to help promote her. LeBoutillier had a new job working for N. W. Ayer, one of the oldest and largest advertising firms in the country. She worked on a lucrative diamond account and had learned how to position products as coveted and desirable. Now McCardell was the product, and one of the few American fashion designers being pitched to the press in this way. LeBoutillier crafted a story for the Paris-starved media, titling her three-page release "The Cult of Claire McCardell."

"Claire McCardell is the crystallized dream of every small town, fashion-career-struck girl," LeBoutillier wrote, and she "rose the hard way. She tramped the blazing pavements for jobs, lived in measly furnished rooms with other ambitious girls," and once "fell ill, returned home for doctoring, and [was] sorely tempted never to return to the fray."

LeBoutillier made her aspirational to American women: "Claire is young, slim, indecently healthy. She skates, she skis, she golfs and swims. But she doesn't do a routine thing to keep lithe and fresh except sleep plenty and down a glass of hot water and lemon juice upon rising."

And she highlighted her prescience: "Claire McCardell is about two years ahead of time in everything she designs and selects for herself. Two years ago, she had a tweed evening coat. Now they are Fords," she wrote, comparing McCardell's design to the popular motor car. "Claire McCardell was the first designer in wholesale to use zippers—the first to cut inexpensive fabric on the bias. . . . Because Claire's basic principle of design is that the wearer should feel comfortable, she puts pockets into almost everything."

The release made McCardell seem edgy, exciting, and outgoing, even as she herself remained shy when it came to self-promotion and the media. She much preferred that her designs do the talking for her. At LeBoutillier's urging, she sat with reporters and patiently answered their questions, even as it made her feel deeply uncomfortable. The newswomen, though, found McCardell easy to talk to. "Modest, retiring, and kind" was how one journalist described her.

McCardell further won them over by allowing her clothes to be sketched and photographed. That season, Seventh Avenue manufacturers guarded their designs even more fervently, so she quickly earned a reputation for being someone whom reporters and editors could count on in a pinch. She lent samples from her new collection to be worn on models for photo shoots, even as others refused to do so. It was a calculated risk, but it paid off. Stories and photos about McCardell and her Win-Sum collection began appearing in magazines and papers across the country.

Each wove descriptions of her clothes with the personal details served up by LeBoutillier. *Vogue* described McCardell as "glowing with health, perfectly turned out, full of laughs, a mind bouncing with ideas, youth and originality shining out in everything she does." For the first time, there were no references to how a suit evoked Chanel or how a heavily padded shoulder took after Schiaparelli. A spate of stories announced that the smartest fashion label of the future would be "Made in the U.S.A." and that Claire McCardell was the person to create it.

Filene's, a major department store based in Boston, bought several of McCardell's rayon dresses. In ads, it promoted her by name and celebrated her as the antithesis of the melodramatic French. She was the perfect designer for women who "love clothes that are casual yet have a distinct personality and flair."

Filene's proved to be the exception, however. Sales of Win-Sum clothes were sluggish that fall, particularly to larger department stores outside New York. McCardell's clothes seemed to sell only at smaller specialty shops whose salespeople had time to explain to customers how the sashes and ties worked or how a limp-looking dress would come to life when it was worn. It didn't matter how many women read about McCardell's collection in the newspapers; if buyers didn't pick up the line for their stores, readers would never have a chance to become customers.

Worse, store buyers lectured McCardell on her designs as they watched models walk the Win-Sum showroom. McCardell was used to that from her years at Townley, where the male buyers, in particular, had questioned a woman's legitimate need for sports clothes. She had once parodied their questions: "Can a female hit a golf ball? Do some wives do their own cooking? Can a girl hook a trout?"

She had believed that this year would be different. One night, she commiserated with fellow designers over drinks. "The buyers came to see our new things, and what happens?" she ranted. "The things that really had new ideas were turned down, one right after the other. All sorts of suggestions—from the buyers—were made to 'improve' the clothes. The result was that the numbers that they bought looked so much like what I and every other designer had made in 1939 and 1938, that I wondered why they had bothered to look at new lines."

The manufacturers behind Win-Sum took the side of the buyers. They told McCardell to incorporate the suggestions moving forward. Design by committee was not what she'd signed up for.

In November, McCardell released a winter resort collection. Sales remained slow, and she grew disheartened. She had a hard time hiding her frustration from Helen Wulbern, a seasoned reporter with *Women's Wear Daily*, who interviewed her at work. Wulbern had been following McCardell since her early days at Townley, and she thought McCardell was a singular talent. Now she was profiling her for a column called "Designers of Today and Tomorrow."

They sat in McCardell's closet-sized office and chatted. Wulbern flipped through the scrapbook that McCardell maintained of her successes. There were articles about her World's Fair win, stories about the Monastic dress, and pictures of her clothes in magazines, only rarely with a credit to her as the designer. The articles that had been glued to the pages had saw-toothed edges. McCardell had cut them out with her pinking shears, which cut woven fabric in zigzags to avoid fraying.

Wulbern complimented McCardell's ingenuity and desire to experiment. McCardell had achieved so many firsts: the Monastic, pockets, the use of men's fabrics such as tweed. McCardell shrugged. The Monastic wasn't so original, she said. The Algerians had thought it up first, she'd just adapted it. She was feeling frustrated and being uncharacteristically dismissive of her work. That surprised Wulbern. She considered McCardell to be keen-sighted and unbridled in her quest for innovation, and Wulbern said that she planned to write just that in her forthcoming profile.

"How do you do it?" Wulbern pressed. "Where do your ideas come from?"

"I design my collections for women like myself and it's too bad that I do because it doesn't appear to be what buyers want."

McCardell's success hinged on buyers seeing the brilliance in her clothes. And they would have to see it soon because the cutthroat bottom line of Seventh Avenue waited for no one.

◆

On a crisp November morning in 1940, not long after her interview with Helen Wulbern, McCardell rushed through the marble lobby of 550 Seventh Avenue on her way to Win-Sum. She made a beeline for a bank of elevators where the morning crush of workers hurried into cars that would zoom them to the twenty-four stories of garment lofts overhead. The building was always buzzing. Designers, buyers, fabric reps, models, and fashion editors rotated in and out all day long, going to the prestigious ready-to-wear firms. Some had taken to calling 550 Seventh

Avenue the "rue Saint-Honoré" of Manhattan, referencing Paris's famous street lined by couture houses.

McCardell squeezed into a crowded elevator, and it wasn't until the doors closed that she realized she was sharing the car with Henry Geiss. What on earth was he doing back on Seventh Avenue?

"Hello, Claire," he said.

Geiss introduced the well-dressed man standing next to him as Adolph Klein. Klein was tall and personable, with a warm smile that emanated easy charm—the opposite of Geiss. They were on their way, Geiss told her, to the company's new loft space. He and Klein were reopening Townley together.

McCardell couldn't believe it. She collected herself quickly, though, and wished Geiss well. She leaned in and gave her former boss a quick hug, a gesture of physical warmth that she usually reserved for friends and family and one that was meant to offer closure on their past tensions.

The elevator opened on every floor and people pushed out and crowded back in. McCardell was halfway out the door to her floor when she heard Adolph Klein speaking. "You should come back to Townley," he said. "Be our head designer."

The gossip that rattled along Seventh Avenue was that Townley had its new designer by the time the brass doors closed again. In truth, the three parted ways saying they would talk again soon.

What McCardell didn't know was that Adolph Klein had been following her career for some time. In fact, he'd already suggested to Geiss that they bring her back as Townley's head designer. "In this business, you have to be exciting or basic," he said. Townley was too small to compete with the bigger companies pumping out basic trends, he reasoned, so they would have to be exciting. Klein understood that the fall of 1940 would bring about a historic restructuring. It wasn't merely about surviving until Paris returned; it was about reinventing fashion infrastructure to elevate New York, and firms such as Townley, along with it. Klein wanted originality, and "nobody ever saw anything like the things Claire dreamed up," he argued. "Why not have my couturiere right here?"

Klein had risen in the garment business by taking big swings. He'd begun his career in millinery in the late 1920s, opening several hat shops in his native Brooklyn before branching out into the dress market. He'd saved $10,000 to invest in a new venture, and he'd convinced Henry Geiss to revive Townley with him. He had a vision of a modern garment firm.

Ultimately, Geiss was a bottom-line guy. If Klein was so bullish on Claire McCardell, he should ask Win-Sum what it thought of her. A few days before bumping into McCardell on the elevator, Klein had done just that. The owner hadn't minced words. "Better you should throw your money out the window," he'd said. "If I were you, I'd go shoot craps with the money. It's not as much of a gamble as Claire McCardell."

Geiss believed that the topic of hiring McCardell was closed. But Klein, a man rarely flustered by the risks of business, had a gut feeling that she was the right call.

After the elevator ride, Geiss insisted that Klein conduct additional due diligence before committing to McCardell. They agreed to seek the opinion of a Boston retailer they both knew. Klein wrote the man to ask his thoughts on McCardell's standing in the marketplace. Days went by, and an answer never arrived. They had to push ahead. A spring collection had to be shown to buyers in January. They had less than two months to go.

Geiss agreed to move forward and offer McCardell the position. What Geiss didn't know was that the letter from Boston had, in fact, arrived. The response had been mailed to Klein's home address, as he'd requested, and not to the office. The Boston retailer had been so disparaging of McCardell's wholesale potential that Klein had chosen not to share it with Geiss. Sometimes a little subterfuge was necessary in business.

McCardell, meanwhile, was weighing her options. She could stay at Win-Sum, where her bosses let the buyers walk all over her, or she could return to the devil she knew in Geiss and the unknowns of the gregarious newcomer, Adolph Klein. After eleven years in the business, she decided it was time to ask for what she deserved. What did she have to lose?

She brainstormed a list of demands for her return to Townley, filling page after page in her work notebook. First, her name would be on the label: Claire McCardell Clothes. Second, she would never water down her designs for owners, sales staff, or buyers. "Claire McCardell clothes will all carry a C Mc label," she wrote in her hurried, looping cursive, and "they will be produced as the sample is made. If you don't like the way it's made, buy something you do like—no changes." Implicit in that was the further mandate that she not be required to copy others' designs even if Parisian couturiers should return after the war.

When the trio met again, McCardell presented her terms, starting with her name on the label. Geiss thought it foolish to tether their business identity to a designer who could leave whenever she wanted. But Klein believed that giving McCardell the respect of her name inside the clothes she designed would foster loyalty. They agreed to her terms with one amendment. The firm name would have to be represented as well. They settled on Claire McCardell Clothes by Townley.

McCardell further demanded complete creative agency over her work and her sample room. Klein promised that he and Geiss would never meddle. Should anyone in the company believe that an item required adjustment, they would discuss it with her first. "Claire gets no surprises in the finished garment," Klein assured her, and he looked directly at Geiss when he said it. In the new iteration of Townley, McCardell would run the creative end, Klein would run the sales team, and Geiss would focus on production.

McCardell practically floated out of the room. Afterward, she told her parents that she'd finally done it. All the hard work, all the heartache, had paid off. Her name—their family name—would be stitched on labels and distributed across the country. The news of McCardell's deal stunned even her closest friends. Joset Walker, who was toiling anonymously for a conservative Garment District manufacturer, admitted to being wildly jealous. Claire McCardell, at the age of thirty-five, became the first designer to get her name on a Seventh Avenue manufacturer's label and the first to be given full control over her designs.

CHAPTER TWELVE

We Admit This Line Is Different

1941

Townley officially reopened on January 8, 1941. *Vogue* magazine heralded McCardell's return to her former firm. McCardell, the editors wrote, "has always dared to do the unusual, at the usual prices. In fact, Claire McCardell, the Typical American Girl, has a taste and designing talent so unusual, that it makes the word Typical turn to irony in the mouth."

The first order of business for Adolph Klein was figuring out how to sell the unusual designs coming out of McCardell's sample room. And the rumor was that she was in there making a wedding gown. Ready-to-wear manufacturers did not make bridal attire, but McCardell had a new problem she wanted to solve. Cold churches occupied her mind.

Four months earlier, the US government had instituted a military draft for men ages twenty-one to forty-five. The country no longer believed it could remain neutral after the Nazis had conquered Paris. It was the first peacetime draft in the country's history. McCardell's three brothers had already registered, as had Irving Harris, who came in just under the wire at the age of forty-four. Men, selected by lottery, were conscripted to do a year of domestic military service. Sudden separations from loved ones and the possibility of having to go to war inspired many young couples to marry quickly, often during the short leave allowed after boot camp. "Furlough brides," as they were called, walked down aisles off-season in chilly, fuel-starved churches.

The United States had begun rationing coal and fuel supplies in anticipation of future shortages.

McCardell, who hated being cold, imagined the discomfort of women on their wedding day. She chose white wool jersey, a decidedly unbridelike but warm material. She gave her wedding dress three-quarter sleeves and a high, round neck. The bodice hugged the torso before dipping into a Basque waist, where two prominent seams formed a downward-facing point. The Basque waist was popular in ball gown design, so it signaled a level of formalism. But it also minimized the hips and provided an hourglass silhouette for a variety of sizes, including for those with fuller figures.

Next, she considered how best to close the dress. Metal hooks and eyes were nothing new—they'd been used on clothing for centuries—but they were traditionally reserved for undergarments, such as corsets and bras. She found a brand of brass hooks and eyes that she thought were as elegant as they were industrial looking. On a wedding gown, they added a subtle sexiness, given their association with bras. McCardell realized that the closure had an additional benefit. Hooks and eyes were more forgiving in fit than zippers or buttons. Furlough brides wouldn't have much time for custom tailoring.

The skirt of the dress fell to the floor, and McCardell topped the ensemble with a detachable wool angora snood, a simple head covering that affixed under the chin with a hook and eye, resembling a hood. She made a warm alternative to a traditional veil or bridal hat.

It was a modern take on the traditional wedding dress, and it announced new territory for the revived Townley and for sportswear in general. There were no limits to what Claire McCardell Clothes might offer. She was in the fine gown business, too. *Vogue* featured her gown in a full-page photo, the model smiling demurely inside a country church.

◆

In the first months of business, Townley bled money. Klein didn't take a salary, and he admitted to his patient, but alarmed, wife that he might be kissing his investment goodbye. But he had a marketing mind that solved problems as skillfully as McCardell's mind did with clothes. Instead of running from his designer's novel ideas, he acknowledged them head-on. "We admit this line is different," he wrote in a release to buyers, "but you will admit that your smartest customers often state they are tired of seeing the same old things." He reminded buyers that McCardell's ideas had seemed odd at first—like tweed and wool for evening wear when Paris had dictated silk and velvet—but women had loved them, and her ideas caught on. Yes, she was years ahead in her thinking, but that was a good thing. "Claire McCardell creates fashions that start far-flung trends," he wrote.

The energy at Townley this go-round was different. Klein and McCardell functioned as a team. A *Vogue* editor observed their rapport and later told Klein that she admired the "many times I heard you laugh together," she said. "That was a wonderful thing—to laugh together when working."

Klein did something other male manufacturers had failed to do when he asked McCardell to walk him through her thinking. A design, she explained, grew out of her current way of life or that of women she knew. Most of her ideas seemed "startlingly self-evident" and she wondered why she hadn't thought of them before.

Take, for instance, her separates idea from 1934. She remained committed to it, even though it hadn't taken off in the marketplace. "It is my experience that a good new idea must be repeated over and over to catch on," she later explained. "You have to sneak up with it, at least in mass-produced clothes." Klein recognized the potential of separates, and he encouraged McCardell to update the idea for 1941.

McCardell worked out of her tall, narrow cubbyhole of an office. One slender window offered a view of the Garment District below.

She spread fabric sample books and notebooks across a big desk, and she sketched using a separate drafting table. Rows of shelves held her collection of scrapbooks, press clippings, archived sketches, and the art and history books she sometimes consulted. Bolts of material were propped against the walls. She pinned fabrics to wallboards, their rich colors and patterns serving as inspirations: wine-dark reds and mustard yellows; rich blues, burnt oranges, and plaids. Boxes overflowed with various types of fasteners. She had splurged on a new dress form that included legs, not just a torso, which helped when designing pants and bathing suits.

A partition separated McCardell's office from the larger sample room next door, where Bessie Sustersic again oversaw the staff. McCardell kept a worktable in there as well so she could be in the mix. Unlike many designers, she rarely passed her sketches on to a sample assistant to be realized without her. She liked to participate in the creation. And she never made samples using muslin, the unbleached, inexpensive cotton that could be mocked up to represent a garment. Fabrics had a life of their own. You couldn't impose a preconceived idea on any fabric, she believed; you had to see what it could do.

Once a sample of a design was completed, it went onto a fit model for further refinement. The ideas that didn't turn out as McCardell had hoped were scrapped. The ones destined for the collection moved across a hall to a workroom where patterns were made. Once orders came in from buyers, Townley used outside contractors to fabricate about 70 percent of the finished garments, minimizing the number of employees it had to house in the loft.

In addition to her sample staff, McCardell had a design assistant. She often hired recent graduates from the fashion program at Parsons, talented women looking to get their start in the same position that McCardell had held under Robert Turk. The Paris campus of Parsons had closed after war had broken out in Europe. The chance to learn from McCardell, who'd studied the French system but was pioneering her own American style, meant that aspiring designers vied for the coveted position. In the coming years, McCardell would mentor many young assistants and support them as they launched their own businesses.

McCardell expanded her original separates line from five to six pieces, including a blouse, slacks, a long dirndl skirt, a shorter skirt, a jersey sweater, and a suit jacket. She mixed silky but washable black rayon with black wool jersey.

Instead of sending male salesmen to introduce the separates to retailers and customers, Klein dispatched McCardell to do a series of trunk shows. Less formal than the semiannual fashion previews in New York, the shows were opportunities to showcase a new design on a store's home turf.

McCardell hopped a commuter flight to Boston one morning wearing three items from her separates collection: a black taffeta blouse, a jersey skirt, and a jacket. She met an audience of customers and buyers on the sixth floor of Filene's department store. She talked about the convenience of having a compact wardrobe when taking a trip. With more and more Americans flying, a duffel bag wardrobe, as she called it, was the future. The jacket she wore included a detachable hood. Originally, she'd paired a hat with the outfit, she said, but on an airplane, a hat was a nuisance. As she spoke, models emerged wearing nine different outfits composed of her separates. McCardell demonstrated how the individual pieces could be rearranged to create the new looks.

Women were used to buying new dresses, not recycling the same pieces, and some in the audience may have been dubious. "Of course, you might get tired of it," McCardell frankly acknowledged, but, she countered, you could refresh the looks "for almost any occasion" with the addition of accessories. She showed them heart-shaped silver earrings, rings, and hatpins, and plastic bracelets and metal necklaces that she'd designed to pair with the clothes. A reporter from *The Christian Science Monitor* covering the trunk show admired McCardell's jubilant approach. "Designing clothes is fun. This was evident from the first moment of conversation with Miss McCardell."

McCardell, wearing her own designs and talking openly about life as a working woman, was precisely the kind of person many attendees aspired to be: confident, casual, smart. McCardell encouraged the women to find their own style, and the audience loved her for it. As one store owner later wrote to Klein, "It has been a most happy experience to come in contact with this charming artist, and her folksy approach to 'mere customers' has been delightful."

Only a few months before, McCardell had complained to Helen Wulbern that designing for herself was a dangerous gamble. But there she was, a walking publicity campaign for her own ideas. Klein doubled down on promoting McCardell as the fashion icon women were looking for. He sent her across the country on a series of personal appearances, not unlike the tours Hollywood stars went on to promote a movie.

Klein further marketed the separates as a dollar-stretching fashion breakthrough for those with "more taste than money." *Vogue* featured them in a spread, heralding these six pieces "that can lead about nine lives. Own it all or parts thereof and do your own juggling."

Seven years after she'd first conceived of the idea, McCardell's mix-and-match separates finally began to gain traction, thanks in part to Klein's marketing savvy.

◆

Townley had an additional stroke of good fortune that year when the phone rang and Marjorie Griswold was on the line. Klein knew of Griswold from her days as the merchandise manager for Macy's. She was a Stanford-educated dynamo who in 1938, at thirty-one years of age, had practically run the entire department store. She had left retail to marry a research chemist and have a baby. Dorothy Shaver at Lord & Taylor had recently lured her back as the store's sportswear buyer. Shaver had promised her a five-day week that would get her home in time to tuck in her son. Griswold quickly earned a reputation for doing as much work in those five days as the average buyer did in ten. And while her colleagues worried about next month's sales tallies, Griswold had the vision to look ahead. She wanted to nurture designers. Among Griswold's future finds would be Lilly Pulitzer and Emilio Pucci.

In 1941, Griswold was just ramping up her business at Lord & Taylor. She told Klein she was making the rounds of manufacturers. Did Townley have anything she should consider? Klein told her that he did have something new and exciting to show her, an original designer she just had to see. They all said that, Griswold thought. Griswold arrived at the Townley showroom with zero expectations, but the minute the first model walked out, she sat up. The woman wore a navy-blue-and-white rayon dress that was revolutionary in its simplicity. And with real pockets no less.

Griswold bought several Claire McCardell designs that day. She went back to Dorothy Shaver and suggested they give McCardell pride of place as one of Lord & Taylor's preferred American designers. Shaver agreed.

At first, Claire McCardell Clothes by Townley didn't sell. Griswold had a hunch, however, that once a woman discovered how the clothes looked on her, she'd be a convert. The unsold clothes were relegated to end-of-season sales racks, where women inspired by the bargain prices took a chance. Sure enough, those same customers later returned, usually with friends, to buy new Claire McCardell Clothes at full price. Within a few years, Townley would be one of Lord & Taylor's biggest accounts. And it would help make McCardell's inventions, such as separates, a staple in women's wardrobes.

Still, Townley needed an immediate hit that year that would bring in some money. It came in the form of McCardell's solution to housework and hostessing.

In 1941, hundreds of factories in New York alone were supplying the war effort in Europe. Women across the country began leaving lower-paying domestic work, such as cleaning, cooking, and taking in laundry, for better-paying factory jobs. Help with domestic chores had been a staple, even among families of lower socioeconomic levels. Now women were left alone to manage these duties.

At the same time, women, particularly those in the middle and upper classes, were pressured to maintain proper decorum when entertaining at home. Emily Post's bestseller *Etiquette: The Blue Book of Social Usage* dedicated pages just to dinner parties. The interior designer Dorothy Draper published a book with the exclamatory title *Entertaining Is Fun!*

How to Be a Popular Hostess. Those books offered mandates for how to invite guests, how to dress, how to set the table, and how to serve drinks while deftly mingling and inspiring small talk. A woman should never seem busy or distracted, and she should always greet her guests in a fresh, stylish dinner dress.

During the week, McCardell was far too absorbed by work to cook and entertain. She took business lunches at the Waldorf Astoria, dinners at the Pierre Hotel. Many nights, she made a sandwich in her tiny apartment kitchen before falling into bed. On weekends in Frenchtown, however, she loved to cook. She found it relaxing to chop, dice, and stir in her tiny kitchen. While the copper pot of stew simmered over the fire in the hearth, she went outside and dug in the dirt with her hands, planting bulbs around the front door in spring, adding herbs to her kitchen garden. In summer, she harvested fresh strawberries from the vines she'd planted. She even enjoyed the overcast days, rain flecking the windows, the earthy smell that emanated after a downpour refreshed the land. When the weather allowed, she set a table outside under a tree in the orchard. She used yards of clean cotton, remnants from her sample room, as tablecloths. Mismatched vases purchased at a nearby flea market held wildflowers. In the tree branches, she strung clean glass jam jars with candles. She would fill her friends' glasses with wine, and they'd talk for hours.

It could have been while preparing her favorite chicken and garlic stew and rushing about in the yard to gather herbs that she conceived of a new idea that spring of 1941: a dress that a woman could wear while cooking and entertaining, without ever having to change. She designed the dress with a matching apron. Instead of using the buttery, soft silks that the French had always dictated for evening wear, she used the thick silk reserved for men's neckties. It was sturdier and easier to clean. She called it the Kitchen Dinner dress.

Women's Wear Daily reported that women "who up to now didn't know a kitchen broom from a vacuum cleaner" were rolling up their sleeves "for all their worth to keep going households that have been evacuated by domestic helpers. We hardly expected that the kitchen milieu, as it were, would make itself felt so soon as an 'influence' in fashions that have social standing." But McCardell was a few steps ahead yet again, they reported, and her Kitchen Dinner dress had done just that. Buyers loved it, as did customers.

◆

Townley survived those first lean seasons, Klein later said, because buyers and customers had begun "catching on to [McCardell's] old things," such as her separates, "while they were laughing at her new ones."

In 1941, though, when her latest "crazy" premiered during the summer press and buyers' preview for her fall collection, even the most adventurous buyers were flummoxed.

McCardell had always preferred minimalist shoes with a low heel, and she'd been looking for the perfect footwear to complement her clothes. It could have been during one of her many evenings spent at the ballet or the theater—or her collaboration with Zorina two years earlier—that got her thinking about ballet slippers. They had a shapely, rounded toe that she liked.

She went to see Ben Sommers, the president of Capezio Ballet Makers. The company had been making ballet slippers for dancers since 1887, and its offices, at Broadway and 49th Street, were close to Townley's. She asked if Capezio would be willing to make ballet slippers in fabrics to match her dresses. Sommers was happy to oblige. McCardell's design included matching fabric ribbons that wound up the calf and tied, similar to the silk ribbons used on a ballerina's pointe shoes.

When McCardell sent her showroom models out in the ballet slippers, "the shocked buyers paid more attention to the shoes than the dresses in the showroom," she later said. "The consensus was that I'd gone mad." Some told her to put her models back into high heels because they made women look better. McCardell didn't think so. She loved the shoes and thought she might use them again.

"With these dames you don't know where they get their inspiration,"

Klein once remarked. "It may be from the crack in the wall." But he kept his promise: He let McCardell make her "crazies," and he did his best to promote them.

♦

Amid all that invention and her rigorous schedule of trunk shows and work travel, McCardell was spending less time with Harris and his son, John. She kept her apartment in Murray Hill, while Harris lived uptown with John and a nanny. She spent as many weekends as she could in Frenchtown, encouraging Harris and John, now eleven, to join her. John, like his father, didn't see the appeal of the farmhouse, where water had to be hauled from a well and candles used for lighting. "We're rough and tough and can enjoy the simple life," McCardell told him.

In time, John came to cherish those weekends in the company of his father's girlfriend. "Claire was the strong and silent type," he later said, much like Roy McCardell and her three brothers. She "wasn't very maternal in her early years," he recalled, and she was "not really in tune with children," but she treated him with respect and care. She was amusing, thoughtful, and kind and had no pretenses.

Harris, on the other hand, held to the adage that children should be seen, not heard. He didn't need to see them much, either. He aimed to make his son a proper man of high society, as Harris wished he himself had been, and he outsourced the task to a series of nannies and boarding schools. Harris had long since fired John's beloved nanny, the one who'd accompanied them from France in 1935, because she wasn't making his son "a man" fast enough. John had been six at the time, and the loss of his one consistent caregiver had devastated him. He grew to know Latin and the plays of Shakespeare; he knew how to tack a sailboat in a strong wind and which sterling silver fork to use for escargot. But he didn't know his mother or his sister, and his mercurial father remained distant. He would later say that McCardell and her family in Frederick had saved him from a very lonely and isolated childhood.

On September 19, 1941, Harris received shocking news from France.

His ex-wife Jean had fallen ill and required surgery and had died while convalescing at the château in Doumy. She was thirty-one years old. She left behind John, Liz, now age eight, and a two-year-old daughter with her second husband.

Harris booked passage to Europe as quickly as he could, given the challenges of intercontinental travel during the war. He went to retrieve Liz. Once there, he began to suspect that Jean's new husband wasn't all he'd claimed to be. It would emerge in the months and years to come that Charles Louis d'Espinay-Durtal had a variety of aliases. In truth, he was a shoemaker's son from Paris. He'd altered his birth records in 1937, the year before marrying Jean. The man's provenance and title would eventually be questioned in the French courts, and Harris would spar with him in US courts for years over Jean's will and trusts that were meant for John and Liz.

On October 26, Harris and his daughter flew out of Lisbon on the Pan American World Airways Atlantic Clipper, landing in New York the following day. Liz was overwhelmed by the sudden loss of her mother and the presence of a father she hardly knew.

John was equally confused by the sudden arrival of his sister. Liz's presence and his mother's death could have pulled up long-buried memories of his parents' divorce. In April 1935, as Harris and Jean's marriage had exploded in front of him through a vicious string of fights, John had been pulled into the living room at the chalet and told to choose which parent he wanted to live with. He was four years old. He had chosen to go to New York with his father.

After that, his mother hadn't communicated directly with him. She had gone through her lawyers for any news of her son, as in one letter written to Harris a few years before she died. Jean's lawyer wrote to Harris about other matters before signing off with a postscript: "Jean has asked me to add that she would still be pleased to have a photograph of John."

Liz, meanwhile, had been weaned on Jean's unflattering stories about her absent father living in America. She didn't know what to make of

McCardell, her father's companion who lived in a separate apartment and conducted a largely independent life. Liz wondered what to call her. Should she refer to McCardell as her new mother? Harris may have been the one to suggest that Liz come up with a different term. Liz began calling McCardell by the British nickname "Mumsy." John followed suit. McCardell accepted the sobriquet, and John and Liz called her Mumsy from then on. They referred to Harris as Popsy.

McCardell didn't attempt to be a replacement mother. She welcomed Liz to New York in the way she knew best: She made her a miniversion of one of her Townley dresses. When she learned that Liz enjoyed ballet, she helped find a class for her in the city. But Liz never fully warmed to McCardell in the same way that John did.

Less than two months after Liz's arrival, in the quiet early morning hours of Sunday, December 7, a radar operator stationed in Oahu, Hawaii, observed a cluster of planes heading toward the island. He called over his superior, who mistook the blips for friendly US B-17 bombers. When 353 Japanese planes unleashed bombs over Pearl Harbor, the attack took Americans by surprise. The next day, President Roosevelt met with a joint session of Congress to formalize the country's response. December 7, 1941, was, he said, a day that would live in infamy. The United States was at war.

CHAPTER THIRTEEN

It's Rather Fun to Have a Limit

1941-43

By the time the Japanese bombed Pearl Harbor in December, New York Mayor Fiorello La Guardia had already been warning Americans of a foreign invasion. Eight months earlier, in May 1941, he had become the director of the Office of Civilian Defense (OCD), a new federal agency tasked with guarding the country from outside threats. He joined first lady Eleanor Roosevelt in building a first-of-its-kind grassroots volunteer defense system. They organized block wardens to assist in air raid and blackout drills; scouts to scan the skies and coastlines for enemy vessels; citizen medics and firefighters to bolster emergency response. Protecting the United States was no "clam bake," La Guardia told the public; it was serious business. The OCD soon mobilized 10 percent of the population to aid in homeland defense.

The quasi militarization of daily life necessitated uniforms. In the summer of 1941, six months before Pearl Harbor, La Guardia asked five New York designers for help, McCardell among them. He requested that each design a uniform for OCD volunteers, and McCardell was tasked with creating one for women.

McCardell was honored to be asked. More, she felt grateful for the ability to do something for the country. Her cousin Lee McCardell was already embedded with the Army in Europe as a war correspondent for *The Baltimore Sun*. Her three brothers had enlisted in the Navy as soon as the United States' entry into the war had seemed inevitable. There was nothing more potent for keeping fear at bay than channeling one's energy into action.

In 1941, creating uniforms for women was a pressing concern, not just for the OCD but for the newly formed auxiliary units of the military. For the first time in US history, women were joining the ranks of the Army, Navy, and Air Force, albeit in noncombat positions. A debate raged among male members of Congress—reflecting the one raging among men in the public at large—about whether women should be in the military at all. Allowing them to serve, some said, compromised marriage, supported lesbianism, and encouraged the disintegration of gender roles. One South Carolina congressman argued that women in the military would undermine the "courageous manhood of the country."

Uniform design became an extension of those arguments. The military forces had little experience dressing women. Now they worried about whether their enlistees should be allowed to wear pants because they were too masculine. The Army vetoed functional breast pockets on a suit jacket after it had run experiments with women carrying necessities in those pockets, such as a pack of cigarettes or a wallet. It was concluded that having real pockets near a woman's breasts resulted in an alarming deformity. The women Army volunteers were given a purse instead.

For the OCD, McCardell was instructed to make a suit with a skirt and no pants. Luckily, she didn't have to contend with the pocket nonsense. She designed a jacket that featured large, functional patch pockets at the hips and the breast. Military tabs fastened by gilt buttons went onto the shoulders and were meant to hold insignia and colored markings identifying various classifications of OCD workers. That fall, she submitted her design for approval. Eleanor Roosevelt suspected that rationing was coming and asked that any excess material be removed. McCardell adjusted her initial design slightly. In December 1941, one week after Congress declared war on Japan, McCardell's OCD uniforms were already making their way to US department stores. Any woman with a certificate showing she'd passed OCD training could purchase one.

By January 1942, the rationing Eleanor Roosevelt had predicted finally arrived. The first thing to go was rubber. Car tires became a precious commodity, and New Yorkers, already a pedestrian population, were forced to walk more than ever. Nylon, a necessity for military parachutes, was rationed soon after. That meant that the new nylon hosiery introduced at the 1939 World's Fair disappeared from store shelves. With stockings in short supply, some women began using eyeliner on the backs of their bare legs to mimic the look of hosiery seams.

The government distributed ration books with coupons. Americans were allowed a limited supply of gas, flour, bacon, and other necessities. Citizens were encouraged to plant Victory Gardens and supplement their food supply with homegrown produce.

By the spring, the War Production Board (WPB) began rationing clothes beyond stockings. The WPB issued a press release on April 8, 1942, that soft-pedaled the new restrictions. It assured American women that their present wardrobes would not be made obsolete by radical fashion changes owing to rationing. But the new regulation, known as Order L-85, included dozens of pages of restrictions and detailed instructions for anyone making clothes, including designers and home sewers.

Wool, rayon, cotton, and linen were prioritized for military use and severely curtailed or eliminated for civilians. Skirt hems and widths were reduced, and the amount of yardage allowed per item of clothing was cut back by about 15 percent. L-85 banned fabric-hungry designs such as pleats and French cuffs on pants. It also eliminated many of the materials and design techniques that McCardell loved to use. No more wool evening wraps or dresses. Belts couldn't be wider than two inches, so her favorite, wide "important belts" had to be replaced with narrower ones. Women's slacks couldn't include a belt at all. Hems had to have less than two inches of extra fabric, limiting the surplus at the hemstitch that she liked to give her customers for easy tailoring. Bias cuts could no longer be employed in some items, because the technique used more material. Aprons were banned, so no more Kitchen Dinner dresses. The size of inset pockets was reduced, and new shoes were rationed.

American women panicked, complaining that the regulations were too drastic. The restrictions "hung like a black velvet pall over the garment industry," as one reporter noted. The rationing did not discourage McCardell. "I think it's rather fun to have a limit," she told a reporter for *The New York Times*. Already inventive and thrifty, she was made for the challenge.

McCardell became the calm voice of reason to the American public. She went on a popular CBS radio show, *Lessons in Loveliness*, to reassure women. "We will have to think harder and work harder to get new style angles—and of course—styles which are flattering," she said, her warm, mellifluous voice a natural for radio. The designers of New York, she said, were certainly up to the task.

She assured home sewers that they were capable as well. When wool became scarce, she participated in a government campaign to show people how to turn old wool blankets into new winter coats. That summer, she channeled the mend-and-make-do aesthetic in her Townley collection with a patchwork dress made of fabric remnants. She called it Salvage Sally. The dress walked the runway during a fashion fair at the Hotel Astor meant to showcase how to construct new clothes from discarded garments.

McCardell bought reams of thick cotton ticking, usually used to cover mattresses, and made pleated slacks that could be worn in the factories and war plants where many women now worked. The practical pants were modeled in the pages of *Harper's Bazaar* by a young Lauren Bacall and wartime women's work wear was being treated as fashion. "Men were favored in their clothes by having plenty of pockets, pleats in trousers, shirt-sleeve shoulders, and so on," a fashion writer remarked about McCardell's designs, "so she took these features from men's clothes for her latest series of casual costumes for women, though they are far from masculine in effect."

Journalists were waking up to the fact that many of their favorite clothes had been made or inspired by McCardell. "Amazing it is to find that many of the silhouettes we have accepted as indispensable American fashion are Miss McCardell's original designs," *The Washington Post* reported.

With the shortage of fabrics and the increase in factory jobs, women needed different clothing options. New York was fast becoming a lab of invention and experimentation, and women designers were at the center. McCardell, along with designers such as Elizabeth Hawes, Clare Potter, Tina Leser, and Vera Maxwell, gave women overalls and pants for work and home. McCardell developed a prototype for a "surprise alert" jumpsuit of red fleece with a belt lined with a new type of phosphorescent-coated reflector buttons. The buttons glowed in the dark, and McCardell may have been remembering those white gloves worn by Parisian women in 1940 so that they could be seen at night during blackouts.

In October 1942, Virginia Pope, the fashion editor at *The New York Times*, launched a new event called Fashions of the Times. The showcase presented new designs using the latest cutting-edge textiles. McCardell and four of her fellow women designers were invited to experiment with laboratory fabrics not yet available for consumer use. The Pacific Lumber Company in California had developed a technique to recover and process the short fibers of redwood tree bark. By mixing them with sheep's wool, it had made a yarn that could be turned into a warm, lightweight fabric. McCardell took the material and made a pilot's suit for women. She later made an outfit with a fabric composed of corn fibers.

On one of her routine visits to see the textile producer Hope Skillman, McCardell learned that the chemical needed to bleach cotton to a crisp white was no longer available. The natural fiber was a dingy off-white, and Skillman apologized. McCardell didn't think it was so bad; she saw it as a creamy, mellow color and began using it, helping establish a trend for the color now known as "bone."

As the year progressed, McCardell joined an initiative to use fewer materials than stipulated under L-85. She also found ways to make use of the opposite problem: unexpected surplus. After the government procured too much balloon fabric—a strong, plain cotton weave used for military balloons and airplanes—McCardell bought the excess and turned it into dresses.

It may have been the L-85 restrictions that got her thinking again about the ballet slippers she'd commissioned for her showroom models. In 1942, the slippers had an added benefit: They used so little material that they didn't violate L-85 restrictions. Fabric ballet slippers, like the ones she'd had Capezio make the year before, could be procured without wasting a precious shoe ration ticket. McCardell wondered if, with design adjustments, a dancer's ballet slipper might become a proper woman's shoe.

Ben Sommers of Capezio admitted to being skeptical. It was one thing to use a ballet slipper as a clever accessory for showroom models, quite another to suggest it as a shoe women would purchase. But "when she believes in something, she doesn't compromise," Sommers later said of McCardell. "She's got an honest feeling, like religion, and it rubs off."

The new shoe design still had a thin sole on the bottom, but the ribbons were gone. McCardell thought that women might wear them as house shoes. They seemed fine for the living room or for cocktails out on a terrace but "not so fine for the subway," she acknowledged.

The shoes were soon spotted, though, on women on the street, and worn in city parks and to dinners in restaurants. Women loved them. They "taught women who had been wearing nothing but high heels for years that no heel or very little heel could be attractive and that the shell shape was flattering," McCardell later said. With the help of Capezio, she had invented the ballet flat.

Sommers thought McCardell was a genius. Her clothes "bring something *out* of you rather than *add* something to you," he once observed. Capezio continued to produce new styles with McCardell as a design consultant. Within a few years, the ballet flat landed the cover of *Vogue*.

◆

In 1942, many in fashion, including Diana Vreeland, sought out McCardell for her ingenuity. That year, Vreeland reveled in her expanded power at *Harper's Bazaar*. With Paris closed, she no longer merely reported on fashion, she *made* it. Vreeland and her editor in chief, Carmel Snow, ever the arbiters of trend, had taken to commissioning clothes from New York designers based on ideas they thought might be relevant to their readers.

She went to McCardell with one such idea. Vreeland glided through the Townley showroom one afternoon on her way to McCardell's office, smoke wafting off the cigarette in her ivory holder and leaving a thin contrail in her wake. Women were suffering, she told McCardell, from the juggling of home and work duties. Not only had domestic help gone to work in the factories; now the men were deployed as well. Women were alone to manage everything. The typical American housedress was dowdy, she said; it was *sad*. Women were *depressed*, she emphasized in her signature melodramatic way. There were all those pesky L-85 restrictions, too. A woman could no longer buy a new apron. The problem was best summarized by one department store executive who later observed that during the war, women hadn't wanted their everyday clothes to look like overalls, but they'd needed them to function like them.

Vreeland believed McCardell was the designer to solve the problem. What about a stylish update to the housedress that would pass muster with the War Production Board?

McCardell was in. Since L-85 prohibited aprons on dresses, she pondered what a woman might don quickly and, if necessary, take off again if it got soiled. An entire dress that could function like an apron, made of a material that was sturdy and easily washable.

She thought about what men wore to do the dirtiest jobs. The answer was denim. In truth, she'd long been obsessed by jeans. She liked the look of topstitching, the outer seams of white thread against the dark indigo, and she loved the brass rivets. Lady Levi's had been released in 1934, but jeans for everyday wear on women were not considered socially acceptable. Even jeans on men wouldn't become popular until Marlon Brando and James Dean wore them in the 1950s films *The Wild One* and *Rebel Without a Cause*. The rare denim being sported by women at the time was a machine-stitched grocery bag emblazoned with a red *V* for Victory and a few pieces of apparel for military uniforms. Denim was not something normally found in a woman's clothing manufacturer.

McCardell ordered samples of various denim materials to test them out. Klein walked in one afternoon to find a veritable mountain of denim piled in the sample room. He gave her one of his *Should I be worried?* looks. She smiled, shrugged, pulled a piece of denim off the pile, and went back to work. Klein was vexed. He'd made promises to stay out of McCardell's way, but that amount of denim alarmed him.

McCardell chose a pressed denim that was preshrunk and softer than what was used in jeans. Since big belts weren't allowed under L-85, she couldn't fit the dress as she had her Monastic. Long sashes or spaghetti string ties weren't practical for a work dress. She landed on a wrap dress instead, one that was oversized enough that the wearer could quickly put it over an existing outfit if necessary. It could be worn alone or over other clothes. By including a set of buttons along the waistline, the dress could be adjusted in size. Wide dolman sleeves made it easier to raise and lower arms for housework and to layer the dress over clothes.

McCardell added one more touch: an oversize patch pocket, just one per the L-85 regulations. It dominated the right side of the skirt. She included a red pot holder that could be attached to the buttons on the waist with a cord, so a woman wouldn't forget where she'd left it.

The patch pocket design surely thrilled Vreeland when she saw it. She shared McCardell's love of pockets. She had shocked the editorial staff at *Harper's Bazaar* when she'd started at the magazine in 1937 and announced her plan to write an article against handbags. "What do I want with a bloody old handbag that one leaves in taxis and so on?" she'd declared to her coworkers. Cigarettes, lipstick, powder, a small comb, money—it should all go into pockets. "Real pockets, like a man has, for goodness' sake," she'd continued. "Of course, you'd have much bigger pockets, and they'd be rather chic." Carmel Snow had had to pull Vreeland aside and explain that much of the magazine's income came from handbag advertising.

Now Vreeland had her big pocket, and it was rather chic. McCardell made it of a quilted denim, a clever solution to help the pocket keep its shape and mask the bulky outline of items stashed inside. It was big enough to hold a small garden trowel for a Victory Garden, a flashlight for blackout drills, or a book.

The wrap dress was multipurpose. It could be worn as an apron, a bathrobe, even a dinner dress when worn with jewelry. The versatility exemplified her philosophy of clothes, which she explained to *The New York Times*. "America is developing honest to goodness clothes made only for the ways and habits of American women and the lives they are living," she said. "Their need of the day is to dress themselves for hard work, a few hours of play on a holiday, and a last-minute party. Their clothes should be made easy and adaptable. The first want is comfort, the second something to suit the time and place."

McCardell thought of the dress as a kind of template, much as she had the Monastic dress silhouette; it was a style that she could update each season. She had learned from her mistake with the Monastic, though. In October 1942, before releasing the design publicly, Townley filed a patent, with McCardell listed as the inventor.

Vreeland chose the wife of a world-renowned American polo player to model the dress in the November 1942 issue of *Harper's Bazaar*. The woman, who before the war would have been pictured in the highest fashions in her Palm Springs home, now leaned against a doorjamb, one hand in her patch pocket, the other encased in the pot holder. "I'm doing my own work," the copy read. "The ideal garment for it, for cooking, dusting, scrubbing, painting, pottering, or any odd job about the house. Note the quilted pocket, big enough for matches, cigarettes, the morning mail and the duster."

On November 5, Klein spoke to a reporter from *Women's Wear Daily*, calling the dress "Miss Busybody." But it was the creative minds in the advertising department at Lord & Taylor who invented the name that stuck. On November 19, an ad for the store called it the Pop-Over, because "you can wear it with or without a dress. It is so becoming you can let your guests see you in it while you do the finishing touches. And it's easy for an amateur to launder." The name was soon shortened to Popover (without the hyphen).

Lord & Taylor gave the Popover its own window display on Fifth Avenue. The dress retailed for $6.95, more than a basic housedress but $13 less than other Townley dresses that fall. Klein had encouraged stores to price the dress in such a way that more women might afford it.

The denim Popover was practical yet so glamorous that "Fifth Avenue and the farm united in their acceptance of it," one fashion journalist enthused.

McCardell introduced women to the potential of denim. Like the Monastic, the Popover became an instant success. Only this time McCardell's name was on the label, and she owned the patent. Letters poured into the Townley offices, addressed to McCardell. Most women wrote to thank her for the life-altering garment; others offered suggestions, including one woman who begged her to please make the dress with a left-handed pocket and oven mitt. A friend of McCardell's in Greenwich Village told her that every writer she knew now wore a Popover to write in. The artist Georgia O'Keeffe painted in the New Mexico desert while wearing her McCardell dress. O'Keeffe became a lifelong fan of McCardell designs.

"Her views on fabric use were unorthodox," as a reporter for *Women's Wear Daily* once observed, and "she could lift a fabric stigmatized by tradition into new uses and fabric houses took advantage of her vision in this connection."

McCardell, duly inspired by denim's potential, returned to the material for a sexy three-piece suit composed of a wrap skirt, a backless halter, and a jacket. "Whee! Look what Claire McCardell's done with denim," one Indianapolis store wrote. "She's whisked it right off the farm; spruced it all up with her own very special brand of cosmopolitan magic; turned it into the neatest little town suits that ever walked down a city street."

By year's end, Townley had sold more than 75,000 Popover dresses. McCardell's denim halter top sparked an industrywide trend for backless clothes. As one magazine reporter later wrote about those prolific years, "Clairvoyant Claire had the subconscious desires of American women cased to perfection." Klein needn't have worried about those piles of denim.

◆

On January 22, 1943, a little over a year after the United States' entry into the war, McCardell walked into the Metropolitan Museum of Art and made her way to the indoor sculpture courtyard. It was one of her favorite spaces in the museum, a soaring, light-filled atrium with an entrance near Central Park. That night, the room glowed in the warmth of a gala party and rang with the voices of hundreds of guests. It was the first official event to honor American designers, the Coty American Fashion Critics' Awards.

The publicist Eleanor Lambert had designed the ceremony to be like Hollywood's Academy Awards. A national selection committee of fashion writers and industry leaders voted on their favorite designer of the previous year. The winner would receive a miniature bronze statue nicknamed "The Winnie," along with a $1,000 war bond. In addition, citations would go to important designs from the previous year. McCardell's Popover earned an award for "outstanding interpretation of fashion trends under the restrictive influences of 1942."

As McCardell wove through the crowd, she saw Hattie Carnegie and Norman Norell. Most Seventh Avenue designers were there, along with prominent actors and politicians. An elevated runway went the length of the courtyard, ready for the evening's fashion show. When the models walked, McCardell's work would be elevated alongside masterpieces of antiquity and modern sculptures by Edgar Degas and Auguste Rodin.

What a long way from her first year as a student, when she'd stood at the penthouse window of one of Frank Alvah Parsons's benefactors, looking down on the museum in the distance. She had wondered then what it might feel like to be a real participant in the cultural life of the city. Now there she was, counted as one of America's greatest designers.

Vogue editor Edna Woolman Chase presented the inaugural Coty Award to Norman Norell. Later, Norell confided to the fashion editor Sally Kirkland that he believed the wrong person had won that night. He was still designing in the European couture tradition, he explained, making evening dresses using hand stitching and promoting exclusivity. But McCardell was inventing within the confines of mass production. "Claire could turn five dollars' worth of common calico into a dress a smart woman could wear anywhere," he told Kirkland. The Winnie, he said, should have gone to her.

In 1943, even with the ongoing rationing and the war, McCardell's inventions had found their audience. Townley's business more than tripled. Adolph Klein could finally take a deep breath; his gamble on McCardell was paying off. Now McCardell prepared to take a gamble of her own—a very personal one.

CHAPTER FOURTEEN

Mr. Claire McCardell

Spring 1943

Old St. Paul's Episcopal Church stood on the crest of a hill in downtown Baltimore, a historic nineteenth-century brick building that commanded sweeping views of the city. To the north, the white marble of the towering Washington Monument glowed amid the brownstone houses and cobblestone streets of the Mount Vernon neighborhood. To the south, ships sluiced the sun-shimmered waters of the city's harbor. March was coming in like a lion, as the proverb promised, and the mournful wail of tugboat horns was carried on the wind along with the brackish scent of the Patapsco River.

On March 10, 1943, a knock came at the heavy wood rectory door. It was Ash Wednesday, the start of the Lenten season leading up to Easter, and the church was busier than usual. The priest opened the door to find a handsome couple standing on the threshold. A man of forty-five, his gray hair flecked with black and a woman with smiling blue eyes, just two months shy of her thirty-eighth birthday.

Irving Harris and Claire McCardell had traveled three hours by train to the historic church to marry, after nearly a decade of dating. They'd come to Baltimore alone, with no friends or family, not even Harris's two children. There had been no engagement announcement, no wedding invitation or breathless society page coverage leading up to the big day. The wedding would be a private affair, save for the strangers who flowed through the church to be marked with a sooty cross on their foreheads. That winter, Germany had declared total war, vowing to sacrifice everything in the name of victory. McCardell lived with a pulsating worry over the safety of her three brothers, Adrian, Bob, and Max. They were serving in the Navy, and Bob and Max were on vessels somewhere in torpedo-heavy waters. The spring of 1943 hardly felt like the time for a celebration, let alone a big wedding.

The church smelled of ashes, burnt palm leaves redolent with incense. It happened that Maryland's Episcopalian bishop, Edward Helfenstein, was observing Ash Wednesday at Old St. Paul's that year, and he readily agreed to allow the ceremony and to serve as a witness. Bishop Helfenstein had lived in Frederick, less than an hour's drive from the church. He knew the McCardell family.

Harris and McCardell stood in the rainbow glow of Tiffany stained-glass windows and vowed to care for each other in sickness and in health. The newlyweds took no honeymoon and returned to New York straightaway. The next day, Harris went to his office at 599 Fifth Avenue, where he'd hung out a shingle as a solo practitioner. Into his typewriter he rolled a sheet of personalized stationery, the one pronouncing that he was Irving Drought Harris, ARCHITECT, in all caps. On this, the second day of Lent, it was time for him to ask for a different kind of forgiveness.

"Dear Mr. McCardell," his letter began. "I hope you will forgive the manner in which the news of our marriage came to you. In discussing the plans, we felt that we should write you, but we feared a big wedding. At any rate it was a beautiful ceremony in St. Paul's Church with Bishop Helfenstein in attendance. He told me more about the importance of the McCardell family than Claire has done in all the years that I have known her.

"I suppose," he continued, "that you would like some of my history."

He described his childhood in Texas and wrote of his father's death in 1901, when he was four years old. He briefly described his service in the first World War, writing "I will never live to be more important."

He explained his divorce from Jean as an unwillingness on his part to live abroad. He did not elaborate on why he had initially brought only his son, John, to New York, leaving Liz behind in France until Jean's death. Harris assured his new father-in-law that his children loved McCardell almost as much as he did. "Claire has brought great happiness to me (and to my children)," he concluded. "I feel certain that I will be able with love and devotion to bring her happiness in full measure."

Roy and Eleanor McCardell were shocked to learn of their daughter's elopement. Harris's letter emphasized just how little they knew about their son-in-law, even after years of his dating their daughter. McCardell openly shared her professional achievements with them, but she had been taciturn when it came to Harris. The extent of her concealment became clear now.

Propriety required that the McCardells snap out of their dismay at being left out of the wedding. A savvy society page writer for *The Frederick News-Post* who kept an eye on the courts had reported in a short announcement on March 12 that "a marriage license was issued in Baltimore this week to Irving Drought Harris, 45, of New York City, and Miss Claire McCardell, 37, of Frederick."

Eleanor quickly printed a formal announcement that went out to family and friends, and she placed a notice in the society news section of the local paper. She also wrote a long letter to the bishop, thanking him for allowing their ceremony to take place on a holy day.

The marriage confounded McCardell's family, as it did many of her friends. Why had she married Harris? And why now, after all these years?

Some in McCardell's social circle believed that it was a marriage of convenience. With Jean's death, Harris needed a mother, at least in name, for his children. For McCardell, ever the problem solver, Harris may have provided a solution to the ongoing scrutiny placed on an unmarried woman nearing forty, even an increasingly famous fashion designer with a thriving business. Unmarried women were second-class citizens. McCardell couldn't get a loan on a house in her own name or open a line of credit. It would be another thirty-one years before women in America could no longer be legally discriminated against by banks based on gender or marital status. After the wedding, Harris bought the farmhouse in Frenchtown that McCardell had long been renting, a thoughtful wedding gift but also a reminder that she couldn't have made the purchase on her own.

Could McCardell have remained unmarried and dating Harris? There were certainly models among the women she knew in New York who lived unconventional domestic lives. Dorothy Shaver had never married. Much like the famous art-collecting Cone sisters of Baltimore, she had made a home with her younger sister, Elsie, who was an artist. They functioned like a traditional married couple, one newspaper profile pointed out, with Shaver going to work at Lord & Taylor each day and Elsie keeping house. Among McCardell's colleagues and friends in New York, there was a variety of relationships that existed outside the traditional rules of matrimony and monogamy.

McCardell rarely discussed her relationship with anyone. She prioritized her privacy, even with her friends and family. Her three brothers were particularly baffled by the union. Harris had "never approved of her career, and he would have been happy if she gave that up," McCardell's middle brother, Bob, believed. Her brothers wondered if Harris had wrongly thought that McCardell would give up working once they married. If that were true, Harris would have been deluding himself. McCardell never wavered on her career. Still, Harris "loathed anyone and anything to do with Seventh Avenue," John Harris later divulged to a *Vanity Fair* reporter. "And he was terrified of being called Mr. McCardell."

Harris may have ignored his wife's career, but their nuptials made news in *Women's Wear Daily*. The trade magazine announced her marriage, using her maiden name and letting readers know that the marriage did not mean the end of her career, as it often did for women. "Miss McCardell is continuing her work with Townley."

McCardell wasn't alone in grappling with tensions that arose between career and marriage. In the 1940s, the women of New York fashion were actively defending—and advocating for—their working lives. *Mademoiselle*, the fashion magazine for college-age women, had been arguing since the late 1930s that women could and should work: "We believe that marriage and a career are compatible; more, we believe that every woman married or single, should be educated for a career when and if necessity or inclination warrants." In 1943, the magazine honored McCardell with a Merit Award.

As millions of women across the country went to work during the war, Hollywood captured the shifting gender roles within American domestic life. Movies featured strong female leads who worked, traveled, and spoke their minds. Katharine Hepburn and Spencer Tracy sparred as two rival reporters in the 1942 film *Woman of the Year*. They struggled mightily after marrying. The wife's career outpaced that of her husband, not unlike the careers of McCardell and Harris. The original ending of the film was reshot because it was deemed too soft on the wife. The new scenes saw Hepburn's character capitulating to her husband. Test audiences believed that she needed to "get her comeuppance for being too strong in a man's world," as the male screenwriter later explained.

Like the fictional lives depicted on screen, Harris reportedly struggled with a marriage of equals. He avoided McCardell's professional life to such a degree that he had yet to meet the other significant man in his wife's life, Adolph Klein.

McCardell's fashion friends knew to tread lightly when Harris was around, according to Sally Kirkland. Kirkland had arrived in New York after graduating from Vassar in 1934 and now worked at *Vogue*. She'd first discovered McCardell clothes on the sales racks at Lord & Taylor, thanks to the promotions of Marjorie Griswold. She and McCardell had become close colleagues, and they regularly lunched together in the city. McCardell respected Kirkland's professional judgment and vice versa. Kirkland was even a little starstruck; whatever McCardell did, she tended to copy, including styling her hair in a similar way. She found Harris to be "a conservative husband, and he didn't much like business-friend types." Kirkland later told McCardell's siblings that she believed their sister had never been much interested in the drama of a big romance. She preferred the stimulation of her career.

John always contended that the marriage between his father and McCardell had come down to love, pure and simple. For all their differences, he believed that they genuinely cared for each other. McCardell was not a woman to expend energy on pursuits or relationships that did not matter to her. McCardell's sister-in-law, Sue, who married McCardell's youngest brother, Max, concluded that McCardell understood and tolerated Harris in a way that others did not. McCardell saw beneath Harris's braggadocio, his unplaceable British-tinged accent, and his bespoke suits. She empathized with the little boy whose father had died when he had been far too young, the boy who'd been raised in a remote town, as she had been, and who had always hungered for a bigger life.

After their marriage, Harris would remain an enigma to the McCardell family. He rarely traveled to Maryland with McCardell for visits, something Eleanor lamented. She would often press McCardell to bring Harris to town with her "so he will get to know how nice Frederick is!"

John and Liz, on the other hand, were frequent visitors to McCardell's childhood home. McCardell's brothers weren't yet married, and Eleanor had been desperate for grandchildren. Eleanor insisted that John and Liz call her Grannie. She doted on her stepgrandchildren, especially John. A boarding student at the prestigious St. George's School in Rhode Island, John was exceedingly polite to both Roy and Eleanor. Eleanor thought John to be a "fine, brilliant, loveable boy." John found Eleanor to be a steady guiding force in his life. He would grow quite close to her in the coming years and visit regularly, particularly in 1945, as Roy McCardell, at age seventy-two, began to have health issues that put him in the hospital. During that year, John would return to Frederick frequently with McCardell.

Liz, on the other hand, never grew close to her stepgrandparents. She would, in her teenage years, alienate her brother. After John left for Princeton University in 1947, he and Liz rarely spoke.

It's worth considering what role marriage played in the larger scheme of McCardell's life. Harris indeed solved problems. At the time, societally, it was simply easier for a woman to be married than to remain single. In addition, Harris had money of his own and could take care of himself and his children. Before marriage, he had kept a housekeeper and a cook, and he could afford to send his children to boarding schools. In marriage, McCardell was not required to fulfill traditional wife-centric domestic duties. She never played the role of the dutiful housebound spouse. She loved to host parties, entertain, and cook, especially in Frenchtown, but she did so on her own terms. When she took cooking classes at Le Cordon Bleu in New York in the 1940s, she did it out of her love of French food. Cooking was a hobby, not a wifely obligation.

Over their many years of dating, Harris had shown that he was willing to let McCardell be absorbed in her work, even if he didn't like it. He did not curtail her career, as evidenced by the fact that McCardell maintained a rigorous and creative professional life that often kept her away from home. Her work came first, and ultimately, Harris did not interfere in it.

McCardell, in turn, respected her husband's discomfort over her success. She never forced him to participate in the many events central to building her fashion empire. She kept her life neatly compartmentalized.

Not long after they married, McCardell gave up living alone for the first time in thirteen years. The family of four moved into an eleven-room co-op at 151 East 79th Street. Harris could afford to buy it thanks to John and Liz's trust fund from Jean, which allowed him to spend money on housing the children. He decorated the interior in a conventional high-WASP masculine style with leather club chairs, traditional furniture, and paintings of sailboats. "Claire seemed content to let Irving's lifestyle set the tone of their home life to a considerable degree," Kirkland observed.

McCardell ceded the interior decoration to him, save one room she kept for herself and which she decorated with modern furniture and khaki linen fabrics. The walls were painted her favorite shade of orangey red, the same color she'd recently selected for her name on the Townley letterhead. Artwork she'd collected and created covered the walls. A large wardrobe held her clothes, and lacquered boxes overflowed with vintage and costume jewelry. She protected her many hats under glass cloches, a clever way to keep them dust-free while also featuring them like the art she believed them to be. Sacrosanct and off-limits to others, the space was hers and hers only. She could close the door to the outside world and be fully alone, content in the privacy of her thoughts.

In her career, McCardell did not seem to crave either the approval or the attention of her spouse. In many ways, she kept her husband in a box—a nice eleven-room box on the Upper East Side—while she went off to work.

CHAPTER FIFTEEN

Make of It What You Will

Spring and Summer 1943

In the weeks following McCardell's elopement, her early summer collection for Townley made news across the country. She'd updated the best-selling Popover dress for warmer months. It now came in men's cotton shirt fabric and with shorter cap sleeves. The pocket was still there, but the attached pot holder was gone. The Popover was ready to leave the kitchen and go out into the world.

As McCardell made her transition into married life, her good friend Mildred Orrick was juggling the realities of two children and a world war. Orrick's husband, Jesse, had been shipped to England to serve as an interpreter of aerial reconnaissance images for the US Army, and Orrick was parenting alone. She woke early to walk her children to school; then she freelanced from home. She designed dress patterns that women could make up; she sold designs to Lord & Taylor; and she drew illustrations for fashion magazines.

At night, she entertained her children with jigsaw puzzles rented from the library for three cents. They sat at the kitchen table, dinner dishes drying in the rack, and listened to *The Jack Benny Program* on the radio while pressing pieces into place. After putting her children to sleep, she collapsed into bed, exhausted, but woke in the middle of the night to sketch. She kept a drawing pad and art supplies on a tray next to her bed. She pulled them onto her lap and worked for several hours before falling back to sleep. She couldn't pursue her work with the singular attention that McCardell could give hers.

Orrick sent several of her late-night sketches to *Harper's Bazaar*. The editors were open to speculative designs now that Paris wasn't supplying the fashion narrative. One of Orrick's hypotheticals took even the seasoned editors by surprise for its edginess. Ballet and modern dance inspired her in much the same way they did McCardell. Orrick had learned a great deal working for the dancer Natacha Rambova after Parsons, and she later illustrated a book that Rambova wrote.

Now she found inspiration in the traditional leotard. It had been designed in 1859 and named for its originator, the French gymnast Jules Léotard. Dancers had soon adopted it as their rehearsal uniform. Orrick sketched a new kind of leotard meant as a cold-weather undergarment for women. Her one-piece wool jersey design had long sleeves and footed tights. She made an ideas board, showing the various ways it might be worn. In one sketch, she drew a sleeveless dress on top, so that the arms and legs of the leotard were visible underneath. She noted that it could be worn as pants, stockings, and an undershirt all in one. She called it a "signposts-to-the-future" design. It might seem odd at first, she admitted, but she saw "no reason why it shouldn't be worn some day soon for general wear."

One editor at *Harper's Bazaar* worried that the idea was too radical even for its advanced readers. But Diana Vreeland decided to give it a whirl. She bought Orrick's drawings, and in January 1943, the magazine ran them under the title "The Leotard Idea."

"It's a new idea, leading toward the twenty-first century and the cosmic costumes of Flash Gordon's supergirl," the accompanying copy read. "It's an old idea based on every ballet dancer's traditional rehearsal costume: the two-piece jersey leotard, warm and all-covering. Mildred Orrick thought it out and sketched it. We present it—make what you will of it."

That spring, Vreeland decided that she would like to make something of it, even though *The New Yorker* had compared the leotard idea to "grandpa's underwear." She had a hunch that leotards would make an excellent addition to college girls' wardrobes. Fuel rationing meant that students were freezing in stone and brick dormitory halls and classrooms. The young college woman was also more willing to take fashion risks with novel sportswear.

To make the leotard a reality, Vreeland went to Claire McCardell, not Mildred Orrick. She may have believed that the leotard concept belonged to the magazine after they'd first published it. And Townley was better positioned to merchandise an idea, in the same way it had done with the Popover. In New York during World War II, *Harper's Bazaar*, and Vreeland in particular, wielded enormous power and influence. McCardell surely knew that Orrick had originated the leotard adaptation but she didn't tell her friend about Vreeland's request, or that she agreed to make it.

Weeks later, in June 1943, McCardell's version of the leotard walked the runway at the Plaza Hotel during the inaugural Press Week, what would later become known as New York Fashion Week. Publicist Eleanor Lambert had brought more than fifty newspaper and magazine editors and newspaper writers from around the country to New York for fashion shows, cocktail parties, and visits with American designers, McCardell chief among them.

McCardell's model wore a one-piece leotard with long sleeves made of striped wool jersey. On top of the leotard, she layered a tabard-style dress—a sleeveless tunic—that looked an awful lot like the sketch Orrick had drawn. But it also had the same spirit as the Popover: a dress that could be thrown over an underlayer. Only this time, the underlayer was meant to be seen.

In July 1943, *Harper's Bazaar* featured a second story on the leotard, this time with models sporting the ones made by McCardell. "In January we tossed out an idea, a new silhouette based on the leotard or ballet school tights. *The New Yorker* ribbed us but fashion followed us. This month we present leotards for the college girl. Under them, wear nothing but brassiere and pantie girdle." The design was credited to Claire McCardell and listed as available at Lord & Taylor.

The article blindsided Orrick. Neither Vreeland nor McCardell had told her it was coming. She had no idea that her good friend had produced her leotard idea. Orrick's mother was livid on her daughter's behalf when she heard the news. McCardell had been like a daughter to her. She'd cared and cooked for her when they had all lived together after the girls had graduated from Parsons. To both women, it felt like a betrayal.

To add insult to injury, Orrick learned that the *Harper's Bazaar* photos of McCardell's leotards would also be featured in a September issue of *Life* magazine. On September 1, 1943, Orrick wrote a letter to Henry Luce, the founder and editor in chief of *Life*. "I have learned that *Life* is planning to publish photographs of the leotard as shown in *Harper's Bazaar* and intends to use the name of Claire McCardell, designer, in their captions. This will imply that Miss McCardell was the originator of the idea which is erroneous." She enclosed a tear sheet from the January issue of *Harper's Bazaar* to prove that she'd been credited with the design. "I am sure *Life* magazine does not want to be guilty of a misrepresentation."

Luce never responded. Even if he received Orrick's letter, chances were good that the issue was already on its way to the printer. The leotard not only made it into *Life* magazine, it landed on the cover of the September 13 issue.

"This is a 'leotard,' new wartime fashion suggested by *Harper's Bazaar* for college girls," the article read. A photo caption identified McCardell as the one who'd made the leotards worn by the models. The article didn't credit her as the originator—that accolade went to *Harper's Bazaar*—but any reader could easily presume that the design was McCardell's, just as Orrick had feared.

In those nascent years of New York running its own creative industry, attributions were often ignored, lost, or misattributed. Babs Simpson, the fashion editor at *Vogue*, would credit Vreeland with the invention of ballet flats, even though the idea had originated with McCardell. Vreeland had simply shown the shoes in the pages of the magazine.

In her own work, McCardell usually distinguished between her originals and her fashion-trend iterations. She filed patent applications for her inventions, such as the Popover. Other creations, though, such as ballet flats, were progressions of existing objects. Similarly, Orrick had taken the existing leotard and reinterpreted it as fashion. Perhaps McCardell had assumed that the idea was open for iteration. One wonders, though, how a designer hell-bent against copying could have failed to mention any of this to Orrick, who was a longtime friend.

Sally Kirkland later noted that "Claire freely admits that the idea of using dancers' leotards as accompaniment to everyday clothes had come from Mildred Orrick originally." Orrick, who was laboring mightily to survive as a solo mother during the war and to maintain her footing in the design world, surely found no solace in that. Worse, Kirkland was among those who had the misconception that Orrick had "temporarily retired" from fashion to focus on family.

In 1943, thanks to *Harper's Bazaar*, *Life* magazine, and the reports coming out of Press Week, McCardell's leotard became a media sensation. But it was not a commercial success. The knitting process required to make the wool jersey was too costly. College students couldn't afford it, and it proved too expensive for Townley's usual price point.

In future seasons, McCardell would evolve the idea. In 1944, she made a striped tweed wrap dress with a matching green bodysuit and tights and matching tweed ballet shoes. Within two years, she evolved the design even further, separating the pieces and creating a pair of footless, body-hugging leggings that were worn by the socialite model Slim Keith in a spread for *Harper's Bazaar*. The leggings were presented as casual pants that could be paired with ballet flats and a sweater or a blouse. In the 1950s, it became the signature look popularized by stars such as Audrey Hepburn.

Over the years, McCardell allowed the design's provenance to remain murky. The leotard was often included on the lists of "firsts" distributed by her publicists. Yes, she was the first to make it, but not the first to think of it. Articles continued to credit her as the original designer of the leotard, and it's unclear if she ever tried to correct them.

In summer 1943, by putting work first, McCardell devastated one of her oldest friends. Mildred Orrick stopped speaking to her. The silence lasted for years. Orrick's anger began to thaw by 1946, when they both returned to Parsons as critics in the fashion department. They wouldn't rekindle their friendship in earnest until 1947. That year, Orrick invited McCardell to lunch. She divulged that she was, at the age of forty-one, expecting another baby, which was a surprise development. McCardell wrote her mother the news, and Eleanor replied with relief that Orrick was back in her life. Then she asked the pressing question: "Will Mildred be able to keep working?"

The answer was yes. Orrick did keep working, building a respected career and a portfolio of acclaimed modern designs, thanks in part to those midnight sketching sessions. Decades later, when that surprise baby, Sarah, was an adult, Orrick told her the story of the leotard. It was a cautionary tale. She spoke candidly about the challenges of balancing friendship, ambition, marriage, work, and children. Growing up, Sarah remembers spending time with her mother's fashion friend Joset Walker. But she doesn't recall meeting her mother's other college friend Claire McCardell.

CHAPTER SIXTEEN

The American Look

1944-45

In 1944, McCardell was fast becoming a household name. That year, *Life* magazine listed her among the country's best designers. A national survey of fifty thousand clothing retailers named McCardell as their preferred designer. McCardell trademarked her name and launched a new business, Claire McCardell Enterprises.

Adolph Klein was her business partner. They would continue to produce clothes under the Townley auspices, while Claire McCardell Enterprises became the umbrella under which McCardell could branch out. In the coming months and years, she would patent a design for a variation on cat's-eye sunglasses, make branded jewelry, gloves, scarves, and raincoats, and produce dress patterns for home sewers. One grateful customer wrote a letter of thanks for the patterns. She couldn't afford a new McCardell from the store, but now, she said, "I am enjoying tremendously the opportunity for the design, the savings, the creativeness, and fun of wearing the dresses I make," adding that such a "big person" as McCardell made "thousands of little persons like myself very happy."

At Townley, McCardell continued to push the boundaries of what women could wear in public, particularly with her athletic playsuits and swimsuits. Her love of swimming and Harris's pastime of sailing helped inspire radical swimwear designs. Most American women in the 1940s continued to wear bathing suits that resembled dresses with skirts. Or the suits had shorts, like the one McCardell had worn as a teenager. McCardell had long since jettisoned her swim stockings, and she always thought about how to make swimming easier. If she could wrap fabric between her legs instead of wearing shorts, it would streamline the suit. She'd begun experimenting with different shapes on the dress form in her office, wrapping fabric between the thighs.

Sally Kirkland, meanwhile, conspired to make the most out of Harris's boating hobby. Kirkland kept a summer house with her husband on Fishers Island, New York, an exclusive enclave for the social set who liked to sail. Kirkland suggested to McCardell that she and Harris dock there one summer day and join them for lunch. Harris fell in love with the island, so much so that he later bought a summer cottage there. Kirkland believed that Harris never realized that she worked in the fashion industry with his wife. On Fishers Island, McCardell, Kirkland, and other fashion friends, such as Vera Maxwell, spent many summer weekends together. "I always have thought that I kind of put one over on him," Kirkland later confessed.

The future fashion editor Polly Mellen was a teenager when McCardell showed off one of her new swimsuits on the beach at Fishers Island. McCardell removed her cover-up, and "she was in a diaper—a diaper!" Mellen later recounted. "Shocking, but she didn't care!"

The suit was made of lightweight, fast-drying wool jersey and cut from one piece of fabric. A woman could wrap it around her body to cover her buttocks and breasts and then tie it behind the neck like a halter, leaving most of her back exposed. McCardell cut the material high on the thighs, and it looked a bit like underwear to those used to a skirted bathing costume. McCardell jokingly called her one-piece halter top the "Diaper Suit." And because she didn't want anything to impede the experience of swimming, or inhibit fast and easy drying of material afterward, she got rid of the linings and bust pads found in most suits. As a result, a woman's nipples might be visible beneath the fabric, causing even more sensation on a 1940s beach.

Swimsuit design had been slowly evolving from the traditional bathing costume, and even two-piece bathing suits were being worn as early as the 1930s. Still, a woman with fabric between her legs and no breast padding in public was considered extremely racy. The design, coupled with the fact that McCardell didn't shave—she thought it a waste of time—gave her the reputation of the rebellious bohemian of Fishers Island. She was "this completely free spirit," Mellen said. "There was no vanity to this woman—a complete absence of narcissism." When criticized for the eroticism of her skirtless designs, McCardell once countered that "Swimsuits are for swimming. If it's a dress you want, I have that, too."

If her dresses had little hanger appeal in a store, her bathing suits were even harder to sell. McCardell's swimsuits proved difficult to display. "Often they were nothing but a bunch of strings," Babs Simpson said. "They looked simple, but they were very complex." Klein once joked about McCardell that "there were times when she'd get an idea and you needed a road map to get into the dress," and now he had to help explain to buyers how McCardell's swimsuits worked. Some fashion magazines offered step-by-step instructions for wrapping them. On Monday mornings during swimsuit season, Marjorie Griswold held a meeting of her floor staff at Lord & Taylor and demonstrated how to put a McCardell bathing suit together. Once a woman learned how to put it on, though, a McCardell suit was easy to wear, wash, and pack.

Over the years, McCardell designed more bathing suits that fit like a second skin. She thought about the water—her suits stayed put when swimming—and she thought about the sun. "I began some years ago taking interest in my sun-burn," she said around this time, referring to her tan. "White streaks from shoulder straps on shoulders and across arms didn't look very well, I thought." She designed some suits with removable straps, or no straps at all, so a woman wouldn't get tan lines. Others she made with her signature brass hook-and-eye closures and a matching wrap skirt, so that they could quickly transform into a sporty outfit that a woman could wear all day, not just to the beach.

As much as she evolved the look of the swimsuit, she similarly innovated with women's athletic wear. She designed a series of playsuits meant for outdoor activities that looked like modernized versions of the bloomer-and-blouse gym uniform she'd worn at Hood. She made a plaid one-piece romper with long sleeves, buttons down the front, and attached shorts that poofed wide before cinching at the thigh. For another playsuit, she designed a one-piece, strapless bubble shape with elastic to cinch it in at the chest and the thighs. Made of cotton calico, that playsuit could go into the water or be paired with a leather belt and worn on land.

McCardell's playsuits and swimwear might not have caught on, though, if not for the artistry of photographer Louise Dahl-Wolfe. Fashion photography was just coming into its own, and Dahl-Wolfe, a *Harper's Bazaar* contributor, was a pioneer. She understood how to capture the sophistication and movement of McCardell's sports clothes. She left the controlled studio and instead went on location with the models. The women stood on jagged sea cliffs, ran on beaches, and stretched into the frame as sailboats bobbed in the background. Powerful, seductive, and athletic, those women could, at any moment, board one of the sailing sloops docked behind them and navigate out to sea solo. They were women of consequence and of action. McCardell's clothes in those photographs evoked the modern, independent American woman. And when Dahl-Wolfe photographed a playsuit-clad model in front of a Frank Lloyd Wright modern house, she put McCardell's designs in conversation with the great American architect. Dahl-Wolfe said that she could never take a bad photo of McCardell clothes. She helped make McCardell's sportswear highly recognizable, even iconic.

The two women became good friends. Dahl-Wolfe and her husband kept a house not far from McCardell's in Frenchtown, New Jersey. They met for drinks and dinners and discussed their art and design work, at least when Harris wasn't around. Those weekends in Frenchtown had the scintillating playfulness of an artist's colony. Dahl-Wolfe sometimes photographed McCardell's latest designs while there. She would pose a model on the dramatic staircase in her modern home.

During the war, as fuel and tires were in short supply, more women rode bicycles year-round. McCardell winterized her playsuits, which Dahl-Wolfe photographed. She designed one winter biking outfit with pants that ended just below the knee. The shorter pants didn't get stuck in the spokes of a bicycle wheel, earning them the nickname "pedal pushers." *Newsweek* later credited McCardell with inventing the style. In truth, her pedal pushers were a modern adaptation of a design that dated back to the invention of the bicycle. In the 1890s, riding a bicycle was considered a defiant act of feminism. "The bicycle is on the way to transforming our way of life more deeply than you might think," the French actress Sarah Bernhardt said at the time. "All these young women and girls who are devouring space are refusing domestic family life." To ride the new velocipede, as it was called, women wore pants similar to men's knickerbockers, which ended just below the knee. Many quickly reverted to long skirts again, though, owing to public harassment.

McCardell now gave women an updated, winter-ready version. By the 1950s, pedal pushers, or Capri pants as they were called in Europe, worn with ballet flats, would become a widespread trend. For her biking outfit, McCardell paired the pedal pushers with a wool jersey sweater that included her signature attached hood. The media dubbed it the "Superman Hood." It would be another few decades before an athletic top with a hood would become known simply as a hoodie.

In the winter of 1944, McCardell's innovative designs earned her the highest honor in American fashion, the award Norman Norell had always believed she deserved. That February, she was called onto the stage at the second annual Coty Awards and handed the bronze Winnie. Even Henry Geiss applauded her in the press, calling her the most advanced designer in the country and crediting her with the massive financial growth at Townley.

In her acceptance speech, McCardell addressed the elephant in the room. The war was turning in favor of the Allied forces, which was a very good development. While everyone longed for peace, concern rippled through the hundreds of guests gathered at the Coty Awards: Could US fashion compete against Parisian fashion?

"We are at last beginning to believe that Americans can give something individual to American women in fashion," she assured the audience. "In the past, I had to blame all my wildest ideas on Paris. Now I can be the American designer thinking for myself. I shall go back to Paris when the time comes to breathe its stimulating air, to see and buy its fine fabrics, to admire the work of talented fingers that produce out of sheer love of beauty and form," she continued, adding, "we are a mass production country; we want to give the best to all people. But the little man and woman with art in his fingertips will always have something to say. The world should be big enough for us all."

Six months after the Coty Awards, on August 24, 1944, the bells of Notre Dame tolled for the first time in years, welcoming the French Resistance army into Paris and announcing the end of Nazi occupation.

◆

That fall, the Museum of Modern Art took up the question of whether American fashion had, like other forms of design, successfully modernized. MoMA staged its first ever fashion exhibition, titled *Are Clothes Modern?* The curator of the show was an expat European living in New York named Bernard Rudofsky. He mounted a history-spanning show in which he concluded that American ready-to-wear had fallen short of fulfilling its potential. Claire McCardell, he believed, was the exception. He lauded the design and cut of her playsuits, saying they represented the future of design.

Vogue refuted Rudofsky's negative assessment of the American fashion industry at large. "Are clothes modern?" the editors asked. "*Vogue* answers, 'emphatically, yes!' and wonders that the bright-eyed, up-to-the-minute Modern Museum could ask such a question seriously."

Vogue's defense of contemporary fashion read like a mission statement for McCardell's approach. "Today's ideal feminine shape is more nearly the natural feminine figure," the editors wrote. "Waists are waists (with no vice-like contraptions). Hips are hips (with no bird-cage bustles)."

They juxtaposed images of Victorian clothes against those of contemporary sportswear designers, like McCardell. "No more stiff boned, constricting collars, no more rigid bust-distorting armour, no more torturing, steel-stay corsets, no more heavy stockings . . . now legs are bare or near-nude in nylons. No more manacling shoes, now flat heels, ballet slippers."

They capped their story with a full-page photo of McCardell wearing one of her newest designs. She called it the Future Dress. She channeled her love of geometric shapes into a gown made of two large triangles of apricot-colored fabric. She sewed them together into a sleeveless dress with a large bow at the neck. White topstitching at the seams created a contrast to the fabric. A thin gold belt sparkled at her waist. She posed with one hand in her pocket, a look of assured confidence on her face. The photographer, Erwin Blumenfeld, had placed her behind a frosted glass door panel so that half of her body was slightly blurred. It was an unwitting, if accurate, presentation of the split life of a woman: Claire versus McCardell; private versus public. The insecurities and the shyness that she felt while doing publicity were nowhere to be seen in the steely, determined look she gave the camera. Claire McCardell was the face of the American fashion revolution.

◆

As *Vogue* photographed McCardell, the Parisian couturiers were announcing plans for their return. The French, now free after years of occupation, were determined to show that couture had survived the Nazis. In the spring of 1945, they would return to the global stage after five years. "A different kind of battle is shaping up in the plush-lined fashion salons of Paris and New York," the Associated Press reported. "It is the struggle between the two cities for the title 'Fashion Capital of the World.'"

On January 11, 1945, two months before Paris staged its comeback, McCardell attended a luncheon and press conference convened by Dorothy Shaver. Shaver had recently become the first female president of Lord & Taylor. She knew it was a critical moment for Americans to go on the offensive. New York would have to define its unique aesthetic and cement its rightful place in global fashion.

Shaver welcomed a world at peace again, she told the press that day, just as she would welcome the creativity of all countries being freely exchanged. But America had come of age, and "this time I believe that the flow of talent will be coming *from* as well as *to* the United States," she said.

Shaver announced a new ad campaign by Lord & Taylor called "The American Look." "I believe that the American Look is, and will continue to be, the most important style trend in the world," she said. The talents of the American designer had been freed from the influence of others, she proclaimed, and now the American Look "stands as a strong, virile influence that is growing and will continue to be vigorous, even with the European market again at our disposal."

The term "American Look" had been bandied about for years in promotion of New York fashion, but in Shaver's handling, it was presented as more than a mere fashion trend; it was a cultural movement, tethered to democracy and the United States' global ascendency. "Just as our way of living and thinking is influencing the entire world, the way the American woman looks is as significant a tendency as any artistic movement or development."

The American Look was nourished, she added, by strong economics, mass production, and a land of milk, green vegetables, orange juice, low-priced beauty parlors, health care, dime-store cosmetics, and women playing sports. The American Look "is young; it is feminine; it emphasizes the American figure, always considered the finest in the world," she enthused. "It enhances the long well-shaped leg; the slim waist; the broad shoulders and natural bust line. It is without artifice, designed for the active, vigorous life lived by American women." Retailers, designers, and manufacturers across the country embraced Shaver's campaign, and it dominated magazine and newspaper coverage for months, including a multipage feature in *Life* magazine.

As Shaver became the outspoken ambassador of the American Look, she simultaneously became a defender of the designers creating it. The American Look was being made predominantly by, and for, women. A reporter asked her whether women might one day be equal to men in the fashion industry; she said yes. "Of course, we must clarify what we mean by the word 'equality,'" she added. "If we mean that women can do most jobs as well as men—though not in exactly the same fashion—then I think it is absolutely true. . . . Every year women are filling more and more jobs in more and more fields." When pressed about the competition with men in retail, she once said, "The best answer to that is that I have survived three changes of management and got a promotion every time."

Embedded within the story of freedom, resourcefulness, and mass-produced style of the American Look, however, were limiting constraints, not the least of which were the whiteness and middle- and upper-class standing of the women who promoted and modeled it. The words *slim* and *young* dominated. Health, athleticism, vitality, and youth were emphasized. It echoed the publicity material Peggy LeBoutillier had created for McCardell, in which she had presented the designer as a lemon water–drinking woman of natural thinness.

McCardell privately fretted when her weight inched above what she believed to be socially acceptable. The delicacies in France had enticed her during her trips to Paris before the war. "I've gained about two pounds in the last week," she once wrote home to her mother. "Guess I'll have to start reducing but French pastry is so good and so cheap." She took to swimming laps in the city's indoor public pools.

A woman's weight and height were routinely included in news articles, even as men escaped such "reporting," and that added pressure to maintain a consistent body size. Even as McCardell aimed to free women from the burdens of proscriptive and fussy attire, escaping the prevailing pressure to be thin proved difficult. The emergence of a body type—lithe, thin, and strong—now signified the archetypal American woman, and *youth* was the watchword. McCardell, on the cusp of turning forty, was regularly described as a "youthful designer." It could make one wonder what would happen when one stopped being young.

Women's magazines brimmed with stories about weight loss and beauty regimes. They suggested slimming diet pills, which would soon include amphetamines, and they pushed tinctures, body oils, hair dyes, and all manner of other products meant to give a woman a healthy glow. "Natural" American good looks apparently took lots of unnatural products to achieve.

Sports culture in America, meanwhile, was evolving into an exercise culture. Joseph and Clara Pilates had earned a large following after opening their studio in New York in the 1920s. Their new exercise program, which later became known as Pilates, was among a growing regimen of indoor classes. McCardell always said that her clothes could be worn without body-shaping undergarments. Yet a woman's body was still being judged against a slender, shapely ideal. The freedom from constricting undergarments didn't release a woman from that judgment. Instead, the boning of corsets was being replaced by musculature. A woman's own body was meant to provide the armature of shapeliness in the form of a taut abdomen.

Fashion—not for the first or last time—sent mixed messages. McCardell grappled with those paradoxes and pressures, as many other women did. Being the face of her brand carried with it a level of power and prestige but also increased public scrutiny. Her relationship to her own body reflected both a desire to liberate herself from cultural norms and a feeling that she had to continue to present herself as the perfect-sized fit model that she'd been at the age of twenty-three. She once said that "tummies are beautiful, like Botticelli's Venus." She believed in the sanctity of the female form. Still, she succumbed to the societal pressure to remain thin, and she encouraged diet and exercise as keys to achieving the American Look.

In its emphasis on sportswear and the mass manufacturing taking place on Seventh Avenue, the American Look also left out a significant group of innovative women designers. The campaign highlighted ready-to-wear, not custom-made, clothes in a deliberate attempt to contrast America to Parisian haute couture. Only, New York had supremely talented made-to-order designers, most notably Ann Lowe and Zelda Wynn Valdes, doing equally unique and signature work for American women.

In her shop on the Upper East Side of New York City, Ann Lowe created couture-quality clothes with a modicum of staff and resources. She had been hand sewing gowns for America's elite for decades, and her debutante and evening dresses were worn at the most exclusive parties around the country. The actress Olivia de Havilland would wear a chiffon blue gown by Lowe as she accepted a 1946 Academy Award. In 1953, Jacqueline Bouvier would marry a promising young senator named John F. Kennedy in a Lowe design. What none of the guests at that well-publicized wedding would know was that ten days prior to the nuptials, a flood in Lowe's shop had destroyed Bouvier's gown along with most of the bridesmaids' dresses. Lowe was so supremely gifted that she was able to remake the wedding gown and dresses on time.

Zelda Wynn Valdes, meanwhile, made sensual, body-hugging dresses for her famous clientele, including artists, actors, and performers such as Josephine Baker, Eartha Kitt, Ella Fitzgerald, and Mae West. From her boutique, Chez Zelda, on 57th Street in Midtown, she turned out exquisitely crafted clothes for women who didn't have the popularized thin American Look.

Lowe and Valdes were doing for custom design what McCardell was doing for ready-to-wear: They were thinking of the female experience and creatively solving problems in couture as surely as McCardell did in mass production.

Many of Lowe's debutante and formal gowns, for instance, had low backs that exposed the skin because Lowe had noticed that dirt and oil would transfer off men's fingers as they danced with their partners. When she made a gown for a young piano player to wear during a concert, she positioned a rear bow to the side of the skirt so that it folded softly over the piano bench and didn't make it uncomfortable for the woman to sit.

Lowe and Valdes were ignored by the broader media campaigns covering the American Look, however. That was partly because they worked in couture rather than ready-to-wear, but it was also because they were Black. In New York, women of color were among the most creative and pioneering in women's fashions at the time, even as they contended with the dual injustices of sexism and racism. It would be decades before anyone would learn that a Black woman had designed Jackie Kennedy's bridal gown or that when Lowe had gone to deliver the dresses on the wedding day, she'd been told to use the service entrance. She refused and walked right through the front door.

In 1945, whether in ready-to-wear or couture, New York fashion had ascended thanks to a group of gifted women designers. Women helmed many of the design departments in Seventh Avenue firms, and they ran the stores lining Fifth Avenue. They were supported by a bevy of fellow women who worked as publicists, buyers, journalists, and editors. The number and influence of women in the New York industry prompted Kenneth Collins, a department store executive, to herald their work in establishing American fashion. "This emancipation of women, this new and more important status of one half of the inhabitants of the globe, will be considered the one significant fact of our times," he said during a meeting of the Fashion Group. "I don't think men will ever again be able to contemptuously refer to the weaker sex and talk about the things that women cannot do."

But Collins, and the women of New York fashion, had yet to reckon with Christian Dior.

PART IV

Women Are What They Wear

(1946–58)

CHAPTER SEVENTEEN

Stay Out of Topeka, You Bum

1946–50

As Dorothy Shaver promoted the American Look, Carmel Snow of *Harper's Bazaar* tried to draw New Yorkers back to Paris. The intrepid editor was one of the first to return to the city after the Nazi retreat. In April of 1946, she stood before the New York Fashion Group's monthly luncheon and assured the crowd that the trip was a breeze. Getting to Paris took just seventeen hours instead of seven days, thanks to air travel. You simply hopped a flight from LaGuardia to Newfoundland, waited to refuel, then went on to Ireland for a layover and breakfast in Shannon. "With my Irish blood I wouldn't have minded being held up there for hours," she said. The airport was like Grand Central Station, and "they make the most wonderful use of Irish tweeds—white tweed coats on the waiters, and red tweed seats in the restaurants! Yes, I'm awfully afraid Ireland is going chic." A third and final flight landed you at Orly Airport outside Paris.

"Since my return, I've been asked over and over again, one question. 'Shall we go over for the next . . . collections?' My answer is an unqualified yes." Snow conceded that couture was still finding its footing, but she mentioned bright spots, including a promising designer she'd met. His name was Christian Dior, and he was full of ideas.

Not long after the meeting, McCardell met Marjorie Griswold of Lord & Taylor and the journalist Sally Kirkland for a quieter lunch at the French restaurant Baroque on East 53rd Street. Every few months, the designer, the buyer, and the magazine editor lingered over glasses of wine and the *sole à la grenobloise* to talk about life and work.

Kirkland relayed further reports from Paris, which had been coming from her *Vogue* colleague Bettina Ballard. The couturiers had miraculously survived the occupation, even defying the Nazis' attempt to move the haute couture trade to Berlin. But they were still struggling to find their way. The war had come to a stunning, shattering end the previous September, and now everyone had to grapple with its aftermath: the horror of the concentration camps, the substantial loss of life, the unbridled power that had decimated Hiroshima and Nagasaki. There was something to be said, however seemingly insignificant, for countering the wrath of war with art and beauty. That was what people needed from Paris right then.

As McCardell's friends discussed Paris, McCardell was preoccupied by personal matters at home. Her father, Roy, had succumbed to a long illness a few months earlier and died at the age of seventy-two. McCardell's oldest brother, Adrian, had been able to join her and their mother at the funeral in Frederick, but her brother Bob, a specialist in the Navy, had still been on a battleship en route from Japan. Her youngest brother, Max, a lieutenant in the Navy, had also been at sea, his location unknown. Now her brothers were home safe, and Adrian had recently married a young Hood graduate. The full grief of her father's death had finally sunk in. She missed him terribly. She had to keep her emotions in check, because she had a new collection to produce. With all that she was going through, she couldn't summon an interest in what the French were plotting.

Kirkland and Griswold turned their attention to McCardell. The L-85 fabric restrictions had just been lifted, and the women were curious: What was she going to design next?

"I never want to see a tight skirt again," she said. "And I think many women feel the same way." It was too late to change her 1946 fall collection, as it had already been designed. But her 1947 spring collection promised to bring a new silhouette. She predicted that women would want longer, fuller skirts.

Kirkland heartily disagreed. Women weren't going to toss out the shorter hemlines and slimmer dresses they'd been wearing through the war and render their wardrobes outdated overnight, she said. They would want slow change. Marjorie Griswold concurred. They both believed McCardell to be a sage predictor of future trends, but in this instance, they told her, she was wrong. McCardell sipped her coffee and didn't argue.

That summer, McCardell sketched her 1947 spring dresses with long, wide skirts that hit the lower calf, a full twelve to fourteen inches below the knee. To balance the broader width at the bottom, she made the bodices snug and nipped them in a bit to emphasize a woman's true waistline. She emphasized natural, rounded shoulders, a slimness at the waist, and a flowing, long skirt that celebrated the hourglass shape. And for the woman who wasn't quite so hourglass, she designed garments with wider sleeves to help give the illusion of a thinner waist.

At Townley, she put one of the outfits in progress onto a fit model, a woman she'd been working with for years. She made a few adjustments and, once satisfied, asked the model to take a walk. The model knew that McCardell wanted to see the outfit in action. She strode through the sample room. She pantomimed, with an actor's flair, as if she were desperately trying to hail a cab. McCardell laughed. Seeing the clothes on a human being was a vital part of her design process. She thought of her fit models as collaborators. They were stand-ins for the customers who would one day wear her clothes. Inviting their feedback led to better solutions.

After the austerity of rationing, after the uniforms and overalls and housedresses, McCardell believed that women were ready for this new silhouette she'd designed. They were ready for some fun and frivolity—restrained, of course, by "intelligent sensibility," as she put it.

◆

Across the ocean in Paris, the new designer Carmel Snow had mentioned worked feverishly on a new silhouette that looked a lot like the one McCardell had come up with. Only, the dresses that Christian Dior sketched were exaggerated in their dimensions. He had in mind the figure eight, an auspicious number to a man who believed in fortune telling and numerology the way others believed in God. In that number, he saw the amplified hourglass of a female body: wide at the shoulders and bosom, extremely slender at the waist, wide again at the hips.

Dior was the same age as McCardell, forty-one, but he was newer to fashion and relatively unknown. He'd been raised in a wealthy industrialist family in Granville, Normandy, in northern France. He and his siblings had been pampered, and they had been pushed to greatness. Dior had defied his parents' wishes for a political career when he'd opened a modern art gallery in Paris in the 1920s. It was a shaky enterprise in the best of times, but one that failed as the world economy collapsed after the 1929 crash. Tragedy further subsumed Dior when his mother died soon after and his father lost the family fortune in the Depression. Dior was poor and directionless, but he could draw. He taught himself to sketch clothes, and his first appearance in *Harper's Bazaar* came early in the war when he illustrated lingerie to accompany an article.

In the winter of 1946, when Carmel Snow first met him, Dior was working as a designer for another couturier. Shortly after, a wealthy French textile entrepreneur gave Dior six million francs to start his own couture house. The investment would quickly climb to over sixty million francs. He founded Maison Dior in October and by the end of 1946 was in a mad rush to complete his first solo collection in time for the spring showings in February.

Life during World War II had been harsh, and Dior believed that people wanted an escape. "In an epoch as somber as ours, luxury must be defended inch by inch," he said. He believed that "deep in every heart slumbers a dream" in which "every woman is a princess." To him, that meant making a woman beguiling to a man. His credo was "Please the ladies by enabling them to please their men."

The Bar Suit, as he called it, emerged as a signature look. A cream silk jacket hugged the body with a "wasp waist," a corseted midsection so thin that it evoked the segmented body of a wasp. A long, pleated black skirt opened with the width and spread of an evening gown. To achieve such girth, Dior padded a woman's hips and lined the skirts with taffeta. He aimed to turn women "into flowers, with soft shoulders, blooming bosoms, waists slim as vine stems, and skirts opening like blossoms," he said.

Dior had over a hundred skilled workers to assist him. He passed his drawings on to teams of seamstresses, each led by a *première*. The seamstresses turned his sketches into a toile, a prototype rendered in less expensive fabric, allowing Dior to refine it to his liking.

That winter, Dior appraised the initial toiles using the industry standard wooden dressmaker's mannequin. He quickly determined something to be wrong. The waist was far too big. He yelled for a hammer. With forceful, passionate blows, Dior carved and reshaped the wooden waist on the dummy into his ideal: eighteen inches. (For comparison, Rita Hayworth, among the most famous Hollywood actresses at the time, had a waist size of twenty-five inches.) Dior didn't aim to celebrate feminine curves as much as construct them. He ordered his premières to make his dresses like buildings, rigid constructions that molded a woman's body. Slowly, each toile came to life, even as one première suffered a nervous breakdown due to the demanding, unrelenting pace.

Next, human models replaced the wooden dummies. The women wore customized corsets and extra padding under their clothes. The additional structure shaped a woman as Dior envisioned. Dior, armed with a gold-tipped cane, pointed, poked, and critiqued the garments. The outfits were snipped, pinned, and adjusted by his assistants, and the models hardly dared breathe lest they be pricked by a needle or by the designer's notorious temper. Those sessions lasted for hours and proved grueling.

One model grew lightheaded from standing and from the restriction of the corset used to shrink her waist. She went limp in Dior's hands. It took him a second to realize that she'd fainted. He tried to grasp her as she slid to the ground in a puddle of fabric, but she passed through his hands. Dior was startled to realize that he still clutched a flesh-colored lump in his hand, and his immediate thought was that he'd somehow taken the woman's breast off as she fell. But it was only padding. "I had completely forgotten that in my desire to give prominence to this most feminine attribute, I had asked those women whom nature had neglected to equip themselves with 'falsies,'" he recounted. That became a favorite anecdote for Dior, one that he retold with relish and later included in his autobiography: the story of the great couturier and the false bosom. Erased from his irreverent recounting was the fate of the nameless woman left unconscious on the ground.

◆

On February 12, 1947, a cold front moved through Paris and froze the Seine River. Even still, members of the international press, the royalty of Europe, and the upper crust of society braved icy streets to line up outside Dior's atelier, their coveted invitations clutched in gloved hands. Inside, models emerged wearing extravagant dresses. Their wide skirts knocked over ashtrays as they sashayed through the crowded showroom. Attendees cheered the decadent, seemingly unending display of tulle, silk organza, and taffeta. Carmel Snow was especially besotted. "It's quite a revolution, dear Christian!" she reportedly gushed after the show. "Your dresses have such a new look! They are simply wonderful."

Dior's "New Look," as it became known, was praised as a much-needed return to femininity after wartime restrictions. Dior believed that the critical raves over his New Look were "due to the fact that I brought back the neglected art of pleasing," and by that he meant pleasing men. The highly constructed silhouette of a single Dior couture dress could take more than eighty hours to fabricate. Coco Chanel was outraged. "Dior doesn't dress women," she said. "He upholsters them."

Frenchwomen protested the excess. One skirt could use as much as fifteen yards of fabric, which seemed excessive, even unpatriotic. France was still recovering from shortages of material, food, and energy. But it was also the superstructure required to achieve the silhouette and the long skirts designed to hamper a woman's movement that especially irked them.

Thanks to Dior, a woman once again needed help getting dressed. The British news organization Pathé filmed the undergarment process in an explanatory newsreel. First came a highly padded, cone-shaped bra. Next came the corset to achieve the figure eight appearance. An assistant had to cinch the laces at the wearer's back and then affix padding to the shoulders and hips, which made the woman "look like a destroyer having its armor plating lay," the Pathé announcer said, "but these are the armaments of beauty."

Dior's New Look hit US shores, and Seventh Avenue rushed to imitate it. It enraged McCardell how quickly the industry went back to copying France. She scrawled in her notebook, "Are we returning to the dark ages when American designers are not allowed to think for themselves?"

A fellow American designer, Bonnie Cashin, also found Dior's fashions retrograde. They lacked any modernity or innovation, she felt, and she mirrored McCardell's beliefs about ease of travel when she said that "you can't stuff a dress weighing twenty pounds into an overnight bag."

Sophie Gimbel, the house designer for Saks Fifth Avenue, lasted less than fifteen minutes in the Dior corset. "I've never been so uncomfortable in my life," she said.

Was the painful scaffolding intentional? A biographer would later describe Dior as "a man of blazing, violent, short-lived passions, and his eroticized imagination may have swayed between tenderness and violence." Who can say how these contradictions contributed to his art? American men put it more succinctly in 1947. "Stay out of Topeka, you bum!" a Kansas man wrote the designer. A man from Idaho complained: "You have disfigured my wife with your genius."

In the summer of 1947, Stanley Marcus, a department store magnate, flew Dior to Dallas to present him with the Neiman Marcus Award for the New Look. Marcus said that he had never seen anything as sensational. In protest, a group of Texas women banded together under the name "Little Below the Knee Club." Their slogan: "The Alamo fell, but our hemlines will not." They argued that Dior was returning them to the fashions of their Victorian grandmothers. Anti–New Look protesters marched with banners reading, "Mr. Dior, we abhor dresses to the floor."

In Louisville, Georgia, meanwhile, a woman named Louise Horn disembarked from a city bus only to have her extremely long and poufy New Look–style skirt catch in the automatic doors. She was dragged for a block before the driver realized what had happened. Horn gathered over 1,200 signatures to insist that skirt widths be reined in for the safety of women.

Dior relished every minute of the controversy. He wrote his business manager that the Americans and their protests had given him wonderful publicity. His name was even more widely known now.

Women in Europe and the United States continued to wear the New Look, despite the burden Dior's clothes presented. At a party one evening, a Dior-clad former model told Carmel Snow how much she loved her outfit, even though she couldn't walk, eat, or sit down in it. *Vogue*'s Bettina Ballard exasperated her husband with a Dior dress fastened with thirty tiny buttons up the back. He struggled to push them all through the delicate buttonholes. They were desperately late for dinner, so he finally yelled to their friend waiting patiently in the other room to come in and help. It was the Spanish designer Cristóbal Balenciaga. "But Christian is mad, mad!" Balenciaga muttered as he fought to close the buttons.

McCardell also thought so. She went on a media blitz to counter the New Look fanaticism and its body deformation. A host on the popular radio show *Three Views of the News* asked her, "Do you believe the old saying that you have to suffer to be beautiful?"

"I certainly don't. When you're uncomfortable you are likely to show it. That's why I make even my most formal dresses as comfortable as a playsuit. Clothes should stay put, too, so there is no temptation to be forever pulling, pinching, and adjusting them which spoils your own fun and makes everyone else fidgety. You never look really well-dressed when you're overconscious of what you have on. Comfort should be a keynote of style."

During another interview in the fall of 1947, McCardell encouraged women to use common sense. "It's not intelligent to follow fashion blindly. Every woman is a separate individual and needs special and separate consideration," she said.

McCardell "prefers comfort to stiff formality," one journalist summarized. "To her, there's no reason to attend a party in a dress that feels like a first cousin to a straitjacket."

Still, the media praised the New Look and all it represented for demure and docile femininity. Only two years earlier, *Vogue* had vociferously defended the natural, corset-free body in its rebuttal to the MoMA show. The editors had proudly embraced Claire McCardell and her ethos. Now they applauded Dior's "waist-indenting *guêpière*," or corset. Every dress was constructed "to give you an exaggeratedly feminine figure, even if nature has not."

Not long after Dior released his New Look, the French philosopher Simone de Beauvoir wrote in *Vogue* about the reversion she was seeing in female sovereignty. Women were being told to quit their jobs and return home. "The French have never been feminists," she wrote, adding that they loved women, but in the way that "ogres love little children—for their consumption." It was easy to see how Dior represented that very idea of women being ogled and consumed by men.

Fashion has always been an excellent bellwether of societal belief, and Dior, with his stated intention to bring femininity back, was a harbinger of broader changes. Women's magazines that had once promoted and advocated careers for women now wrote stories about the bliss of staying home and raising families. With the war over, federal and civilian policies again prioritized male workers over women, in much the same way federal laws had biased jobs in favor of husbands during the Depression. In times of conflict—world wars, the Great Depression—women were asked to use their intelligence, resourcefulness, and muscle to save the country. After the conflict was resolved, they were told to return home again and to limit their ambitions to family making. The public image of women was shifting from Rosie the Riveter confidence to New Look submissiveness.

If McCardell was being honest, she could see the brewing backlash to women's autonomy already forming in 1945, as soon as peace had been won. The editors of *Vogue* had asked to use clothes from her collection for an editorial photo spread. They chose a pair of tapered green wool trousers and a black turtleneck blouse. A year earlier, the model wearing McCardell's clothes might have been pictured active in the workplace or moving freely about the city. Now she stood by the fireplace, the proverbial hearth, her elbow on the mantelpiece, her head resting in her hand, as she looked benevolently at her husband sitting in a living room chair. He was dark haired, handsome, still wearing his khaki-colored Army uniform as if he had just walked through the door fresh from battle. He looked not at his wife but straight ahead, blankly watching the roaring flames of the fire. "He's back," the copy read. "Unbelievably, back for good. Life together begins again—with your vow that home and you will stay as attractive as he dreamed." On the model's lips and fingernails, a caption noted, the woman wore Revlon's newest color of deep, rich red—Fatal Apple, a reference to Snow White. Two years before Dior unleashed his fairy-tale princess fantasies, the world was already primed for them.

Fashion in the late 1940s became, not for the first or last time, a dichotomy between the self-determination and naturalness of the American Look and the structured prettiness of the New Look. In 1948, a year after Stanley Marcus feted Christian Dior in Dallas, he handed the Neiman Marcus Award to McCardell. Marcus lauded her "refreshing creative spirit and her completely American approach towards fashion." He told an auditorium full of industry professionals that she was "one of the few truly creative designers this country has produced, borrowing nothing from other designers. She is to America what Vionnet was . . . to France."

In 1948, women did earn one minor concession from Dior. He let out his extraordinarily tight waistlines ever so slightly, perhaps in response to the months of backlash. They were no longer "as small as last year's extremes which kept many women from breathing in public," one report noted, "so the trend is away from slow strangulation."

CHAPTER EIGHTEEN

Society Is an Awful Chore, Isn't It?

1950–52

Golden sunlight illuminated the glass-and-steel skyscrapers of Manhattan. McCardell gathered her bag and switched off the lamp in her office at Townley. It was well after 6:00 p.m., and the rest of the staff had left for the day.

Most evenings, she didn't go straight home. She attended fashion industry events or classes at Parsons, where she remained a guest lecturer and critic. She kept a rigorous schedule. Come February, though, once the spring/summer season was completed, she could take her annual vacation. Some years, Harris joined her and her friends from Frederick at a lodge in Canada's Laurentian Mountains. But just as frequently, she traveled without her husband.

That winter of 1950, she and Harris were arguing more than usual. Her husband seemed itching for a fight. It may have been the pressure of ongoing legal battles over his children's inherited trusts from Jean. He had spent years in court battling lawsuits lodged by Jean's second husband. Or it could have been owing to McCardell's mounting accomplishments. Even Eleanor picked up on the tensions from Frederick. After McCardell was featured in *Holiday*, a popular arts and culture magazine, Eleanor wrote, "Claire, dearest, Why didn't you tell me your picture would be in *Holiday*? I was so thrilled to see you in it this month. Certainly, is a tribute to you and your work," adding, "Hope Irving doesn't mind!"

In mid-February, McCardell escaped for Europe without her husband. She joined friends on a ski trip to the Austrian Alps. A letter from John Harris arrived for her at the Grand Hotel in Kitzbühel a week later. John, a junior at Princeton, wrote McCardell to say that Eleanor was worried about her. Eleanor had gone through John to inquire about McCardell's travel plans, rather than reach out to her son-in-law directly. "The first I knew of your trip was a letter from Grannie the day before yesterday saying why did you have to go *all* the way to Austria? Where are you staying? And did I think you'd be coming back on a plane? I'm afraid she picked the wrong department for information about you. *Harper's Bazaar* probably has the inside story, but I never shall."

McCardell replied and explained the last-minute nature of her travel. "I decided at noon on a Friday," to join her friends, "and sailed at 4 o'clock so even *Harper's Bazaar* hadn't heard about it."

Two months later, on Saturday, April 15, 1950, McCardell was home in New York, but preparing to take another solo journey, this time to Washington, DC. She dressed in her room, choosing one of her newest designs, an ankle-length pleated evening dress with a wrap-front halter top. A long sash tied at the waist and flowed down to her calves.

McCardell walked into the living room, where Liz, age sixteen, cast a confused glance at her. Liz had thought they were leaving for Frenchtown. "Why do you have your city clothes on?" she asked.

"I have some business to take care of and will be back tomorrow. We'll leave then."

McCardell took a train to Union Station in Washington, DC, and then a cab to the Hotel Statler on 16th Street. The modernist hotel had played host to foreign dignitaries and Hollywood royalty, such as Judy Garland. That night, McCardell was the star.

The Women's Press Club was honoring six women with its annual achievement award, among them Martha Graham, who'd pioneered modern dance; Olivia de Havilland, a two-time Academy Award winner; and Mildred Rebstock, a scientist being recognized for her critical research into antibiotics. The Women's Press Club had been founded in

1919 as an answer to the all-male club, which barred women. McCardell became the first fashion designer to earn the honor. President Harry Truman handed her a framed certificate. To her, the award represented not only the importance of American fashion but the continued elevation of women in society.

After the ceremony and dinner, Press Club members entertained the crowd with skits lampooning the reasons why Americans hadn't yet elected a woman to the White House.

On Sunday, McCardell joined Harris and Liz in Frenchtown. Liz learned of her stepmother's award only when she later heard the news on the radio. She chalked the omission up to McCardell's modesty. But it also could have been due to the firewall that McCardell kept between her marriage and her career. She knew her husband's deep reluctance to be Mr. Claire McCardell. Whether Harris chose to ignore the event or McCardell never invited him, the fact is that he didn't join the other male spouses at the gala as they feted their wives.

As the calendar turned to 1951, however, Harris wanted McCardell to play the role of Mrs. Irving Drought Harris. Liz would turn eighteen in September, and Harris had decided that his only daughter should be formally introduced to New York society. The debutante year in New York was an exacting tradition composed of dance lessons, teas, and dinner parties that culminated in elaborate debutante balls in November and December. Harris announced to the family that he'd secured Liz an invitation to the prestigious Grosvenor Debutante Ball, to be held Thanksgiving weekend at the Plaza Hotel.

Parents, namely mothers, were expected to participate in the yearlong activities. They chaired the volunteer committees that planned the dances and hosted formal dinners. They navigated their daughters through a minefield of explicit rules about what to wear and how to perform, as well as the unspoken nuances of societal maneuvering. A successful season was thought to solidify a woman's prospects in life by ensuring a husband and cementing the right connections. A tepid coming out meant ridicule at best; at worst, a girl would be ostracized.

The debutante system of 1950s New York harkened back to its origins in eighteenth-century England. The tradition had been invented as a way for the upper class to broker auspicious partnerships for their daughters. Women became currency in a ritual to marry them off. Debutante balls presented marriage-ready daughters to society while also demonstrating a family's wealth and social currency.

In the centuries since its inception, countless women had detailed the trials of being a debutante. Edith Wharton, the great scribe of Gilded Age America, described her season as a "long, cold agony of shyness." Eleanor Roosevelt, who was presented at a debutante ball at the Waldorf Astoria in 1902, called the experience "utter agony." Or, as McCardell's mother, Eleanor, succinctly put it when she heard about Liz's debutante rigmarole, "Society is an awful chore, isn't it?"

To a modern woman like McCardell, the ritual seemed absolute lunacy. She complained heartily to Peggy LeBoutillier. Her friend was sympathetic. Not much had changed since LeBoutillier had railed against the debutante system in her 1933 essay for *Collier's* magazine. At the 1951 Grosvenor Debutante Ball, Liz would be presented with eleven other debutantes who hailed from some of the wealthiest families in New York. McCardell worried about how Liz might fare in that punishing system.

Liz and her father had already been fighting about her future. Liz wanted to be a modern dancer, like Martha Graham, but Harris thought it a tawdry profession. Now they argued over the coming out. Liz felt deeply uncomfortable with the high-stakes pressure of the debutante season. But when Harris made up his mind, there was little anyone could do to persuade him otherwise.

McCardell was experiencing her own pressure from public performance. In 1951, she was a household name. She and Klein had brokered high-profile endorsements and affiliate deals through Claire McCardell Enterprises. Her clothes and face advertised everything from bourbon, beer, and playing cards to helicopter charter services, motor oil, and cars. In the coming months, her cat's-eye sunglasses, released under the name

SunSpecs, would become popular among celebrities including Ginger Rogers. McCardell would soon become the face of Clairol hair dye.

Increasingly, publicity for those products required television appearances. In 1945, there were fewer than ten thousand television sets in the United States. By 1950, that number had grown to over 6 million, and within the decade, 90 percent of Americans would own a set. McCardell's visage was now broadcast into homes all over the country, and she regularly appeared on national news and variety shows. "I'm going to have to keep T.V. on *all* the time!" Eleanor once joked. McCardell's mother lamented the signal strength in Frederick and the fact that she couldn't get as many programs as her friends who lived in bigger cities, but even so, she routinely saw her daughter on TV.

In her televised appearances, McCardell presented as confident. Producers loved her seemingly easy banter and engaged demeanor. Her assured television persona, however, hid a deep anxiety. She suffered from near-debilitating stage fright that she had to overcome every time the cameras began rolling. She spent days in the lead-up to the shows memorizing and editing the scripts given her by producers and in preparing anecdotes that might seem off the cuff when she was interviewed. She confessed in letters to her mother how deeply insecure she felt about going on television. Eleanor reassured her. "They *want* you or they wouldn't ask you and you must stop thinkin' you aren't good at it. Please get over the notion that you aren't good. You *are*."

McCardell understood the stress that came with performing for an audience. So she likely empathized with Liz, who was being asked to be the center of attention in a societal show. Even though McCardell vehemently disagreed with Harris's decision, she supported her stepdaughter.

McCardell's obligations began on May 21, 1951, a full six months before Liz's coming out. She had to leave work early and attend a tea in the Park Avenue home of a Mrs. James H. Wickersham, the chair of that year's Grosvenor Debutante Ball. She spent the afternoon with the mothers of Liz's fellow debutantes, discussing plans for cocktail parties and dance lessons. A slew of events ran through the summer, with dinners hosted at yacht and country clubs. Each time, McCardell's name appeared in the society pages as Mrs. Irving Harris.

The morning of Liz's debutante ball, November 24, 1951, McCardell went to the ABC television studio downtown and taped an episode of *Betty Crocker Star Matinee*. The half-hour show included interviews with stars, short dramatic readings, and food demonstrations. McCardell stood next to the actress who played the role of the fictional Betty Crocker, a General Mills character originally devised to sell flour. They were joined by an English-born actor named Roland Young.

That night, she and Harris hosted cocktails for guests at the headquarters of the New York Junior League before moving to the Plaza. White chrysanthemums and pink carnations filled the hotel's main ballroom. Liz entered with her fellow debutantes, each in a white gown and long white gloves. Their dresses, frothed by crinoline and layered with sheer white organza, were as clean and bubbly as the champagne that would later fizz in the debutantes' throats. The young women bowed to the room. Liz and Harris took part in the traditional debutante waltz for fathers and daughters. The night proceeded in an unbroken veneer of forced gaiety.

McCardell came out of the affair with a terrible head cold. She looked forward to a quiet holiday and some much needed rest in December, but her attention was quickly subsumed by John. Her stepson had graduated from Princeton the previous spring, just as the Korean War had entered its second year. John assumed he would be drafted. He chose to preemptively join the Marines. He later said that he believed enlisting would offer him better control over his destiny versus waiting to be drafted. Some McCardell family members wondered if John wanted to prove his mettle to his father. Harris was intent on making John "a man," and he often spoke of his own service in World War I as the most important time in his life.

In December, John learned that he would go to a military base in California after the new year. Eleanor hoped John could visit her in Frederick first. "I'm praying he won't have to go to Korea. I've lost all respect for the Marine Corps if it doesn't give him a job he is so well fitted for, instead of making cannon fodder of all that brilliant mind." Eleanor admitted to being happy to hear that John had caught McCardell's cold over the Christmas holiday. "I hope my step-grandson is well again, but I also hope not well enough to be sent to Korea. What a waste of a fine, brilliant, loveable boy. But of course, each person thinks that of one she loves."

That spring of 1952, John did deploy to Korea. Eleanor was incensed. "I wish to Heavens that the old men who *make* wars could be made to do the fighting," she wrote.

McCardell channeled her anxiety over John's safety into making elaborate care packages. She went to John's favorite Manhattan gourmet food shop, Maison Glass, and ordered everything she knew he liked: dates, figs, plums, cheeses, cakes, dried sausages. She tried to locate a container capable of shipping him fresh maple syrup, and she wrote to him in March 1952 that she was "also tempted to try olive oil, but your father disagrees with me. We hear from the Postmaster that the [packages] may go through air mail from California . . . and after that anything can happen."

McCardell ordered John a copy of Evelyn Waugh's new novel, *Men at Arms*, to be shipped via airmail, "not that I've read it but because you like all his others." She worried that the items she sent would be "a bit heavy to carry around in a foxhole," but she couldn't help herself.

On a hot Monday afternoon in June, McCardell shut herself in her office at Townley and wrote John a long letter to catch him up on the news from home. They'd been in Frenchtown over the weekend, and she had spent her time "struggling with this strawberry situation as is the usual procedure for June," she joked. Liz had been visiting from Bradford College in Haverhill, Massachusetts, and McCardell updated him on her progress at school, knowing that the siblings weren't on good terms. "Hate to think you missed seeing Liz dance at Bradford two weeks ago. She really had talent and poise and a touch all her own. I think Popsy is finally convinced, and I think it is wonderful that she has found something she really wants to do. She's grown up a lot this year at Bradford." She closed her letter with love and asked him to please write when he could.

In September, McCardell updated John on the gossip from the summer. She'd thrown a cocktail party in July for their neighbors on Fishers Island. The island's wealthiest resident, Lammot du Pont, had died days earlier, and the rumor was that he had left upward of $70 million to his heirs. Now that they'd closed the house for the season and were back in New York, she told him that Harris was in a dark mood. "Popsy and I are in the midst of a battle at the moment," she admitted. "He is so bitter about so many things, and I do get very mean in arguments sometimes. We keep hoping that the fighting is not getting worse and well [we're] just hoping you'll be home soon without any scratches."

As she once had done with her father, McCardell traded letters with John about politics. John favored Republican Dwight D. Eisenhower, who was running against the Democratic Illinois governor, Adlai Stevenson, in the 1952 presidential election. "Your candidate Eisenhower seems to be doing remarkably well. Popsy is surprised," McCardell wrote. The Eisenhower campaign actively courted women voters, promising increased women's rights should he win. McCardell found herself leaning toward Eisenhower as well, though she signed off her letter to John without divulging it just yet.

In early October, McCardell and Harris were spending the weekend in Frenchtown when a telegram arrived. John's unit had come under heavy fire in Korea. Several men had died, but John had survived. He was in serious condition, recovering in a military hospital. On October 17, 1951, McCardell wrote to John in the hospital. "Don't you think you've done your share now?" she wrote. She hoped that would mean the end of her stepson's military service. His leadership in battle and his injuries would earn him the Purple Heart.

John was on his way home by November, as Americans went to the polls for the presidential election. In 1952, many people presumed that a woman should vote the way her husband did. In the lead-up to the election, McCardell learned that models and female employees working on Seventh Avenue were being harassed for wearing Eisenhower buttons in the Democrat-heavy city. There were also whisper campaigns telling women that their vote would not be secret, so even those who kept their voting preference private felt threatened. McCardell grew alarmed; soon, she was incensed. She went on a popular radio program and publicly endorsed Dwight D. Eisenhower much to the chagrin of her Southern Democrat mother.

Days before the election, she also sent letters to newspapers, including one to the city editor of *The New York Times*: "Reports have come in from various phases of industry, notably the garment section, that people feel their jobs might be in jeopardy because of the way they vote. We would appreciate it so much if your paper would remind the voters that the ballot is secret and no one can check on how one votes."

Amid that roller-coaster year for her family and for politics, McCardell quietly ascended to a new professional height. In 1952, Henry Geiss finally retired from Seventh Avenue. McCardell bought his shares in Townley and became one of the only women in the country to be a partner in a garment firm. "Although Claire was getting more famous by the minute," her friend Sally Kirkland later observed, "Irving managed to ignore the whole thing."

CHAPTER NINETEEN

Ah, Men

1953-55

On April 7, 1953, as dusk descended on Beverly Hills, California, and palm trees rustled in a gentle breeze, actors, art collectors, and fashion icons arrived at the Frank Perls Gallery on North Camden Drive. Perls was respected in the art world for his cutting-edge exhibitions. Most recently, he'd presented the inaugural West Coast show of the modern artist Joan Miró. Now he had organized another vanguard event: the first solo retrospective of a living American fashion designer, Claire McCardell.

The opening had all the hallmarks of a Hollywood movie premiere, including searchlights and Greta Garbo. Perls was a mission-driven gallerist, determined to promote his favorite contemporary artists. "I like to have people fall in love with the work of a particular artist," Perls once said, and he had first fallen in love with McCardell after the war, when he'd seen one of her dresses displayed at MoMA in New York. He'd bought a McCardell dress for his wife, and had remained enchanted by her work ever since. He believed she deserved to be recognized as one of the country's foremost creators.

McCardell wasn't altogether sure what to make of the splashy opening and the attention. Earlier, a reporter had told her that "if you ask almost any designer, from Paducah to Paris, he will say the most creative genius in American fashion today is Miss Claire McCardell." She'd blushed. Direct compliments embarrassed her. "That's very pleasant to hear," McCardell had replied.

Inside the gallery, Perls displayed twenty McCardell garments from the past twenty years, including the Monastic, the Popover, the separates, and her bathing suits. Dorothy Jeakins, an Academy Award–winning costume designer for 20th Century Fox, had installed the show and mounted the clothes on specially made wire dress forms suspended from the eighteen-foot ceiling so they seemed to dance amid the partygoers. Several of the pieces were on loan from the Costume Institute at the Metropolitan Museum of Art in New York. McCardell was being recognized as the leader of a significant school of design, and museums were acquiring her clothes.

Stanley Marcus had contributed an essay for the show's catalogue. "Claire McCardell's designs are unlike those of any other designer," he wrote. "Most American apparel designers work on a formula—Paris inspiration watered down to meet the production capabilities of the manufacturing industry," but "Claire McCardell, as much as any designer I've ever known, designs as she pleases."

More than one guest told her that her clothes looked as if they could walk a runway the next day. They had never gone out of style. A reporter later asked her how she managed to stay so original and relevant. "I don't intentionally go against trends. I just try to look at things with common sense and predict a change before it gets here," she said. "A wardrobe should be an accumulation of clothes chosen through the years for comfort and good looks," she added. "Only a silly woman would toss out all her clothes once or twice a year and buy an entirely new wardrobe from the ground up." She made her point that night at the opening by wearing a red damask evening dress that she'd designed ten years before.

The following day, Greta Garbo returned to the Perls Gallery with a seamstress. She asked for permission to copy McCardell's 1934 halter-back top and culottes from her original separates line.

◆

The same year that Perls celebrated the ingenuity and longevity of Claire McCardell designs, Christian Dior fully abandoned the hourglass figure of his New Look. Years of Dior-mandated voluptuousness disappeared with his new H-Line, a slim, short-skirted tubular silhouette that erased the bust, shoulders, and hips. "Christian Dior, tyrant of the hemlines, decrees short skirts for American women," *The Saturday Evening Post* reported. "Can he bend the female world to his will again?" Dior put his own fashion out of fashion in a head-spinning game meant to keep women guessing and men intrigued.

Women cheered the death of his New Look corset, but Dior hadn't removed it for them. He'd done it, he said, because men were tired of feeling the rigidity of the corset as they danced with women.

"In the minds of many Americans, there is a strong suspicion that the reason Paris's male fashion designers turn out such often-grotesque styles is that, subconsciously at least, they despise women," the fashion journalist Phyllis Battelle later wrote. McCardell, conversely, "has presented us with our most long-wearable styles. Her secret: She ignored Paris. And perhaps most important, she liked and respected women."

Once again, McCardell became the defender of a woman's body. "I am not in favor of any silhouette that compresses the figure, either in the waistline, hipline or the bosom," she told one reporter about the H-Line. "I think real fashion is always a design that lets the natural figure show to best advantage."

In January of 1954, Hope Johnson of the *New York World-Telegram* reached out to McCardell about a different French couturier, a man named Jacques Fath. He was a self-taught designer, a "brash boy with slightly theatrical fashion ideas," as Bettina Ballard described Fath, and he'd become the new darling of Paris. Christian Dior was still "the head man, so to speak," as *Life* magazine explained, "but Fath has recently had a spectacular rise in prestige. It is likely that the next look to confront and impoverish the U.S. male will be the Fath look."

Confident and boisterous, Fath was as famous for his elaborate parties as he was for his clothes. He liked to costume his clients more than dress them for real life. He made women's swimsuits using suede and steel, two materials that couldn't go anywhere near water.

Johnson hoped that McCardell would respond to something incendiary Fath had just said in the press, namely, that women shouldn't be fashion designers. "Women are poor creators because they try to dress every other woman in the type of clothes they themselves like," he'd said. "Fashion is art. Art is creative and men are the creators. Look at the great painters, the great sculptors, the great writers. The woman designers see fashion as she likes it. But a man will see it as hundreds of women like it. There'll come a day when all the great designers are men."

He'd added, as a final dig, that men had better heads for business. It was a supreme irony, given that Fath often admitted to barely surviving financially from collection to collection. McCardell, meanwhile, was selling over $3 million in wholesale annually on top of what she brought in through Claire McCardell Enterprises.

Johnson mailed a copy of Fath's quote to McCardell and asked for a statement. McCardell never went on the record besmirching a fellow designer. With Dior, she'd focused on the facts of his clothes, not on the man. And she rarely took the bait of sexist taunts. If she reacted each time a man disregarded a woman's work, she'd never design again.

Lately, though, she had noticed the increasing backlash against women working in her profession. The question of whether a woman should work at all after the war was far from settled; in fact, it had once again become a vigorous debate. The attack by Fath may have felt to her like more than a spat between male and female designers and more than the long-standing France versus America rivalry. It represented so many filaments bound together into a larger, formidable mass, a skein of misogyny that attempted to hamper women.

McCardell rolled a sheet of paper into her typewriter. "Ah, men," her response began. "They never understand the way clothes feel. Their lines are often harsh and masculine. When Chanel gave them soft feminine simplicity it was Chanel they loved. Men designers all must go to a woman for final judgment. She may be a model, she may be a première, she may be a wife. There is always a woman behind the throne. Some day all designers will be women. Men, I hope, will be busy with masculine things."

Several months later, in the summer of 1954, McCardell elaborated on her beliefs about women and clothes. The publishers at Time Inc. asked her to join the advisory board of a new magazine to be called *Sports Illustrated*. She accepted, and the editors invited her to contribute an essay for the inaugural issue, set to come out that August. They wrote that "with the right to vote—and the right to share in so many other activities that had formerly been labeled 'for men only'—came a tremendous change in the way women dressed," and McCardell had pioneered that change.

Sportswear, she began, "changed our lives because they changed our thinking about clothes. Perhaps they, more than anything else, made us independent women. . . . In these so-called sports clothes, a woman could move and walk and forget her clothes for the first time in her life. She was at ease and able to take care of herself. Her preoccupation with clothes and its problems solved, she had time for many things. She could handle a job and a house at the same time." McCardell titled her essay "Women Are What They Wear."

◆

McCardell's idea of a woman being allowed to handle both a career and a family intrigued the journalist Betty Friedan. Popular opinion in the United States contended that a woman should not work because she should focus solely on raising a family. In the summer of 1955, as Friedan reached out to Townley about interviewing McCardell for a profile in *The Town Journal* magazine, she had only recently returned to her writing career. She left her children in the care of a babysitter, and she defended her choice in a magazine essay titled "I Went Back to Work."

In June 1955, Friedan sat in the mirrored showroom at Townley as McCardell previewed her fall line to a hundred buyers and reporters. She caught a glimpse of McCardell half hidden in a doorway, keeping an eye on the show from a distance.

A model walked out in a red-and-brown cotton flannel dress called a "sleeper" in the program. The woman circled the room as an announcer explained that the dress could be worn overnight while traveling on a train, and then, with the addition of a belt, continue to be worn the next day. The audience burst into applause. Friedan overheard a buyer murmur that McCardell was one of the few designers who didn't worry about what Paris was doing.

After the show, McCardell emerged to answer questions. One buyer rushed over to ask about a new dress, "Darling, what do you call that divine color?"

McCardell laughed. "Why, I just call it red."

The fashion world buzzed over Dior's new H-Line, but at Townley, McCardell "ignored such nonsense," Friedan wrote.

Friedan went back another day to shadow McCardell at work, using the opportunity to watch her and her staff in action. Women filled many of the positions on McCardell's design team. Starting in the 1940s, she and Mildred Orrick had created an informal support system for women pursuing fashion careers. They mentored female students in their role as visiting critics at Parsons, and they helped orient newcomers to the city. Orrick and her husband, Jesse, had turned the first floor of their brownstone into an apartment that they leased to women designers and artists in need of safe, inexpensive housing. Some tenants were McCardell's mentees, such as a young fashion designer named Adri Steckling-Coen. (And when she moved out, her friend, the writer Joan Didion, moved in.)

Friedan interviewed McCardell's current staff, as well as some of her former employees, including a young designer named Mona Roset. Roset had been a student at Parsons, and McCardell had hired her after graduation to be a fit model and assistant. Over the years, McCardell had developed a list she called her Essential Eleven that she shared with students and her staff, like Roset. Learning to sew and learning to drape topped the list. They should learn anatomy, as McCardell had in her fine arts training, in order to really see and understand the human body. Beyond the technical skill of the craft, McCardell advised her mentees to study history—fashion and otherwise. They had to know what came before to envision what might come next.

McCardell further encouraged the women she mentored to forge their own careers, even if it meant that they might become direct competitors, as was the case with Roset. She'd recently been hired as a designer for a Seventh Avenue manufacturer. Roset admitted to Friedan that she'd been terrified about going out on her own. She had been packing up her desk on her last day at Townley. It was after six, and everyone had already gone home. But McCardell stayed late to say goodbye. She came to Roset's desk and gave her a twenty-minute pep talk. She told Roset that whatever she did with her career, she should never forget to honor her own judgment. Don't worry about what others are doing, McCardell had reminded her, always be your own best advocate.

Perhaps the best testament to how women at Townley felt about their boss was evidenced by McCardell's longtime sample room head, Bessie Sustersic. When Sustersic had a daughter, she named her Claire.

As Friedan reported her profile on McCardell, she also began gathering data about women and work. The average marriage age of women in the 1950s had shot back down to twenty. More than 14 million teenage girls got engaged by age seventeen each year. The proportion of women attending college had shrunk from 47 percent in 1920 to 35 percent in the 1950s. Of those who did enroll in higher education, 60 percent dropped out to marry, sparking the joke that women now attended college to hunt for a husband and earn an MRS degree or, once married, a PhT—putting husband through. That research would undergird her best-selling book *The Feminine Mystique*. The book wouldn't be published until 1963, but it was rooted in the stifling misogynies Friedan saw emerging in the 1950s.

A baby boom was in full effect, so much so that McCardell had launched a short-lived line for toddlers called Baby McCardell. The rigorous home economics science courses that she had taken in the 1920s were devolving into high school and college classes on keeping a husband happy. Home ec was no longer seen as a back door for women to enter a career as it had once been.

More women were being funneled into the white picket fence ideal of postwar America, and many admitted to being deeply unhappy. One housewife told *Life* magazine that she wanted more than a husband and children. She equated the swift regression of female independence to being "trapped in a squirrel cage."

As forthcoming as McCardell was about her design process and as open as she was in discussing her feelings about the rights of women, their careers, and their need for freedom in clothes, she didn't appear to discuss her marriage in depth with Friedan. Friedan made no notes to that effect in her reporting, and there was only a cursory mention of her private life in the article. That would be in keeping with the many interviews McCardell had given over the years. She never expounded on life with Harris or on being a stepmother to John and Liz. The closest she came to talking about her home life was in describing a new T-neck tunic she had made for Townley. She told a reporter that she'd been inspired by a T-square sitting on the drafting table of her architect husband. Even then, the brief insight into her personal life was in service to her work.

Harris, for his part, never went on record about his wife's career. "When, as often happened, someone would congratulate him or want to interview him on Claire's accomplishments, his response was one of unabashed ignorance," Sally Kirkland later wrote. "Whatever his wife did, and he understood that she did it very well, he would say, it was entirely her own achievement and her own affair."

It's remarkable, then, that McCardell let Friedan into her apartment on East 79th Street for a follow-up interview. It's not clear what made her break her long-standing tacit agreement with Harris not to bring work home. He was there that evening.

The two women retreated to McCardell's red-painted room and sat in front of the white marble fireplace. Sheer organdy curtains shimmered at the windows, lit by a summer sun now setting behind the Manhattan skyline. McCardell talked to Friedan about her many inventions. She then pulled out a box of letters. In it were hundreds of notes that women had written her over the years, including a 1952 letter from the actress Joan Crawford who asked McCardell to design clothes for her.

It wasn't the letters from the rich and the famous, though, that McCardell wanted to share with Friedan that night; it was the ones from her customers. She gave Friedan a twelve-page handwritten letter from a woman in upstate New York. "Dear Miss McCardell," the letter began, "I spilled [dye] on my favorite dress and put an end to the career of a most remarkable garment."

The customer explained that her Claire McCardell dress, bought years prior at Lord & Taylor, had originally been worn as a gown when she was pregnant with her third child. After giving birth, she had taken in the seams and it "served me just as well in my natural shape as it had as a maternity dress." The garment became a "traveling uniform" when her husband's work required that they trek through Peru and Guatemala. It looked nice even without ironing, she wrote, and had been worn as a housedress, a beach robe, and an evening gown with "lots of bracelets and my hair combed." The dress had survived yet another journey along the Amazon River in a small, filthy wood-burning river steamer, where it had held up to being washed in the Rio Negro and being pawed by curious monkeys. If not for her clumsy handling of the dye, she believed, the dress could have lasted years longer. "It has been so useful to me, and so becoming in every situation and so thoroughly satisfactory in every way, that I've wanted for a long time to write you an appreciation," she explained. "Thank you for the very good dress."

While Dior's women couldn't walk, eat, sit, or breathe, McCardell's women were exploring the Amazon on river boats. "Does Dior get letters like that?" McCardell asked Friedan.

It grew dark outside McCardell's apartment, and it was time for Friedan to catch the subway back to Queens, to her husband and children. She had one last question before she left. She'd noticed that McCardell had worn the same denim suit with blue jean topstitching several times over the last few weeks. McCardell explained that she had a habit of wearing a uniform when busy. It eliminated the need to make unnecessary choices. That was, after all, the point of fashion. Freedom sometimes meant donning the same suit so that you could get on with your life. Nevertheless, it made Friedan curious.

"Do you still find clothes exciting?" she asked.

"The longer I live, the more things I want to design. I'd like to play around with light and color," McCardell answered. "I'd like to dress women from the skin out, there's no logical reason for women's underwear." She felt particular ire about the new push-up bra, which had "a lot to apologize for" as she would later write. She believed it had "distorted so many American bodies it should be ashamed of itself. All emphasis had been concentrated in one place."

McCardell was designing all sorts of new ideas that are "really none of my business," she told Friedan, and she broke into her rich, deep laugh, the one that had become so familiar to those who heard her on the radio and watched her on TV. "Probably forty years from now I'll be sitting in a wheelchair designing a dress for a great-great-grandmother to look as young as she feels." She assured Friedan that she was only getting started.

CHAPTER TWENTY

McCardellisms

1955-56

A few weeks after her interview with Betty Friedan, McCardell was on a plane with Sally Kirkland to the south of France. Kirkland was now an editor at *Life* magazine, and she'd planned an ambitious editorial spread to report on a fashion first, a cross-promotion between Claire McCardell, an American textile firm, and five of the twentieth century's most prestigious European artists: Marc Chagall, Raoul Dufy, Fernand Léger, Joan Miró, and Pablo Picasso.

Dan Fuller, the president of New York–based Fuller Fabrics, had already spent two years collaborating with the artists. Each had selected motifs from his work, and Fuller's textile designers had translated them into repeating patterns for mass-produced cotton fabric. Fuller called it the "Modern Masters Series." For less than $2 a yard, a woman could wear a Picasso.

That fall, a documentary and exhibition at the Brooklyn Museum would launch the line. And an accompanying fashion feature in *Life* magazine would showcase the fabrics as used by McCardell in a collection of new clothes.

In her luggage, McCardell carried several outfits she'd designed using the material. Kirkland had spent months planning for each artist to be photographed in their studios, along with a model wearing McCardell's creations. When they landed in Europe, though, Chagall and others stalled. Kirkland came to believe that they were waiting for Picasso to bless the project. Only now, Picasso wasn't returning Kirkland's calls. That summer, he had purchased a 1920s villa in Cannes. Through an assistant, he told Kirkland that he'd changed his mind. He was far too busy for a photo shoot.

Kirkland took her crew to Cannes, where she rented rooms in a hotel near Picasso's villa. In addition to McCardell, there were a photographer, several assistants, and top European models, including Jacques Fath's favorite, the French Bettina Graziani.

Now they waited for Picasso. Everyone, it seemed, waited for Picasso. Each day, Kirkland or her staff went to his villa. Each day they were turned away. Picasso was not a man known for his time awareness, a characteristic that irked the punctilious McCardell.

McCardell busied herself with work in her terra-cotta-tiled hotel room. She opened the louvered patio doors to the sunshine and sea breezes of the French Riviera and continued refining the outfits she'd designed, making small adjustments with needle and thread.

Someone in Cannes tipped off Kirkland that the way to Picasso was through Graziani. If the highly respected French couture model liked the American's ready-to-wear clothes, it might hurry things along.

Only Graziani was dubious when she first saw the modest cotton clothes that McCardell had made. As soon as she started trying on the outfits, though, she became a convert. McCardell's American Look won over haute couture's most famous model.

Graziani approved the clothes, Kirkland made sure that news made it to Picasso, and soon after, he invited them to his villa. The photos, which ran in a November issue of *Life*, featured Graziani in a pair of ruby red pants and a shirt featuring a Picasso still life. The fedora-clad Picasso posed next to her, wielding a saber. He thought it made a fun prop. Stateside, Lord & Taylor sold McCardell's art-inspired clothes along with a collection of beaded jewelry McCardell had designed to accompany the line.

◆

High-profile cross-promotion was becoming standard for the female fashion designers of America. They were in demand to endorse products. Joset Walker smiled out from a Camel cigarette ad; Clare Potter and Lilly Daché promoted Chrysler. But few were as sought-after as McCardell. In the spring of 1955, a drawing of her face dominated the cover of *Time* magazine. "The person who understands best how American women want to look is a shy Manhattan designer named Claire McCardell," the journalist Osborn Elliott wrote. McCardell's media ubiquity put her in high demand. Adolph Klein brokered so many endorsements and licensing deals that year that McCardell couldn't keep track of them. Her designs were becoming as recognizable as her face, and brands wanted to use both to bring attention to their products.

In his rush to turn McCardell into a full-fledged brand, Klein sometimes confused consumers about what was being sold. Photos of models wearing Claire McCardell Clothes ran inside a catalogue for home cleaning supplies—the images were only meant to lend verve to the domestic items for sale—but perplexed broom salesmen fielded hundreds of calls from women looking to order dresses. Klein apologized for the misrepresentation in a statement that ran in *Women's Wear Daily*. In a rare argument with Klein, McCardell confronted him about the number of endorsement and product deals and questioned whether the royalties were being split evenly with her. The argument "was a beauty," Klein later acknowledged. He must have reassured her that the finances were in order, because they quickly returned to their usual easygoing work rapport.

Amid the flood of interest, it may have been Eleanor Lambert, now McCardell's publicist, who suggested that McCardell write a book. It would be a logical next step in expanding her brand and an opportunity for her to reach even more women. Drafting the occasional essay for a magazine was one thing, but McCardell was far too busy to write a book. Her brother Adrian later joked that his sister had been "long on dresses, but short on words." Lambert could have also been the one to suggest a ghostwriter. McCardell was paired with a seasoned author named Edith Heal.

There were already books on the market that dictated rules for etiquette, style, and fashion, but McCardell envisioned one that would, like her clothes, free women from strict mandates. She wanted a practical, inspirational guide that could help readers locate their own style, manage their clothing budgets, and find joy while living within their means.

Throughout her hectic workdays, she grabbed whatever scrap paper was at hand and began writing out her fashion philosophy. She also sat for interviews with Heal, who took copious notes. Heal further gathered McCardell's published essays and the transcripts of her speeches over the years.

McCardell suggested the title should be *Fashion Is Fun*, but when the book was published in 1956, it was called *What Shall I Wear? The What, Where, When, and How Much of Fashion*. Still, she opened the book espousing her core belief that getting dressed should be an enjoyable act. "Fashion should be fun, and whenever I am tempted to take it too seriously, if I design something that asks for a pedestal in the Museum of Modern Art, I am tumbled down to earth by the blunt voice of a buyer: 'Where would you wear it?' And mentally I applaud because I believe that clothes are for real, live women, not for pedestals. They are made to be worn, to be lived in. Not to walk around on models with perfect figures."

She incorporated personal details about her own wardrobe, and divulged that her biggest secret for timeless style was to ignore fashion when it didn't suit her. "People without a sense of fun, of dash, of whim, may misunderstand Fashion," she wrote, purposefully capitalizing the word "fashion" to signify the industry's emphasis of its power over women. "Fashion puts in shoulder pads—then takes them away. I never had so much fun as the year I ripped them all out."

She encouraged her readers to assert their own independence. "First of all, stay firmly you. And if Fashion seems to be saying something that isn't right for you, ignore it."

McCardell coalesced her signature design elements—pockets, sashes, spaghetti ties, wrap dresses, brass hooks and eyes, and more—into a list she called "McCardellisms." She'd developed these over the years, she explained, to encourage the versatile elegance that she hoped her reader would embrace. "A part of the beauty of clothes is the freedom I've talked so much about."

On November 12, 1956, a review of *What Shall I Wear?* ran in the Frederick newspaper. "It is a book that certainly will receive as prominent a place in the lady's home library as Emily Post's rules on etiquette for Miss McCardell deals completely with fashion," the reporter wrote, adding that "her appeal to the average woman can be sensed in her value of fashion." Her small-town thrift had never left her, which was further noted in an article in *The Baltimore Sun*: "One important factor in her success may well have been that she never lost sight of Frederick."

The book was chock full of sensible and freeing advice for the average woman, even as it was painfully blunt about weight and body type. In one passage, McCardell wrote frankly about whether a woman should wear a sleeveless dress. "Yes, if your arms are slender. No, if you have overdeveloped arm muscles or any sign of flabbiness."

She encouraged readers to stop comparing themselves to models "unless Nature gave you a head start and you are willing to starve, exercise, go to bed early, learn a special walk." But she also claimed that "you can learn self-discipline from her." Your figure, she continued "is adjustable—through diet and exercise. Instead of struggling from one size to another, you will save time and frustration, by banishing potatoes." It is difficult to reconcile these passages with McCardell's long-standing embrace of women's figures. She was a designer who worked hard to create dresses capable of fitting different body types.

The book further advises a woman to adjust her outfits to her husband's tastes. "When you buy shoes, you are not just buying for your own feet," she wrote. "You are buying for your husband's tastes, for the things you are going to walk to. Does he take big steps? Would he rather help poor delicate little you into a taxi?"

She wrote of not just pleasing a husband, but paying attention to how your friends apprise you, and even considering how your children expect you to dress. In 1953, McCardell told a reporter, "I don't believe a woman dresses for men or for other women. I think a woman dresses for herself, that is, for her own pleasure and her own peace or comfort of mind." Yet in the book, she encourages readers to dress up when going grocery shopping because "your most critical woman friends may be eyeing you bounce a melon."

It's hard to imagine the independent McCardell, known for shocking in her diaper bathing suit on the beaches of Fishers Island, to have written those lines. The passages are out of step, too, with many of McCardell's public statements and private beliefs. She wasn't one to extol the virtues of dressing for anyone but yourself.

It's possible that at least some of the statements were the result of Edith Heal's influence. In 1948, Heal had published a book titled *Teen-Age Manual: A Guide to Popularity and Success*. As she co-wrote McCardell's book, she simultaneously worked on another one titled *The Young Executive's Wife: You and Your Husband's Job*.

What Shall I Wear? was a "highly collaborative effort," according to McCardell's brother Bob. The book became a patchwork of McCardell's ideals and those of her ghostwriter, Heal. McCardell's more radical feminist ideas may have been purposefully tamped down in deference to the 1950s housewife narrative. A later critique of the book suggested that it was "more of a McCardell product than a McCardell manifesto."

Ultimately, the book was a testament to the competing and contradictory truths of a woman's life in 1956 America. McCardell was ahead of her time while also being a product of her time, and that dichotomy is reflected in the text.

Still, the primary message that threads through the book is pure McCardell. She advocated for women to be themselves, to be comfortable, to be honest about their needs and desires, and not to fall victim to the whims of fashion. A woman "must dress for her temperament. She must dress for her life. Physical ease is important; and even more important, mental ease."

In the penultimate chapter, she told her reader to be brave. If a dress no longer fit or if one was on sale and a great bargain but too small, do a little detective work. Turn the garment inside out. Can you rework it? What do the seams tell you? Letting out a dress requires just a half inch if that half inch is in the right place, she explained. You can always take a dress apart and rebuild it for your body. McCardell encouraged women to become their own seamstresses, their own premières. Take what designers have given you, what I have given you, she wrote, and make it your own.

It was a simple but empowering message coming from one of the world's most famous fashion designers. Nothing, least of all a dress, is overly precious. Take a seam ripper to it and be free. Remember: Fashion can be fickle, she wrote, and it changes constantly. It never stands still. Take advantage, then, and make your own rules. McCardell believed above all that "your job is not so much tracking down the clothes as tracking down yourself."

CHAPTER TWENTY-ONE

The Quiet Genius

1956–58

In 1956, Diana Vreeland began seeing evidence of McCardell's growing international influence. "It is the most curious thing as I look at the French dresses of 1956," she wrote to McCardell. "I recognize so many of the dresses you made in 1946 and so do many other people." It had taken a decade for them to catch up to her, but European designers were now copying McCardell. Even Christian Dior acknowledged her. He had branched out into ready-to-wear and opened a boutique in New York. He let Marjorie Griswold of Lord & Taylor and others in the fashion industry know how much he admired McCardell's work, calling her "a creative genius."

"Have you ever wondered what the European's typical idea of the American girl is?" a CBS radio announcer asked. "Well, in the fashion worlds of Paris and London, there's a unanimous vote for Claire McCardell."

That year, Adolph Klein and McCardell went for drinks to talk about the future. Klein likened McCardell to the spark plug of the organization, the one who energized Townley and Claire McCardell Enterprises with her brilliance and creative courage. He suggested that McCardell, now fifty-one, might elevate herself to more of an oversight role and take more time to enjoy her success. "Become the executive designer and hire a couple of kids to relieve you," he said. It was meant to be a promotion. She could be the boss at the top, giving directions to those beneath her, not unlike the way a French designer like Dior ran his ateliers.

McCardell wasn't interested. She was a hands-on creator, an artist. She liked making her clothes. Instead, she doubled down on work. As the calendar turned to 1957, it was shaping up to be a banner year. She had several projects going under Claire McCardell Enterprises. In a nod to her childhood, she released a booklet of Claire McCardell paper dolls. They included cutouts of her playsuits, bathing suits, and wrap dresses. She was also deep into the development of her first signature perfume, a scent called White Sash. She designed the packaging to resemble the light blue box ruling on graph paper, harkening back to her love of geometry. Edith Heal wrote the marketing copy, extolling how the bottle's graph paper label had "clean-cut checks looking as cool and fresh as polished cotton." The tagline: Perfume is Fashion, too.

For her Townley line, McCardell had been playing with big blocks of vibrant color, not unlike the new pop art coming out of the United Kingdom. And she'd begun fashioning shorter skirts of yet another surprising material: leather. It would be another decade before leather skirts really took off in women's fashion. "The busiest drawing board in the U.S. fashion industry belongs to Claire McCardell," *Life* magazine reported.

That winter, at the height of it all, McCardell felt unusually run down. She'd lost her appetite. She'd lost weight. She may have blamed her fatigue and upset stomach on her busy schedule. She rarely complained about her health, so when she mentioned how awful she'd been feeling to her mother, Eleanor was worried. "I know you make light of any ailment," she wrote. She encouraged McCardell to take care of herself.

By late spring, fatigue and stomach ailments hobbled McCardell. She could no longer make light of her health. She went to see her doctor, who immediately sent her for tests.

The diagnosis came as a shock. McCardell had colon cancer. An oncologist told her it was imperative they act fast. The cancer, he believed, was advanced. She would need surgery, and she would require radiation treatment. But even with the most aggressive plan, the best-case prognosis was that she had a year to live, and more likely six months.

The idea of death seemed preposterous to McCardell. She'd been told countless times that she couldn't do what she said she would. But she'd proved everyone wrong. She'd built a career through unrelenting determination, and now she marshaled that same stubborn will and prayed that it would come through for her once more. She'd always beaten the odds, so why not now?

McCardell found a specialist in colon cancer, a surgeon at New York Hospital who'd helped pioneer radiation treatment. In early June, Eleanor traveled to New York. She accompanied her daughter to the hospital for the operation. Eleanor prayed, fervent, beseeching entreaties to God to deliver her daughter through the procedure. After surgery, she stayed by her daughter's bedside as she recuperated and prayed for her to survive the cancer, too.

McCardell began radiation treatment later that summer. The pain was so severe that it felt "as though my stomach will fall on the floor at times," she described. Still, she kept working.

In September, her brothers, Adrian, Bob, and Max, met her in Frenchtown for the weekend. "I'm glad my family likes one another," Eleanor had once said of her children. She may have been thinking about her stepgrandchildren when she'd made that observation. The tensions between John and Liz and their strained relationship with their father had only heightened over the years. Eleanor's assessment of her children was accurate; they truly cared for one another. In Frenchtown, the siblings reminisced and talked about the future, as though the future were certain.

One of her brothers picked up McCardell's Kodak Brownie camera and snapped a photo of her. She had her back to the lens, her body far thinner than usual. She stood in front of the fireplace, the firebox tall enough that she could practically walk into it. The French copper pots that she'd bought decades earlier to cook stews for her friends still hung on the walls. Now she could hardly manage to keep down broth.

Back in New York, she pulled herself out of bed each morning and took a car to Townley. She couldn't imagine not working, not being creative, when that had been the central focus of her life. Klein had called

McCardell the spark plug of the organization, but the electric current went both ways. She needed the work as much as it needed her. Without it, she wasn't sure who she was.

In October, surprising news arrived from Europe. While on vacation in Italy, Christian Dior had collapsed and died. He was just three months older than McCardell. Dior's multimillion-dollar brand would continue under his name with a new head designer, a twenty-one-year-old protégé named Yves Saint Laurent. Dior had seen to it that his brand wouldn't die with him.

As the fashion world mourned Dior, only a select few knew the extent of McCardell's illness. Vreeland was among them. She couldn't believe McCardell's stamina and purpose as she continued working on her next collection. Klein took over all traveling duties so that McCardell could focus on her health. He went to trunk shows and department store openings across the country in her stead. He did his best to remain positive and brush off any concerns over McCardell's absence. Hope Skillman saw the toll it took on him. "All these sad months you have answered queries, 'How's Claire?' with such dignity and hope but I know how heavy your heart is," Skillman wrote to Klein. "And I have tried not to ask you anymore."

In December, McCardell collapsed at work and was admitted to the hospital for a few days. She needed someone she could trust and who truly understood her. She needed Mildred Orrick. Orrick had made a name for herself working as a head designer for other labels, but when McCardell called, she came. Orrick sat with her friend as she grew weaker. They talked about the next collection, the 1958 resort and summer seasons for Townley. Orrick sketched, and McCardell marked up the drawings with notes as her energy allowed.

McCardell had maintained a cursory relationship with church and religion over her busy life. But as her illness progressed, she found herself thinking of those long-ago sermons of Robert Norwood, who had been the rector of St. Bartholomew's Church during her Parsons years. His sermons, with their themes of art, creativity, and human purpose, had resonated in her twenties, and they continued to do so in 1957. At Christmas, Harris gifted her an anthology of Norwood's writings. McCardell kept the book by her bed and read from it most days. She underlined meaningful passages and made notes in the margins.

When New York Fashion Week kicked off in January 1958, McCardell was back in the hospital. She called Orrick for another favor. Orrick arrived in her room on a cold winter morning and helped McCardell into a red denim suit, which had to be pinned in to fit. McCardell wasn't supposed to leave the hospital, so the two friends sneaked by the nurses' station to a car that was waiting to take them to the Pierre Hotel. Townley was holding a media preview of the collection that Orrick had helped design.

More than a hundred journalists from around the country milled about the lobby of the hotel. McCardell's arrival caused a stir of excitement. Many had been told by now that McCardell was sick with cancer. The fashion writer Dorothy Parnell ran over. "We hadn't expected to see you!" she said.

"The best friends I've had in my career are the newspaper women," McCardell told her. "I wouldn't miss seeing them for anything."

By 1958, fashion shows had matured. The models who wore Townley clothes walked a proper runway through a ballroom of guests. It was a long way from her first buyer's preview with Robert Turk in 1929, when she'd helped model his sample clothes and changed in the back of a grimy warehouse. Three decades after McCardell had begun working on Seventh Avenue, the Garment District had ascended. No longer the needle trade, it was now the *fashion industry*. In her lifetime, McCardell had imagined and worked hard to create the profession of the American fashion designer. "Everybody in the fashion world just worshiped her," McCardell's former fit model Connie Wald said. "They recognized her value. Claire was *the* American designer."

The last model walked the runway for Townley. McCardell then did something that she'd never done in all her years of fashion shows: She came out and waved to the crowd. The audience, composed of the editors and writers and buyers who'd championed her career, leapt to their feet. They gave her a long standing ovation.

♦

On March 22, 1958, the phone rang at Mildred Orrick's brownstone on the Upper East Side. Orrick answered as her youngest daughter, Sarah, age ten, stood nearby. Sarah watched her mother's face go pale. Orrick said a few words into the receiver and then hung up. Sarah tiptoed over, having heard snippets of the conversation. "Mama, who's Claire?"

McCardell had died that morning at New York Hospital, two months shy of her fifty-third birthday. In Frederick, Eleanor McCardell refused to believe it. "I think Mumsy's death came as a real shock to her," John Harris wrote to McCardell's aunt Courtenay. "More so than to us who had seen it coming for so long." The McCardells held a private funeral in Frederick. McCardell was buried in Mount Olivet Cemetery in the family plot near her father and grandfather.

On March 26, a public memorial was held in New York. Hundreds of people poured into St. James' Church on Madison Avenue and 71st Street, including Irving, John, and Liz Harris and McCardell's three brothers. Eleanor had been too weak with grief to make the trip. The church pews quickly filled with McCardell's friends, who had been, along with her, the pioneers of American fashion: Adolph Klein and Eleanor Lambert; Peggy LeBoutillier, Joset Walker, and Mildred Orrick; Dorothy Shaver and Marjorie Griswold from Lord & Taylor; the journalists and editors Bettina Ballard, Sally Kirkland, Diana Vreeland, Carmel Snow; and Hope Skillman and the fabric and textile salesmen and workers who had so loved their visits to McCardell.

McCardell had left instructions: No flowers. Any gifts in her memory should go to cancer research. Checks had already begun arriving at Townley for that purpose. Instead, two simple sprays of daffodils, Easter lilies, pink carnations, and stock had been placed on the altar steps. They had been McCardell's favorite flowers.

The officiant stood in front of the congregation. He opened McCardell's dog-eared book of Robert Norwood sermons and went to passages McCardell had marked for him to read. "Somewhere in the universe," Norwood had written, "the beauty of all art down through the ages is fully manifested in a beautiful, royal Selfhood. What we call beauty, love, goodness, courage, contentment: all these manifested from some central sun of glory and of beauty, and that central sun is the living God." McCardell had always been in thrall to the larger questions of beauty and art. In the final weeks of her life, that was what she'd been contemplating.

"Even of this service," the pastor said from the pulpit, "she was the designer."

◆

The world at large was stunned by McCardell's untimely death. Many hadn't known how serious her illness had been or that she had been sick at all. Hundreds of letters flooded into Townley.

"I can't tell you how deeply distressed I am," Emilio Pucci wrote. "I know that her disappearance has deprived the world of one of its very great designers of all times."

The president of the May Company department store in Los Angeles had read the news in his morning paper. "I just couldn't believe it," he told Klein. "To me there was an indestructible quality about her as a person, the same as her clothes, and to adjust to her not being with us will take more than a few short months or years."

The president of a Denver department store summed up the feelings of many when he said that McCardell had been this country's greatest original designer, "but so much more than that she was a really great person. She was a square shooter with no pretense about her and that's a rare type in the world we live in."

Obituaries and tributes ran in newspapers across the country and in Europe. The fashion journalist Inez Robb published an impassioned tribute. McCardell's untimely departure, she wrote, "has pinpointed the worm in America's fashion rose." Too many American fashion designers lacked the courage of their own talent. McCardell "had faith in herself and her gifts, and it paid off in fame and fortune. She did not attempt to cage women in 18-inch waists one season and in barrels the next. She knew the anatomy and she neither insulted nor flouted it. She stood on her own feet on her native soil, and she was good. No tricks, no fads, no stunts. When Paris sneezed, Miss McCardell did not slap a mustard plaster on her customers! And I mourn her passing and salute her courage."

The customers who had worn McCardell's clothes wrote many of the most heartfelt letters. "I must tell you what a great loss I feel at the death of Claire McCardell," one woman from Maryland wrote to Klein. "It has always peeved me to hear Paris given all the credit for furnishing the inspiration for fashions when I know that Miss McCardell's quiet genius furnished far more than any of them could afford to admit. I congratulate you for respecting a real artist. I have worn and loved her clothes since the first she designed for you. My collection fills three closets and I would not exchange them for a houseful of Dior's."

◆

No sooner had the news of McCardell's death circulated than the question turned to what would happen to her label. "Replacing Claire McCardell is the tough, sad problem Adolph Klein, Townley Frocks President, has been considering for several months," the *New York Post* reported on March 25, 1958.

As in life, McCardell's death was juxtaposed against that of Christian Dior. "I feel that her contribution to American fashion is a lasting one and that the traditions she established can be carried on by her associates, just as the Dior traditions are being carried on," a radio host in upstate New York told Klein.

"I do hope that she had prepared and trained a successor-designer, who, like Christian Dior's young man, can carry on," a Florida store owner wrote.

McCardell had not named a successor. The woman who'd planned her own memorial had left no instructions about the continuance of her name, or her label.

Adolph Klein had to bury his grief and address the future. He assured *The New York Times* that McCardell's fashion philosophy would continue under his guard, "not just for purely sentimental reasons—although it is the only memorial I can offer—but simply because she was such a great designer and so prophetic that we have a substantial heritage to work with."

As forward-thinking as Klein had been about marketing McCardell's inventive work when she was alive, he struggled to figure out what to do after she died. It wasn't until two months after her death that he announced that Mildred Orrick had agreed to help, at least in the short term. Klein kept Claire McCardell Clothes by Townley alive, thanks to Orrick, for two more seasons. But by the spring of 1959, he discontinued the label.

It's unclear why Klein didn't hire Orrick as a permanent replacement. Orrick, who had a thriving career of her own, may have indicated that she wasn't interested in forever working under McCardell's label. Klein could certainly have turned to one of the many mentees or assistants McCardell had trained and nurtured over the years. There were several possible candidates, including Adri Steckling-Coen. She would go on to have a successful clothing line in the McCardell style. Klein's decision may have come down to precedent. In 1958, a New York manufacturer did not continue the label of a deceased designer. The Claire McCardell trademark reverted to the McCardell family. "We decided to let the name die with her," her brother Adrian later told *The Baltimore Sun*. "It wasn't that difficult. Claire's ideas were always her own."

In Adrian's answer, then, is a clue to why Klein and the family may have let the label die. No one quite knew how to continue without McCardell. As the journalist Alice Hughes told Klein, "It is completely impossible to think of any designer who could replace Claire."

◆

Shortly after the memorial, Irving Harris flew to England. It fell to John Harris to handle the affairs of McCardell's death. "My father asked me particularly to convey to you his thanks for your kind letter, which touched him very much," he wrote to McCardell's aunt Courtenay. John wrote that his father "has gone off to England to stay with old friends and get a bit of rest and a change of scene."

John necessarily kept his correspondence polite, but inside he roiled with a mix of grief and a deep anger over his father's selfishness. Harris should have been there, writing those letters. Years later, John would tell his children that the McCardells had felt more like family than his own father. And now that his stepmother was gone, there was little to tether him to his father.

He went to Harris and McCardell's apartment on 79th Street to help box up his stepmother's things. Walking through the quiet home, he had the out-of-time feeling particular to grief. He felt that McCardell was still there in another room, ready to come out and join him at any moment. "It will not be the same place without her," he wrote to McCardell's family. "But that only makes me realize more keenly how grateful I am for the fifteen years in which she was with us. Somehow conventions prevented my ever telling her that in so many words. I hope she knew. Now there is no one to thank but God."

McCardell's brothers were the ones to box up the farmhouse in Frenchtown. They carefully packed the brass pots and pans, the oversized metal spinning top their sister had bought to entertain John and Liz when they were young, and the many photos showing happier times: McCardell and Harris in the garden, McCardell laughing under the big tree in the yard, friends circling the table, a shaker of martinis being poured into glasses. McCardell's brother Adrian was the executor of her will, which hadn't been updated since the 1940s. The bulk of the shared marital wealth resided with Harris in the form of the two houses and the apartment in New York. McCardell had $20,000 in savings, diligently set aside over her years of work. Half was left to Harris; the other half was evenly split among her brothers and mother.

Eleanor, now seventy-eight, was showing her age. John promised to visit her soon, but in the meantime, he wrote her letters. "Only now that my duties are almost finished do I begin to realize how much I shall miss

Mumsy," John wrote after he finished boxing up her things. "How much we all counted on her without ever really thinking about it. Gratitude in human terms always seems to be a little late."

Marjorie Griswold also wrote to Eleanor that spring: "You have great reason to be proud of Claire, not only as the greatest designer America has ever had, but also because she remained a fine, lovely person, unaffected by her success. She had a rare ability to keep her thinking clear and straight, something very difficult to do in the fashion whirl of New York. The most famous European designers such as Dior, Emilio [Pucci] and Fath told me that Claire meant creative American designing to them. And here, all the sportswear designers acknowledged her leadership."

In the months following her death, those who had worked closely with McCardell tried to cement her legacy. They donated McCardell clothes to the Costume Institute at the Metropolitan Museum of Art and the Brooklyn Museum, among others. Klein and Orrick collected her Townley sketches and donated them to Parsons for an archive. A group of Parsons alumni raised funds for a scholarship in her name. Coty gave McCardell a posthumous lifetime achievement award, which it presented to Eleanor and Adrian in New York in the fall of 1958. Staff at Capezio, with Orrick's help, created a gallery honoring McCardell's ballet flat designs in the shoemaker's Manhattan headquarters.

One wonders what McCardell would have made of all the memorializing. She maintained that there was but one measure of a designer's legacy. "Good fashion," she believed, "somehow earns the right to survive."

In 1958, a textile designer named Mimi Blaker sent a letter to Adolph Klein. She had known McCardell for decades, and she credited the designer with helping her launch her own career. She captured what so many felt about McCardell at the time. "There is one thing sure," she wrote. "The women of America will long remember what she did."

Epilogue

The year McCardell died marked the end of an era in many ways. In 1958, Carmel Snow left *Harper's Bazaar*, closing her long reign as the queen of fashion coverage. The photographer Louise Dahl-Wolfe, McCardell's collaborator and friend, quit the magazine soon after, saying that fashion had lost its appeal. In December, Dorothy Shaver suffered a stroke. She died in June 1959 at the age of sixty-five, but not before bringing Lord & Taylor's annual sales to an unprecedented $100 million. Diana Vreeland would leave fashion journalism and dedicate her time to curating exhibitions at the Met's Costume Institute.

After Townley, Mildred Orrick went on to work for several designers in the 1950s, including Anne Fogarty, who became well known in 1959 for her book titled *Wife Dressing: The Fine Art of Being a Well-Dressed Wife*. In 1963, Orrick became the head designer for Villager Clothes, a successful line of sportswear that operated out of Philadelphia. In retirement, she and Jesse lived again in the Virginia house that they'd renovated during the Depression. She died in 1994 at the age of eighty-eight.

Joset Walker continued designing until she retired in her fifties and bought an eighteenth-century house in New Jersey with her second husband. In the 1970s, she said in a newspaper interview that she didn't think women should go into fashion anymore. Second-wave feminism had taken hold in the United States, thanks to writers such as Betty Friedan, but the second wave of American ready-to-wear had been overtaken by men. Fashion didn't provide the same career possibilities for a woman that it once had.

In fact, the story of American fashion became constructed on the subsequent generation of men: Halston, Ralph Lauren, Calvin Klein, and Tommy Hilfiger—men who, it should be noted, credit Claire McCardell as their inspiration. "She really invented sportswear, which is this country's major contribution to fashion," Calvin Klein said. "She realized that and did it in the 1940s." It may seem simple, he added, but what McCardell did "was very difficult." In the 1970s, Sally Kirkland aimed to revive McCardell's name and remind people of her legacy by writing a short biography of her friend in an anthology of fashion design.

Eleanor Lambert remained central to New York fashion until her death in 2003 at one hundred years old. She became best known for staging the 1973 Battle of Versailles, which famously pitted American designers such as Halston, against French couturiers.

After McCardell's death, Irving Harris stopped communicating with her family. He quickly remarried. His new wife came with teenage sons, who Harris had believed would be shipped off to boarding school as he'd done with his own children. When he realized that his bride expected him to parent, the marriage ended. He married a fifth wife, and they moved to Santa Barbara, California, where they lived together until he died in his eighties.

John stopped speaking to his father not long after his stepmother's death. Harris had begun treating John's young son in the same harsh manner in which John had been raised. John didn't want to expose his children to such behavior. John would only discover that he had a half sister living in France when he took his wife and two children on a trip to Paris and made a side trip to see his childhood home in Doumy.

Liz moved west after graduating from college. She went first to San Francisco, the city where her grandmother Emma Spreckels had once lived and where her great-grandfather Claus had made his fortune. She later moved to New Mexico. Liz and John remained estranged, and the siblings followed in the Spreckels/Harris tradition of resolving familial disputes through the courts. Today, John Harris's two children have a pact. "We promised to be the first generation of our family not to sue one another," Emily Harris Jones told me.

It took decades for the McCardell brothers to sort through their sister's artwork, sketchbooks, notebooks, and clothes. It was a slow and difficult process. Beginning in the 1980s, they established two archives in her name, one at the Library of the Fashion Institute of Technology in New York, the other at the Maryland Center for History and Culture in Baltimore.

By then, Claire McCardell's name had receded from public memory. Hers was not the only one. The names of her contemporaries—the many women of the 1930s and 1940s who birthed American fashion—were also forgotten.

Yet McCardell has never been forgotten by the world's fashion designers and curators or by vintage clothing experts and enthusiasts. In 2022, the fashion designer Tory Burch, with the help of the Maryland Center for History and Culture and the fashion curator Allison Tolman, reissued McCardell's book, *What Shall I Wear?* Burch created a spring collection that year inspired by McCardell designs. In 2023, the Costume Institute at the Met mounted its "Women Dressing Women" exhibition highlighting pioneering female designers, and a giant banner of McCardell graced the side of the museum. Nearly a century after she'd climbed those same steps with her Parsons class and eight decades after she had accepted the Coty Award in its sculpture garden, McCardell's face shone out from the Met's limestone facade. She was pictured in her Future Dress of 1945.

Today, it is difficult to find a pristine, original Claire McCardell outside a museum. Over the years, women rarely mothballed her clothes; they wore them to threads. Yet McCardell's work is all around us. Her fashions have survived, even if her brand did not. They can be seen in our everyday lives: in our houses, in our workplaces, in the street as we move about in our flat-heeled ballet shoes, our wrap dresses and denim, our separates and our playsuits, better known today as athletic wear. Claire

McCardell's innovations have seeped into the culture at large and are so prevalent now that their revolutionary origins are invisible. We are the inheritors of her brave risks, her experiments, and her singular focus.

As we dress in the clothes that McCardell bequeathed us, we might also choose to ponder the wisdom she proffered. We can, as she counseled her mentees, become better students of history, knowing that the past informs our present. Hard-won freedoms can be stripped away again. We can find the courage to defy and overturn the rules and dress codes meant to keep us controlled and confined. And we can understand that our clothes are far more than vehicles for adornment; they can and should be the foundation for pursuing our fulfilled and purposeful lives. As the historian Einav Rabinovitch-Fox reminded us, Claire McCardell "did not see feminist ideas of freedom and independence as abstract but sought to turn them into an everyday practice."

McCardell understood that the most powerful aspect of clothes is in how they inform our experience. Our right to choose how to dress is a sartorial symbol of our right to choose the way we live. "It wasn't me in the clothes, or just wearing them, that interested me," McCardell once said, "it was the clothes in relation to me—how changed I felt once in them."

Acknowledgments

This book has been years in the making, and it exists thanks to the support of many extraordinary people.

Marya Spence is a brilliant agent whose guidance helped shape this book from the beginning. As did the crucial input of Mackenzie Williams. I want to thank everyone at Janklow + Nesbit for their support, as well as Will Watkins at CAA.

To my editor, Tzipora Chein, whose enthusiasm and diligent care took this book to the next level. And to everyone at Simon & Schuster, including Chonise Bass, Ingrid Carabulea, Lauren Gomez, Jonathan Karp, Irene Kheradi, Annalea Manalili, Sean Manning, Amanda Mulholland, Olivia Perrault, and Jackie Seow.

The only reason this book exists is because of the McCardell family, past and present. I would like to thank all of them, but especially John and Bonnie McCardell for their hospitality and research help; Katie McCardell Webb for her early support and many hours spent talking with me about her aunt. To Lee McCardell, Steve McCardell, and Mac Kennedy.

Sarah Orrick brought her amazing mother, Mildred, to life for me through interviews and her own exceptional writing. Emily Harris Jones patiently answered my many questions about the Harris family.

I am grateful to the Maryland Center for History and Culture in Baltimore. Former curators Allison Tolman and Alexandra Deutsch supported my research in 2018. I have further benefited from the help of curators, archivists, and staff, including Catherine Rogers Arthur, David Belew, Katie Caljean, Micah Connor, Sandra Glascock, Chloe Green, Martina Kado, Margot Kopera, Julia Nadeau, and Debbie Orlove. Leslie Eames, this means I will finally stop emailing you!

At the Fashion Institute of Technology in New York, where McCardell's professional archive is housed, I want to thank April Calahan who helped me enormously when she was the archivist there. She further assisted me with her tutorials on fashion history produced through her podcast, *Dressed*. Also at FIT, a thank you to Valerie Steele for discussing McCardell, and Tiffany Nixon for answering research questions.

To the stellar research archivists and librarians at the Brooke Russell Astor Reading Room for Rare Books and Manuscripts at the New York Public Library; the Smithsonian Institution Archives of American Art; and the Smithsonian's National Museum of American History archive. To Gillian Mahoney at the Library of Congress. Mary Mannix and Derek Gee at the Frederick County Public Library; and the staff of the Maryland Room at the Enoch Pratt. To all those at Heritage Frederick, in particular Jody Brummage and Amy Hunt. At Parsons, a special thanks to Jenny Swadosh. At Hood College, archivist Mary Atwell is a researcher's best friend. On Fishers Island, Pierce Rafferty; and to the archivists at New York-Presbyterian/Weill Cornell Medical Center.

I was inordinately lucky to be writing for *The Washington Post Magazine* when Richard Just and David Rowell were editors there, and I wrote my first story about Claire for them. Antoinette LaFarge and Maya Gurantz underwrote early research with their Out of the Archive Project grant. Adam Higgs further reminded me of why Claire's story remains vital, and it was a very lucky day when our paths crossed.

I am grateful to McCardell researchers who came before me, in particular the late Nancy Nolf, the late Sally Kirkland, and the curator Kohle Yohannon. I'd also like to thank the pioneering scholars and writers of women's history and fashion who recognized this period as being about far more than fashion. Among them Rebecca Arnold, Keren

Ben-Horin, Einav Rabinovitch-Fox, Julie Satow, and Avery Trufelman. Historian Sandra Bonura and writer Vincent Dicks illuminated the lives of Jean Harris and the Spreckels family with their excellent books, and they gave generously of their time. And to Penelope Rowlands for chatting about Carmel Snow.

To historian and dear friend Melissa Blair for the many hours of counsel and editing help, and for taking me to the woods to work when I needed it most. To Thea Webb, who helped with research in 2018, and to Daphne Gabb, Robyn Levy, and Arya Royal for additional research assistance. To Hilary McClellan, ace fact checker, as well as Sameen Gauhar for her early assistance. To Vicky Pass for talking sportswear and the history of stockings. To Julia Ridley Smith for being an exceptional reader, editor, and friend. A lot of life happened while I worked on this book, and you were present for much of it. Your wisdom and humor got me through. To George and Lulu Kauffman for the meals and fine company.

To Tory Burch for championing Claire McCardell and women entrepreneurs, and the team at Tory Burch, including Frances Pennington and Emily Farra.

I'd also like to thank—with zero hyperbole—the state of Maryland. Where I live is not only the birthplace of Claire McCardell, but also the reason I can write. I availed myself of our public park systems. I received funding from the Maryland State Arts Council. The Baker Artist Award and the Greater Baltimore Cultural Alliance supported me in ways I cannot even begin to articulate. To Jeannie Howe, Connie Imboden, Alix Fenhagen, David London, and Melissa Warlow, I will never forget what you've done for me. And to Steve Ziger and Jamie Snead for the surprise gift on my doorstep when I needed a boost.

And then there are the writers, artists, editors, and literary boosters of Baltimore, who helped me along the way, including: Josephine Bergin, Cleve Corner, Jane Delury, Elisabeth Dahl, Julia Fleischaker, Kristina Gaddy, Alec MacGillis, Emma Snyder, Jeannie Vanasco, and Jung Yun. To Ron Tanner and his magical Good Contrivance Farm. To

Ann Stiller for the tea and proofing. To Wendy Ward and Joe MacLeod for brainstorm sessions; Joe Rubino for videos; Stefani Foster LaBrecque for her friendship and photography skills. The support of the arts and of artists in Baltimore is exceptional, and I am proud to call this city home.

To my own crew of exceptional women: Emily Evans, Erika Goldwater, Yalda Nikoomanesh, and Sonia Sorensen. You understood I was a writer even before I did, and your friendship over the decades has sustained me. You four are my compass home no matter where I am.

And to my family. My brother, Mike Evitts, for sparking my love of storytelling back when we made up entire worlds on the basement stairs. I couldn't have done this without you. To Anne Faulkner for giving me a home when I needed it most and for building a new one with my brother. To the extended Faulkner crew—Lara, Frank, Katie, Bill, and Joe. To Sharon and Charlie Sorrentino, Bryan and Julie Cook, Sarah and Dave Denham. To Tom and Nancy Dickinson. To Cat Mihos, my angel investor, for your wisdom and grace. And to my mom and dad, William and Carole Evitts, who aren't here to see this book but whose spirit imbues every page.

Finally, to Matt, the man "who lives it." There truly aren't enough words. Your unwavering patience and humor are the rarest of gifts. And to Nola, my brave and kindhearted girl. This one's for you. I hope it makes you as proud as I am of you.

Notes

A NOTE ON SOURCES

All quotes in this book have been pulled directly from primary sources. In some instances, scenes were written using the primary accounts of sources recounting these moments via letters, notebooks, articles, journals, and interviews.

LIST OF ABBREVIATIONS

The abbreviations below are used for frequently cited libraries, archives, manuscript collections, names, and published sources. Additional published sources referenced in this book are listed in a select bibliography. For the endnotes, a full citation is given on first use, and subsequent uses are cited using the abbreviated title.

Libraries, Archives, and Museums

BFP: Betty Friedan Papers, 1933–1985. MC 575, Schlesinger Library, Radcliffe Institute, Harvard University

DSP: Dorothy Shaver Papers, Archives Center, National Museum of American History

FGI: Fashion Group International records, Manuscripts and Archives Division, The New York Public Library, Astor, Lenox, and Tilden Foundations

FIT: Fashion Institute of Technology–SUNY, Gladys Marcus Library, Special Collections and College Archives, Claire McCardell collection, 1927–1975, SC.38

HF: Heritage Frederick Archive, The Historical Society of Frederick County

Hood Archive: Beneficial-Hodson Library, Archives and Special Collections, Hood

College publications collection; Beneficial-Hodson Library, Archives and Special Collections, Nancy Nolf Collection, 2013.47
MCHC: Claire McCardell Collection, 1923–1995, MS 3066. H. Furlong Baldwin Library, Maryland Center for History and Culture
Parsons: Claire McCardell Fashion Sketches, KA.0082, New School Archives and Special Collections, The New School, New York, New York

Private Family Collections and Sources

IDH: Irving Drought Harris Family
MFA: McCardell Family Archive
OFP: Orrick Family Papers

Books, Articles, and Publications

AF: Sarah Tomerlin Lee, ed., *American Fashion: The Life and Lines of Adrian, Mainbocher, McCardell, Norell, Trigère* (Quadrangle, 1975)
Dior: Marie-France Pochna, *Christian Dior: Destiny: The Authorized Biography* (Flammarion, 2021)
FIOB: Beryl Williams, *Fashion Is Our Business* (John Gifford, 1948)
GWDD: Betty Friedan, "The Gal Who Defied Dior," *Town Journal*, October 1955, 33
RM: Kohle Yohannan and Nancy Nolf, *Claire McCardell: Redefining Modernism* (Henry N. Abrams, 1998)
WSIW: Claire McCardell, *What Shall I Wear? The What, Where, When, and How Much of Fashion* (Abrams Image, 2022)
WWD: *Women's Wear Daily*

Introduction: Dressing for a Revolution

1 *The journalist was equally surprised*: Betty Friedan interview with Peggy LeBoutillier, BFP.
1 *"something is very wrong"*: Betty Friedan, *The Feminine Mystique* (W. W. Norton, 2013), xxi.
1 *Friedan had told her editor*: GWDD.
2 *McCardell didn't look anything like*: GWDD.
2 *"I've always designed things"*: Osborn Elliott, "The American Look," *Time*, May 2, 1955.
2 *"continuous experiment"*: WSIW, 14.
3 *He wanted to*: Francine Du Plessix Gray, "Prophets of Seduction," *New Yorker*, November 4, 1996, 90.
3 *"You can't go back"*: GWDD.
3 *"She changed the world's meaning"*: GWDD.

One: The Practice House

11 *The neighborhood kids*: Nancy Nolf interview with Adrian McCardell, September 1997, Hood Archive.

11 *The wide, oak-lined boulevard*: *FIOB*, 65.
11 *McCardell's mother, Eleanor*: Nancy Nolf, interview with Bob McCardell, August 1997, Hood Archive.
12 *After church, the family gathered*: Lee McCardell, "Two Centuries of Frederick Town," *Baltimore Sun*, August 19, 1945.
13 *Why couldn't a girl's clothes*: Claire McCardell, Coty Awards speech, February 1944, MCHC.
13 *McCardell sometimes entertained*: McCardell, Coty Awards speech.
13 *Eleanor was as fashionable*: *RM*, 16.
14 *By elementary school*: "Pastor-Hunter Gives Lecture," *Frederick News*, August 22, 1914, 5.
14 *McCardell played the lovable*: "100 Appear in Benefit Play," *Frederick News-Post*, March 10, 1917, 5.
14 *Eleanor said these dresses*: Sally Kirkland, "Claire McCardell," in *AF*, 215.
15 *In the 1860s, Mary Walker*: Anika Burgess, "The Unconventional Life of Mary Walker," Atlas Obscura, September 27, 2017, https://www.atlasobscura.com/articles/mary-walker-feminist-dress-reform-equal-rights.
15 *decency laws*: Clare Sears, *Arresting Dress: Cross-Dressing, Law, and Fascination in Nineteenth-Century San Francisco* (Duke University Press, 2015), 2.
15 *One person pelted her*: Burgess, "The Unconventional Life of Mary Walker."
15 *They were slimmer*: Author interview with fashion historian Allison Tolman, 2024.
16 *Dormer windows pierced*: *RM*, 16.
16 *Rarely satisfied with what she saw*: *RM*, 16.
16 *As she cut her custom*: McCardell, Coty Awards speech.
17 *Eleanor selected her new clothes*: *WSIW*, 105.
17 *Before marrying Roy*: Eleanor McCardell, letter to Claire McCardell, January 24, 1951, MFA.
17 *When the sewing machine*: Nancy Nolf, interview with Adrian McCardell, September 1997, Hood Archive.
18 *She had learned to sew*: "Irma's Quilt," Technical Writer, June 20, 2013, https://techwriter.typepad.com/technical_writing_at_dahm/people.
18 *McCardell sat*: McCardell, Coty Awards speech.
18 *She thought a pretty grosgrain*: *RM*, 15.
18 *Koogle asked if she*: Betty Friedan, draft notes for "Gal Who Defied Dior," article, BFP.
19 *Each semester, McCardell*: Claire McCardell, report cards, MFA, 1919.
19 *"is just my way"*: McCardell, Coty Awards speech.
19 *Apart from geometry class*: Nancy Nolf interview with Adrian McCardell, September 1997, Hood Archive.
20 *She noticed that*: *WSIW*, 141.
20 *But McCardell never settled*: Nancy Nolf, interview with Bob McCardell, 1997, Hood Archive.
20 *McCardell, who was once*: *Vogue* article, n.d., FIT.
20 *But over breakfast*: Kitty Ross, "At Big Pool," *Frederick News-Post*, June 23, 1920, p. 3.
20 *He could handily swim*: Kevin L. Jones and Christina M. Johnson with Kirstin Purtich, *Sporting Fashion: Outdoor Girls 1800–1960* (Prestel Verlag, 2021), 150.

21 *The skirtless one-piece*: Richard Thompson Ford, *Dress Codes: How the Laws of Fashion Made History* (Simon & Schuster, 2021), 282.
21 *When pressed on a matter*: Claire McCardell frequently used this phrase in her personal correspondence; MCHC.
22 *They wanted to partake in*: Richard C. Bell, "A History of Women in Sport Prior to Title IX," *The Sport Journal*, March 14, 2008, https://thesportjournal.org/article/a-history-of-women-in-sport-prior-to-title-ix.
22 *"The result of all this activity"*: Marquise de Sourdy, "The Baise-Main: From the Point of View of a Tilted French Woman," *Vogue*, October 31, 1895.
22 *Their punishment for taking*: Kitty Ross, "At Big Pool," *Frederick News-Post*, June 23, 1920, 3.
22 *Anna Koogle scolded*: FIOB, 66.
22 *"I didn't sew very well"*: McCardell, Coty Awards speech.
23 *"our lives are tuned to"*: WSIW, 104.
23 *She was "determined to save"*: RM, 20.
23 *That city was*: Nancy Nolf, interview with Bob McCardell, 1997, Hood Archive.
23 *On September 20*: 1923 Hood student handbook, 7, Hood Archive.
24 *"The real purpose"*: Untitled editorial, *The Blue and Grey*, September 1923, Hood Archive.
25 *A healthy diet*: Patricia Campbell Warner, *When the Girls Came Out to Play: The Birth of American Sportswear* (University of Massachusetts Press, 2006), 164–165.
25 *One 1880s manual*: Cornelia M. Clapp, *Manual of Gymnastics: Prepared for the Use of Students of Mt. Holyoke Seminary*, 1883, 33.
25 *The poofed legs resembled*: Warner, *When the Girls Came Out to Play*, 203.
25 *But when women began*: Warner, *When the Girls Came Out to Play*, 204–06.
25 *"Due to their indulgence"*: *Frederick County Almanac*, 1925, 16.
25 *Those were the same clothiers*: *The Blue and Grey*, 1923, Hood Archive.
26 *McCardell refused to wear*: WSIW, 35.
26 *"I don't hate crinolines"*: Multiple versions of this quote can be found in McCardell's letters, speeches, and papers in the MCHC archive.
26 *McCardell's pursuit of*: 1924–25 Hood College catalogue, Hood Archive.
26 *Student grades were sent*: Nancy Nolf, interview with Bob McCardell, 1997, Hood Archive.
26 *"The burns on my hands"*: McCardell, Coty Awards speech, February 1944, MCHC.
26 *He looked his stunned daughter*: Betty Friedan, draft and interview notes, 1955, BFP.
27 *Instead, she asked for*: RM, 21.

Two: An Army of Brave Women

29 *Young women chatted*: "A Club for Girl Art Students," *New York Times*, May 15, 1904.
30 *Women began flocking*: "A Club for Girl Art Students," *New York Times*, May 15, 1904.
30 *In 1902, Hall founded*: *The Designer*, March 1905, quoted in "The Three Arts Club—New York 1905," The Paper Sunflower, August 13, 2017, https://thepapersunflower.blogspot.com/2017/08/the-three-arts-club-new-york-1905.html.
30 *Only a handful*: Paulina Bren, *The Barbizon: The Hotel That Set Women Free* (Simon & Schuster, 2022), 24–25.

30 *McCardell's roommate that year*: Author interview with Sarah Orrick, 2023.
31 *The primary objective*: Adam Lewis, *Van Day Truex: The Man Who Defined Twentieth-Century Taste and Style* (Viking Studio, 2001), 26–27.
31 *The school's current president*: Lewis, *Van Day Truex*, 24.
32 *"As a nation we now"*: Report of Commission to International Exposition of Modern Decorative and Industrial Art in Paris, 1925. Washington, DC: US Department of Commerce, 1925.
33 *Fiorello La Guardia*: "Fiorello LaGuardia on Prohibition," Ohio State University, https://prohibition.osu.edu/american-prohibition-1920/fiorello-laguardia-prohibition, accessed October 11, 2024.
33 *"It's funny how all"*: Claire McCardell, letter to Eleanor McCardell, undated, MCHC.
33 *"Mildred and the other girls"*: Claire McCardell, letter to her parents, undated, 1925, MCHC.
33 *That autumn, one of Slack's friends*: Claire McCardell, letter to her parents, undated, 1925, MCHC.
33 *But she soon had*: Claire McCardell, letters to her parents, 1925, MCHC.
34 *But really, the term* flapper: Richard Thompson Ford, *Dress Codes: How the Laws of Fashion Made History* (Simon & Schuster, 2021), 148–150.
35 *McCardell, once described*: GWDD, 33; *Vogue* magazine, undated article, FIT.
35 *An elderly friend*: Claire McCardell, letter to her parents, 1926, MCHC.
35 *On a weekend trip home*: Nancy Nolf, interview with Adrian McCardell, 1997, Hood Archive.
36 *McCardell painstakingly copied*: As evidenced in McCardell's student work, HF.
37 *"The ladies of the board"*: Claire McCardell, letter to her parents, 1926, MCHC.
37 *It floored her, too*: Claire McCardell, letters to her parents, 1926, MCHC.
37 *McCardell made a series*: Claire McCardell, student sketches, HF.
37 *"I love modern art"*: Claire McCardell, letter to her parents, 1926, MCHC.
38 *"Suppose you've gotten"*: Claire McCardell, various letters to her parents, 1926, MCHC.
38 *Not long after*: Bible, MFA.
39 *New York was*: "City Called Bowl of 'a Heady Drink,'" *New York Times*, November 30, 1926.
39 *He routinely talked*: Robert Norwood, collected writing, compiled by St. Mark's Church, New York, MFA.
39 *McCardell felt desperate*: Claire McCardell, various letters to her parents, 1926, MCHC.
39 *Selling even one*: Claire McCardell, various letters to her parents, 1926, MCHC.
40 *How one made a living*: Claire McCardell, letter to her parents, undated, 1926, MCHC.

Three: This Clothes Business Certainly Is a Gamble

41 *It would speed her*: "Souvenir log of the S.S. 'Leviathan,' Students and Veterans Tours, 1925," United States Lines, https://www.ggarchives.com/OceanTravel/Passengers/USL/Leviathan-PassengerList-StudentLog-1925-08-25.html, accessed June 2023.
41 *It was a luxury hotel*: "The Steamship Leviathan," brochure, 1923, https://www.ggarchives.com/OceanTravel/Brochures/USL-1923-TheSteamshipLeviathan.html, accessed June 2023.

41 *McCardell took in*: Claire McCardell, letters to her parents, undated, 1926, MCHC.
42 *McCardell would live*: Claire McCardell, Coty Awards speech, 1944, MCHC.
42 *Frank Alvah Parsons understood*: Adam Lewis, *Van Day Truex: The Man Who Defined Twentieth-Century Taste and Style* (Viking Studio, 2001), 33.
42 *Their neighborhood teemed*: Hazel B. Reavis, "The Old Latin Quarter Has Bowed to New Ideas," *New York Times*, May 16, 1926.
43 *"The scum of Greenwich Village"*: Ernest Hemingway, "American Bohemians in Paris a Weird Lot," *Toronto Star Weekly*, March 25, 1922.
43 *"wore a slipover jersey"*: Ernest Hemingway, *The Sun Also Rises* (New York, NY: Scribner), 1926, 30.
43 *Where she wore*: *WSIW*, 29.
44 *Worth laid the foundation*: Robin Givhan, *The Battle of Versailles: The Night American Fashion Stumbled into the Spotlight and Made History* (Flatiron Books, 2015), 11–14.
44 *At the House of Worth*: Claire McCardell, letter to her parents, February 3, 1927, MCHC.
45 *She'd packed an iron*: Claire McCardell, letter to her parents, Saturday, October 16, 1926, MCHC.
45 *The* vendeuses, *or saleswomen*: Claire McCardell, letter to her parents, undated, 1926, MCHC.
45 *McCardell was suddenly surrounded*: Claire McCardell, letter to her parents, undated, 1926, MCHC.
46 *The effortless elegance*: "Vionnet, Couturier, Dies at 98; Innovator Created the Bias Cut," *New York Times*, March 5, 1975, 42.
46 *She believed*: Madeleine Vionnet, "Introducing the Winter Mode," *The Delineator*, November 1927, 27.
46 *Orrick took her time*: Author interview with Sarah Orrick, 2023. Also evidenced in the Mildred Orrick Fashion and Costume Sketches, KA.0067, New School Archives and Special Collections, The New School, New York, NY.
46 *McCardell rushed*: Many sources speak about McCardell's quick sketches. Mildred Orrick said as much to Betty Friedan in the 1955 article "The Gal Who Defied Dior." Bessie Sustersic, McCardell's longtime assistant at Townley, referred to her drawings as "stick figures." The archives of Parsons, FIT, MCHC, Heritage Frederick, and the McCardell family also have a wealth of her sketches, beginning in 1925, when she was a student at Parsons.
46 *Her college French was improving*: Claire McCardell, various letters to her parents, 1926, MCHC.
47 *Other nights, they attended*: Claire McCardell, various letters to her parents, 1926, MCHC.
48 *They often ended their nights*: Claire McCardell, various letters to her parents, 1926–27, MCHC.
48 *"For goodness' sake"*: Claire McCardell, letter to her parents, September 19, 1926, MCHC.
48 *McCardell had grown wise*: Claire McCardell, various letters to her parents, 1926–27, MCHC.
48 *The trio of McCardell, Orrick, and Walker*: Sally Kirkland, "Claire McCardell," in *AF*, 217.
48 *For one assignment*: *AF*, 217–18.

49 *With all the walking*: Claire McCardell, various letters to her parents, 1926–27, MCHC.
49 *"She certainly was a"*: Claire McCardell, letter to her parents, November 1926, MCHC.
50 *The French, she noticed*: Claire McCardell, letter to her parents, September 27, 1926, MCHC.
51 *She meticulously disassembled*: Peggy LeBoutillier, press material, undated, FIT.
51 *She gleaned all she could*: RM, 26.
51 *"learning important things"*: Claire McCardell, Coty Awards speech, February 1944, MCHC.
51 *A few weeks later*: Claire McCardell, various letters to her parents, 1927, MCHC.
51 *The pay was paltry*: Claire McCardell, various letters to her parents, 1927, MCHC.
52 *By the end of the evening*: Claire McCardell, undated letter to her parents, winter 1927, MCHC.
52 *The legitimate way*: Samuel Hopkins Adams, "The Dishonest Paris Label," *Ladies' Home Journal*, March 1913, 7.
52 *One swindle involved*: Véronique Pouillard, "Design Piracy in the Fashion Industries of Paris and New York in the Interwar Years," *Business History Review* 85, no. 2 (spring 2011): 319–44.
53 *"Copying, a fancy name"*: Elizabeth Hawes, *Fashion Is Spinach* (Random House, 1938), 38.
54 *One apocryphal tale*: Lois Gould, *Mommy Dressing: A Love Story, After a Fashion* (Doubleday, 1998), 31.
54 *I've learned more about*: Claire McCardell, letter to her parents, January 17, 1927, MCHC.
54 *A warm spring washed over*: *AF*, 218.
55 *"Well, are you coming?"*: Both Mildred Orrick and Claire McCardell wrote accounts of this evening in their letters. This account is pulled from their personal papers, MCHC and OFP.
56 *The engine's roar*: Claire McCardell, letter to her parents, Monday, May 23, 1927, MCHC.
56 *She again clasped*: The story of that day was recounted by McCardell in several sources, including letters home to her family and in a story printed in *The Frederick News*. Mildred Orrick also wrote in her personal correspondence about the details of that day. McCardell and Orrick further recounted the details of the landing to Betty Friedan over a lunch interview in 1955.
56 *A few days later*: Claire McCardell, letter to her parents, May 23, 1927, MCHC.
56 *He had circled*: A. Scott Berg, "The Spirit of St. Louis' Amazing Journey," *Smithsonian Magazine*, November 2013.
57 *McCardell and Orrick sailed home*: Claire McCardell, various letters to her parents, 1927, MCHC.

Four: This Town Doesn't Pity a Soul

60 *Others suggested that she accept*: Claire McCardell, various letters to her parents, 1928-1929, MCHC.
60 *"I don't know"*: Claire McCardell, letter to her parents, undated, 1928, MCHC.

Notes

- 60 *The dormlike atmosphere*: Claire McCardell, letter to her parents, undated, 1929, MCHC.
- 60 *"Why don't you go home"*: Claire McCardell, letter to her parents, undated, 1928, MCHC.
- 61 *"the nerve"*: Claire McCardell, letter to her parents, undated, 1928, MCHC.
- 61 *By the 1920s*: Susan Porter Benson, *Counter Cultures: Saleswomen, Managers, and Customers in American Department Stores, 1890–1904* (University of Illinois Press, 1988), 84.
- 61 *The stores provided*: Benson, *Counter Cultures*, 85.
- 61 *The modern department store*: Benson, *Counter Cultures*, 76.
- 61 *The male owners appreciated*: For more on the role of women in department stores at the time, see Julie Satow, *When Women Ran Fifth Avenue: Glamour and Power at the Dawn of American Fashion* (Doubleday, 2024).
- 62 *At Macy's, the man*: Claire McCardell, various letters to her parents, 1928, MCHC.
- 62 *Most evenings, McCardell returned*: Claire McCardell, various letters to her parents, 1928, MCHC.
- 63 *"preferred a Demon"*: Esther Forbes, *A Mirror for Witches* (Houghton Mifflin, 1928).
- 63 *She thought so much*: Claire McCardell letter to her mother, undated, 1928, MCHC.
- 63 *Anytime "one reads of a witch"*: Virginia Woolf, *A Room of One's Own* (Harbinger, 1957), 48–49.
- 63 *McCardell had been thinking*: Claire McCardell, letter to her parents, undated, 1928, MCHC.
- 64 *Carmel Snow, the firebrand*: Penelope Rowlands, *A Dash of Daring: Carmel Snow and Her Life in Fashion, Art, and Letters* (Atria Books, 2005), Kindle edition, 94.
- 64 *City codes for public buildings*: Nicole Garner, "11 Things Women Couldn't Do in the 1920s," Mental Floss, March 22, 2023, https://www.mentalfloss.com/article/520324/11-things-women-couldnt-do-1920s.
- 64 *"This town"*: Claire McCardell, letter to her parents, undated, 1928, MCHC.
- 64 *By the end of June*: Claire McCardell, letter to her parents, undated, 1928, MCHC.
- 64 *The dentist delivered the news*: Claire McCardell, various letters to her parents, 1928, MCHC.
- 64 *A few days before McCardell*: Claire McCardell, various letters to her parents, 1928, MCHC.
- 65 *After her husband had died*: Author's interview with Sarah Orrick, 2023.
- 66 *They moved in*: Claire McCardell, various letters to her parents, 1928, MCHC.
- 66 *The woman knew of*: Claire McCardell, various letters to her parents, 1928, MCHC.
- 67 *"I don't want to do"*: Claire McCardell, letter to her parents, undated, 1928, MCHC.
- 67 *The garment business*: Nancy L. Green, *Ready-to-Wear and Ready-to-Work* (Duke University Press, 1997), 2.
- 67 *Mass production and ready-to-wear*: "Historical Overview," The Gotham Center for New York City History, https://www.gothamcenter.org/garment-industry-history-project, accessed on June 1, 2023.
- 68 *"I learned a new sound"*: David Von Drehle, *Triangle: The Fire That Changed America* (Atlantic Monthly Press, 2003), 125.
- 68 *It was time to return*: RM, 29.
- 69 *"It occurs to me"*: Dorothy Parker, "My Home Town," *McCall's*, January 1928, 4.

69 *"I am sure I am going"*: Claire McCardell, letter to her parents, undated, 1928, MCHC.
69 *Eleanor believed in*: Nancy Nolf interview with Adrian McCardell, September 1997, Hood Archive.
69 *"I hope I can pay"*: Claire McCardell, letter to her parents, undated, 1928, MCHC.
69 *For $25 a week*: Claire McCardell, letter to her parents, undated, 1928, MCHC.
70 *An American woman looked*: F. Scott Fitzgerald, *The Great Gatsby* (Scribner, 1925), 55.
70 *She clocked in*: Claire McCardell, various letters to her parents, 1928, MCHC.
70 *The zeppelin achieved*: "Airship Hypnotizes City Gazing Upward," *New York Times*, October 16, 1928, 1.
70 *It was almost as thrilling*: Claire McCardell, letter to her parents, October, 1928, MCHC.
71 *Roy McCardell had entered politics*: "McCardell Named to State Tax Post," *Baltimore Sun*, July 9, 1930, 24.
71 *"Wasn't nearly as gay"*: Claire McCardell, letter to her father, November, 1928, MCHC.
71 *Among the regulars*: Claire McCardell, letter to her parents, 1928, MCHC.
72 *"If my clothes suit you"*: Claire McCardell, letter to her parents, 1928, MCHC.
72 *As Pollack's assistant*: Claire McCardell, various letters to her parents, 1928, MCHC.
72 *"I can't see why Gay"*: Claire McCardell, letter to her parents, 1928, MCHC.
72 *At many New York dress houses*: "America Comes to Seventh Avenue," *Fortune*, July 1939, 122.
73 *The precision and strength*: David Von Drehle, *Triangle: The Fire That Changed America* (Atlantic Monthly Press, 2003), 62.
73 *It was believed*: David Von Drehle, *Triangle: The Fire That Changed America* (Atlantic Monthly Press, 2003), 119.
73 *Pollack later remembered McCardell*: *AF*, 219.
73 *In March 1929*: Claire McCardell, various letters to her parents, 1929, MCHC.
74 *He needed an experienced*: *FIOB*, 72–73.
74 *He fired her*: *AF*, 219.
74 *She would later describe*: *FIOB*, 72.

Five: Let the Girl Do It

77 *McCardell slipped into*: McCardell frequently spoke of copying at Bergdorf during her early months working for Robert Turk, including during a speech she made in 1944, to the journalist Murray Robinson for an article titled "She Designed Her Career" in *New York World-Telegram* and in Betty Friedan's article "The Gal Who Defied Dior."
78 *"I didn't sweep the floors"*: Claire McCardell, draft of Coty Awards speech, February 1944, MCHC.
78 *He needed fresh ideas*: McCardell, Coty Awards speech, February 1944, MCHC.
78 *Turk wasn't a particularly talented*: Amy Fine Collins, "The Queen of Yankee Chic," *Vanity Fair*, October 1998.
79 *It wasn't just Americans*: Julie Satow, *When Women Ran Fifth Avenue*, chap. 3.
79 *The dress he had "designed"*: Murray Robinson, "She Designed Her Career," *New York World-Telegram*, undated.
80 *Only the wealthiest and most*: Booton Herndon, *Bergdorf's on the Plaza: The Story of Bergdorf Goodman and a Half-Century of American Fashion* (Alfred A. Knopf, 1945), 159.

Notes

80 *The United States was*: Undated press release, MCHC.
80 *She knew enough*: McCardell, Coty Awards speech, February 1944, MCHC.
80 *Whether he saw*: McCardell, Coty Awards speech, February 1944, MCHC.
81 *The Seventh Avenue*: Louise Dahl-Wolfe, *A Photographer's Scrapbook* (St. Martin's Press, 1984), xi.
81 *Manufacturers feared being copied*: Sandra Stansbery Buckland and Gwendolyn S. O'Neal, "'We Publish Fashions Because They Are News': *The New York Times* 1940 Through 1945," *Dress* 25, no. 1 (198): 33–41.
81 *Each piece of apparel*: An excellent account of how fashion shows worked at the time appears in an interview with Eleanor Lambert for the Fashion Institute of Technology, Oral History Project of The Fashion Industries, 14.
82 *"If the resident buyers"*: "America Comes to Seventh Avenue," *Fortune*, July 1939.
82 *his 1929 fall season*: As discussed in several articles, including "Circular and Pleated Themes Cleverly United in Fall Collection of Sportswear," *WWD*, June 26, 1929, 8; "Jacket Themes and Details in Second Sportswear Group," *WWD*, October 8, 1929, 16.
82 *Turk held tight*: "Sportswear Knitted Fashions: Linker & Klein Reorganizes Robert Turk Unit," *WWD*, April 22, 1931, 10.
83 *The man in charge*: Osborn Elliott, "The American Look," *Time*, May 2, 1955.
83 *A bluster of a man*: GWDD.
83 *An employee named*: *AF*, 221; Bernadine Morris, "Looking Back at McCardell: It's a Lot Like Looking at Today," *New York Times*, May 24, 1972, 58.
83 *McCardell still wore*: "McCardell Fashions Earned Their Survival," *Baltimore Sun*, May 16, 1976.
83 *She continued to go*: "McCardell Fashions Earned Their Survival."
83 *It exasperated her*: *RM*, 40.
83 *she acknowledged*: Betty Friedan, interview and draft notes, BFP.
84 *Once a month*: Rebecca Arnold, *The American Look: Fashion, Sportswear and the Image of Women in 1930s and 1940s New York* (I. B. Tauris, 2021), 93.
85 *"I have been completely confused"*: Transcript of Paul Mazur speech, April 7, 1931, Fashion Group International records, Manuscripts and Archives Division, The New York Public Library, Astor, Lenox, and Tilden Foundations.
85 *By the winter of 1932*: "Robert Turk to Leave Paris Feb. 8," *WWD*, February 1, 1932, 112.
86 *He was now*: "Towbin Leaves Townley Frocks," *WWD*, May 23, 1932, 15.
86 *the day before*: "Boro Man Drowns Rescuing Brother," *The Brooklyn Times-Union*, June 6, 1932, 65.
87 *McCardell couldn't make sense*: *FIOB*, 74.
87 *On Tuesday, June 7*: "Robt. Turk Funeral Set for Tomorrow," *WWD*, June 6, 1932, 24.
87 *"Let the girl do it"*: Betty Friedan, interview notes, BFP.
87 *"I don't know"*: Eleanor McCardell, letter to Claire McCardell, undated, MFA.
88 *According to one source*: *AF*, 227.
88 *She had no time*: *FIOB*, 75.
89 *As one fashion journalist*: *FIOB*, 74–75.

Six: Everyone Deserves Pockets

91 *She designed her collections*: Claire McCardell, Coty Awards speech, February 1944, MCHC.
91 *giving a woman a place*: *WSIW*, 91.
91 *Geiss, like most male manufacturers*: *RM*, 51.
92 *As Geiss made his arguments*: Hannah Carlson, *Pockets: An Intimate History of How We Keep Things Close* (Algonquin Books of Chapel Hill, 2023), Kindle edition, 118.
92 *"dragging the pocket"*: Carlson, *Pockets*, 110.
92 *By 1915*: Carlson, *Pockets*, 118–22.
92 *They guessed at*: Osborn Elliott, "The American Look," *Time*, May 2, 1955.
93 *Around that time*: "The Cult of Claire McCardell," press release, n.d., MCHC.
93 *A woman may live*: *WSIW*, 85.
93 *As* Fortune *magazine explained*: "Model Women," *Fortune*, September 1930.
94 *"Men are free"*: Claire McCardell, "Women Are What They Wear," *Sports Illustrated*, August 1954.
94 *"follow the instinctive demand"*: Claire McCardell, Coty Awards speech, February 1944, MCHC.
94 *"As we all know"*: Claire McCardell, as cited in the curatorial material for the exhibition "Claire/McCardell," 2022, MCHC.
94 Vogue *captured*: "Vogue's Eye View: Of the Mode," *Vogue*, April 15, 1933, 27.
95 *"We have gotten away"*: Jane Driscoll, "Woman's Dress Should Reveal Natural Beauty, Maintains Designer Who Emphasizes Curves," *Washington Post*, March 2, 1942, 11.
95 *He put shoulder pads*: *AF*, 236.
95 *"A short year ago"*: "Vogue's Eye View: Of the Mode."
95 *Geiss further challenged*: Helen Wulbern, "Claire McCardell: A Discourse on Designing for Oneself," *WWD*, November 1940, FIT.
95 *In McCardell's closet*: Photo of McCardell in the tweed suit in the 1930s, MCHC.
96 *"This awful anachronism"*: Claire McCardell, Coty Awards speech, February 1944, MCHC.
96 *Women, she said*: Typed statement on Townley letterhead, December 19, 1945, MCHC.
96 *She aimed to make*: McCardell, "Women Are What They Wear."
96 *"I wondered"*: McCardell, Coty Awards speech, February 1944, MCHC.
96 *"The buyers very often"*: McCardell, Coty Awards speech, February 1944, MCHC.
96 *McCardell happily appropriated*: Claire McCardell, letters to her parents, 1933–1934, MCHC.
97 *"The comfort and ease"*: Claire McCardell, Coty Awards speech, February 1944, MCHC.
97 *McCardell began to wonder*: McCardell, "Women Are What They Wear."
97 *Wouldn't it be wonderful*: *WSIW*, 104.
97 *"Clothes without glitter"*: Claire McCardell, note, December 1945, MCHC.
98 *Stores did not sell*: *AF*, 224.
99 *She chose women*: Undated newspaper article, DSP.
99 *Shaver launched*: "American Designers Create Clothes for the Average American Woman," *Daily Herald*, September 1940; DSP.

99 *"Long entrenched and highly organized"*: Undated news article, DSP.
99 *Shaver assured the public*: Alice Hughes, "Designers of the U.S. Take Bows," *New York World-Telegram*, April 10, 1933, DSP.
99 *spring of 1934, the retailer*: Claire McCardell, scrapbook, source unattributed, FIT.
100 *In 1930, a fortune teller*: Sarah Orrick, unpublished biography of Mildred Orrick, OFP.
100 *Fortune-telling thrived*: Travis Hoke, "The Heyday of the Fortune Tellers," *Harper's Monthly Magazine*, January 1, 1932, 237.
100 *One man assured*: "700 Ways Found to Kill Spare Time," *New York Times*, April 18, 1934, 21.
100 *Horoscopes began*: Nick Levine, "The Dignity of an Exact Science: Evangeline Adams, Astrology, and the Professions of the Probable, 1890–1940," senior thesis, [unknown institution, date].
100 *McCardell received*: Astrological report for Claire McCardell, 1934, MCHC.

Seven: Abdication

101 *Luckily, McCardell had*: Claire McCardell, various letters to her parents, 1936, MCHC.
101 *In 1931, she had been*: Joset Walker Fashion Design Scrapbooks, The New School Archives and Special Collections digital collections, https://digital.archives.newschool.edu/index.php/Detail/objects/KA0045_b01_f01_02, accessed October 10, 2024.
102 *In the mid-1930s*: Various ships' manifests, 1934–38.
102 *Gentlemen were told*: "Games at Sea," Gjenvik-Gjønvik Archives, https://www.ggarchives.com/OceanTravel/TravelGuide/22-GamesAtSea.html, accessed October 13, 2024.
102 *There were other games*: Claire McCardell, various letters to her parents, 1930s, MCHC.
102 *On the Italian ship*: Claire McCardell, various letters to her parents, 1934, MCHC.
103 *He opened his love letters*: Letter and photo to Claire McCardell, July 17, 1934, MCHC.
103 *By 1920, at age twenty-two*: The 1920 federal census has Irving Drought Harris listed as divorced.
104 *Her grandfather*: Sandra E. Bonura, *The Sugar King of California: The Life of Claus Spreckels* (Nebraska University Press, 2024), 312.
104 *The Spreckels family*: Bonura, *The Sugar King of California*, 118.
104 *When he'd built*: Bonura, *The Sugar King of California*, 195.
105 *She was away*: "Spreckels Heiress Gets Only $2,500,000," *New York Times*, January 8, 1926, 19.
105 *Jean visited her uncle*: It is likely that Irving Drought Harris's boss at the time, the eminent architect James Gamble Rogers, introduced Harris to Spreckels.
105 *Their son, John Wakefield Harris*: Amy Fine Collins, "The Queen of Yankee Chic," *Vanity Fair*, October 1998, 162.
105 *Jean was said*: Quoted in "Jean Harris Marries Charles d'Espinay in 1938," Fairford, May 18, 2018, https://lynhuntingford.blogspot.com/2018/05/jean-harris-marries-charles-despinay-in.html.
105 *Whatever the case*: Robert M. McBride, testimony, Supreme Court Appellate Division, First Judicial Department, p. 449; "Spreckels Heiress and Husband Reunited," *New York Times*, January 14, 1932.

106 *As his daughter, Liz*: Elizabeth Harris, interview with Nancy Nolf, 1997, Hood Archive.
106 *Six months later*: Respondent Harris, Exhibit 18, copy of custody agreement dated April 17, 1935, Supreme Court Appellate Division.
106 *In October 1935*: Court transcript, Supreme Court Appellate Division, 1935, p. 1481.
106 *In May 1937*: *WWD, 100 Years special supplement*, 47.
106 *The boat traveled so swiftly*: Claire McCardell, various letters to her parents, 1937, MCHC.
107 *"certainly can be perfect"*: Claire McCardell, letter to her parents, 1937, MCHC.
107 *"Paris is really"*: Claire McCardell, letter to her parents, undated, 1937, MCHC.
108 *As Dorothy Shaver told*: "Stylists War Over Well Dressed," *Washington Herald*, July 3, 1937, DSP.
108 *"I don't want to look"*: *WSIW*, 103.
109 *She realized that*: According to various archival interviews with the McCardell family, as well as Nancy Nolf interview with Elizabeth Harris, 1997, Hood Archive.
109 *McCardell had also seen*: Sarah Orrick, unpublished family biography of Mildred Orrick, OFP.
110 *"The woman 'pin-money worker'"*: Erin Blakemore, "Why Many Married Women Were Banned from Working During the Great Depression," History.com, November 8, 2021.
111 *"In the days of dependent women"*: Claire McCardell, "Women Are What They Wear," *Sports Illustrated*, August 1954.
111 *On May 11, 1937*: Claire McCardell, various letters to her parents, May 1937, MCHC, as well as ephemera saved from the coronation.
112 *"You're too old"*: Claire McCardell, personal notebooks, MCHC.
112 *"It's good to be home"*: Claire McCardell, letter to her parents, undated, 1937, MCHC.

Eight: Hanger Appeal

113 *The annual Beaux-Arts Ball*: Virginia Pope, "Beaux Arts Ball for Fiery Moderns," *New York Times*, January 18, 1931, 81.
114 *McCardell had attended*: Claire McCardell, various letters to her parents, 1927, MCHC.
114 *McCardell had sewn*: *RM*, 41.
114 *She added her favorite detail*: *AF*, 223.
114 *Inside, the exhibition hall*: "Architects Hold Mi-Careme Dance," *New York Times*, March 25, 1938, 16.
115 *Her boyfriend, on the other hand*: Nancy Nolf, interviews with John Harris, 1997, Hood Archive; author interviews with Emily Harris, 2024.
115 *John, even at his young age*: Nancy Nolf, interview with John Harris, 1997, Hood Archive.
116 *"It's lovely"*: Claire McCardell, letter to her parents, undated, 1926, MCHC.
116 *The society pages always covered*: "Architects Hold Mi-Careme Dance."
117 *McCardell often found*: *WSIW*, 37.
117 *In Austria, she admired*: *AF*, 224.
117 *In the 1930s, a woman*: Abbott Kahler, "'The Hatpin Peril' Terrorized Men Who

Couldn't Handle the 20th-Century Woman," *Smithsonian Magazine*, April 24, 2014, https://www.smithsonianmag.com/history/hatpin-peril-terrorized-men-who-couldnt-handle-20th-century-woman-180951219/.
118 *Her wardrobe*: Helen Wulbern, "Claire McCardell: A Discourse on Designing for Oneself," *WWD*, November, 1940.
118 *A newspaper sketch depicted*: "Week-End Snow Birds," *WWD*, February 2, 1937, 8.
118 *"Mass production, wonderful"*: Claire McCardell, Statement on Mass Production, undated, MCHC.
118 *She didn't have*: *FIOB*, 10.
119 *No such data*: Sofi Thanhauser, "A Brief History of Mass-Manufactured Clothing," Literary Hub, January 27, 2022, https://lithub.com/a-brief-history-of-mass-manufactured-clothing/.
119 *Women had to add*: Ruth O'Brien, *Women's Measurements for Garment and Pattern Construction* (US Government Printing Office, 1941), 1.
119 *In the 1930s*: O'Brien, *Women's Measurements for Garment and Pattern Construction*, 1.
119 *McCardell had long considered*: Richard Martin, *American Ingenuity: Sportswear 1930s–1970s* (The Metropolitan Museum of Art, 2004), 21.
120 *Sustersic, in making*: *AF*, 302.
120 *Geiss had no such vision*: Claire McCardell, letter to her parents, undated, 1938, MCHC.
120 *Four years earlier*: "Mrs. Odlum Marks 5th Year with Store," *New York Times*, September 29, 1939.
120 *Before the event*: Dale Carnegie, speech, March 31, 1938, FGI.
120 *Carnegie jokingly titled*: Dale Carnegie, speech, March 31, 1938, FGI.
121 *The first night*: Claire McCardell, various letters to her parents, 1938, MCHC.
121 *At the next meeting*: Claire McCardell, various letters to her parents, 1938, MCHC.
122 *Let's do it in a way*: Dale Carnegie, speech, March 31, 1938, FGI.
122 *Her moment came*: "Fair Warning" advertisement, *WWD*, October 14, 1938, 2.
122 *He was in a constant*: undated article, MCHC.
122 *As one report*: *RM*, 41. There are several versions of how the Monastic dress was discovered that day at Townley, but this account is based on the author's research in McCardell's archive, as well as the research of Kohle Yohannan and Nancy Nolf in their book *Redefining Modernism*.
123 *"I finally designed a dress"*: MCHC, Claire McCardell letter to her parents, undated, 1938.
123 *"Not only is it becoming"*: Alice Hughes, "The Bias Dress," *New York World-Telegram*, n.d.
123 *That year, the least expensive*: Margaret Dana, "Fashion Is Spinach by Elizabeth Hawes," *Atlantic*, May 1938.
123 *McCardell's dress was*: Mary Corey, "Thoroughly Modern McCardell," *Baltimore Sun*, October 4, 1998.
124 *The industry soon dubbed it*: Best & Co. advertisement, Claire McCardell, scrapbook, FIT.
124 *In 1938, dress codes*: Scott Harrison, "From the Archives: Wear Slacks to Court and Go to Jail," *Los Angeles Times*, November 15, 2019.
124 *The Monastic provided the comfort*: Margaretta Byers, *Designing Women: The Art, Technique, and Cost of Being Beautiful* (Simon & Schuster, 1938), 193–94.

124 *"Her costume, if advisedly chosen"*: Byers, *Designing Women*, vii.
124 *Best & Co. created*: Best & Co. advertisement, 1938, Claire McCardell scrapbook, FIT.
125 *American design had long been derided*: Cecile Gilmore, "Gowns of Medieval Beauty Look Custom Cut," *New York Times*, September 11, 1938, FIT.
125 *The women behind the counters*: RM, 41–42.
125 *The thing that frightens me*: MCHC, Claire McCardell letter to her parents, undated, 1938.
125 *"There's a girl up the street"*: AF, 211.
125 *An exposé in* Fortune: "America Comes to Seventh Avenue," *Fortune*, July 1939, 122.
126 *Seventh Avenue began copying*: BFP.
126 *A large percentage*: MFA, "The Fashion Originators' Guild of America," *Fashion Art Magazine*, 1934, 32.
126 *He bought ad space*: "Fair Warning" advertisement, *WWD*, October 14, 1938, 2.
127 *The dress had been*: Best & Co. Monastic advertisements, 1938, Claire McCardell scrapbook, FIT.
128 *The dress that had revolutionized*: Osborn Elliott, "The American Look," *Time*, May 2, 1955.

Nine: Gushing Nitwits

129 *And like many*: John A. Tiffany, *Eleanor Lambert: Still Here* (Pointed Leaf Press, 2011), 18–30.
130 *McCardell invited LeBoutillier*: Claire McCardell, various letters to her parents, 1938, MCHC.
130 *LeBoutillier understood*: "Margaret LeBoutillier, Debutante of 1930, Becomes Engaged to N. Bronson Williams," *New York Times*, April 7, 1936, 29.
130 *In 1933, she announced*: Virginia Cowles and Peggy LeBoutillier, "Society Girl," *Collier's*, September 16, 1933.
130 *LeBoutillier had a talent*: "Telephoto Is Used as Commercial Aid," *New York Times*, January 10, 1937, 41.
131 *"Peggy did it!"*: Claire McCardell, letter to her parents, 1938, MCHC.
132 *She jokingly called it*: Claire McCardell, "Women Are What They Wear," *Sports Illustrated*, August 1954.
132 *At a time when*: Marian Young, "Bought Now, They'll Serve Through into Summer," *New York World-Telegram*, January 1939, FIT.
132 *Afterward, McCardell could*: Claire McCardell, letter to her parents, 1938, MCHC.
132 *In the coming weeks*: Claire McCardell, various letters to her parents, 1938, MCHC.
132 *McCardell went to Zorina's apartment*: Claire McCardell, letter to her parents, 1938, MCHC.
133 *With the Zorina line*: Rebecca Arnold, "Movement and Modernity: New York Sportswear, Dance, and Exercise in the 1930s and 1940s," *Fashion Theory* 12, no. 3 (2008): 341–57.
133 *That winter, Zorina was spotted*: Carolyn Crew, "Fashion Takes Wing," [unknown publication], 1939, FIT.

133 *The exercise suit*: Marian Young, "Fall Creations Show U.S. Designers Worthy of Fashion Crown They Inherited," [unknown publication], n.d., FIT.
133 *McCardell suspected*: Claire McCardell, various letters to her parents, 1939, MCHC.
135 *Carnegie liked to say*: "People and Ideas: Miss Hattie Carnegie," *Vogue*, April 1, 1951, 142–43.
136 *In return, they received*: Nancy Hardin and Lois Long, "Luxury, Inc.," *New Yorker*, March 31, 1934, 26.
137 *McCardell would create*: Display ad, *New York Times*, September 17, 1939.
137 *She wished she could talk it over*: Claire McCardell, letters to Eleanor McCardell, 1939, MCHC.
138 *Mildred Orrick, meanwhile*: Sarah Orrick, unpublished family biography, OFP.
138 *With her mind finally made up*: Claire McCardell, various letters to her parents, 1939, MCHC.
138 *She gave Geiss notice*: "Claire McCardell Resigns Townley Post," *WWD*, March 21, 1939, 24.
138 *In her new position*: Claire McCardell, various letters to her parents, 1939, MCHC.
139 *She had barely set up*: FIOB, p. 59.
139 *Norman Norell became a fast friend*: Bernadine Morris, "Norell," in *AF*, 343.
139 *She had once discovered*: FIOB, p. 54.
140 *McCardell made a careful study*: Claire McCardell, letter to her parents, August 1939, MCHC.
140 *"How many more times"*: Claire McCardell, various letters to her parents, 1939, MCHC.
143 *the couple had finally gone public*: Betty Friedan, interview with Peggy LeBoutillier, 1955, BFP.
143 *Harris assiduously avoided*: Nancy Nolf and Kohle Yohannan, interviews with Bob McCardell and John Harris, 1997, Hood Archive.
143 *"He had a strong personality"*: Nancy Nolf, interview with John Harris, August 1997, Hood Archive.
144 *She noticed that people*: Claire McCardell, various letters to her parents, 1939, MCHC.
144 *The story, as Vreeland*: *AF*, 232.
145 *She thought her to be*: Diana Vreeland, letter to Adolph Klein, 1958, MFA.
145 *Not everyone was as impressed*: *AF*, 231.
145 *Hattie Carnegie customers*: *AF*, 232.
146 *Carnegie returned from France*: "Fashions Viewed as Plea for Peace," *New York Times*, August 29, 1939, 22.

Ten: The Specter of War

147 *McCardell waited until*: Claire McCardell, letter to her parents, January 9, 1940, MCHC.
148 *Carnegie reluctantly agreed*: Claire McCardell, letter to her parents, January 1940, MCHC.
149 *A New York Times journalist*: "94 Americans Off on the Washington," *New York Times*, January 14, 1940, 36.
149 *An attaché at the French Embassy*: "94 Americans Off on the Washington."
149 *The seas churned*: Claire McCardell, letter to her parents, January 1940, MCHC.

150 *Those aboard reported a feeling*: "Arrived Safely . . . Good Crossing," *Harper's Bazaar*, February 1940, 44–45.
151 *And finally disembarked*: Claire McCardell, letter to her parents, January 1940, MCHC.
151 *McCardell rode for several hours*: Claire McCardell, letter to her parents, January 1940, MCHC.
151 *Snow prided herself*: Penelope Rowlands, *A Dash of Daring: Carmel Snow and Her Life in Fashion, Art, and Letters* (Atria Books, 2005).
151 *After twenty-four long hours*: Claire McCardell, letter to her parents, January 1940, MCHC.
151 *Most buses, taxis, and even private cars*: Bettina Ballard, *In My Fashion* (David Mackay, 1960), 145.
152 *"I'd forgotten how gloomy"*: Claire McCardell, letter to her parents, January 1940, MCHC.
152 *Bettina Ballard*: Ballard, *In My Fashion*, 154.
152 *darkness drenched the City of Light*: Ballard, *In My Fashion*, 148–49.
153 *It was difficult*: Claire McCardell, various letters to her parents, 1940, MCHC.
153 *Four weeks after Paris fell*: Transcript of meeting, June 26, 1940, FGI.
154 *"Let us highlight"*: Transcript of meeting, June 26, 1940, FGI.

Eleven: Shooting Craps

157 *McCardell admitted*: RM, 46.
157 *She didn't enjoy*: Betty Friedan reporting notes, BFP.
157 *McCardell's ambition had grown*: Claire McCardell, handwritten notes and sketches, MCHC.
158 *The rumor was that*: AF, 243.
158 *The country's retailers assured*: Sandra Stansbery Buckland and Gwendolyn S. O'Neal, "'We Publish Fashions Because They Are News': *The New York Times* 1940 through 1945," *Dress* 25, no. 1 (1998): 33–41.
158 *The fashion reporter Marian Young*: Unattributed article, 1940, FIT.
159 *On that day*: Virginia Pope, "Mayor Has Plan to Aid Fashion Bid," *New York Times*, August 22, 1940, 22.
159 *The women explained*: Elizabeth Hawes, *Fashion Is Spinach* (Random House, 1938), p. 14.
160 *La Guardia now understood:* Pope, "Mayor Has Plan to Aid Fashion Bid."
160 *La Guardia would approach*: Unattributed article, July 8, 1944, FIT.
160 *Skillman was impressed that*: GWDD.
161 *LeBoutillier crafted a story*: Peggy LeBoutillier, "The Cult of Claire McCardell," MCHC and FIT.
162 *"Modest, retiring, and kind"*: Undated letter to Adolph Klein, MFA.
162 *Vogue described McCardell*: "Claire McCardell of Townley Frocks," *Vogue*, May 1, 1941.
162 *Filene's, a major department store*: Filene's ad, 1940, FIT.
163 *She had once parodied*: Claire McCardell, "Women Are What They Wear," *Sports Illustrated*, August 1954.

298 ♦ Notes

163 *She had believed that this year*: "Please Make Buyers Buy NEW Fashions," [unknown publication], 1940, FIT.
163 *She had a hard time hiding*: Helen Wulbern, "Designers of Today and Tomorrow," *WWD*, November 14, 1940, 4.
164 *The building was always buzzing*: Lisa Lockwood, "550 Seventh Avenue: End of a Fashion Era," *WWD*, November 28, 2018, https://wwd.com/feature/550-seventh-avenue-end-of-a-fashion-era-1202911750.
165 *McCardell squeezed*: *AF*, 236.
165 *She leaned in*: *RM*, 49.
165 *"In this business"*: Osborn Elliott, "The American Look," *Time*, May 2, 1955.
165 *Klein wanted originality*: Elliott, "The American Look."
166 *"Better you should throw"*: *AF*, 236.
166 *"If I were you"*: Elliott, "The American Look."
166 *But Klein, a man*: Elliott, "The American Look."
166 *Sometimes a little subterfuge*: *AF*, 239.
167 *She brainstormed a list*: Claire McCardell, personal notebooks, MCHC.
167 *Geiss thought it foolish*: *RM*, 50.
167 *"Claire gets no surprises"*: *AF*, 239.
167 *Joset Walker, who was toiling*: *AF*, 239.

Twelve: We Admit This Line Is Different

169 Vogue *magazine heralded*: "American Designer: Claire McCardell of Townley Frocks," *Vogue*, 1941, MCHC.
170 *She made a*: *RM*, p. 61.
170 *In the first months*: GWDD.
171 *"We admit this line"*: "Merchandising Information of Unusual Importance," Townley Press release for buyers, FIT.
171 *A* Vogue *editor observed*: Janet Chatfield-Taylor, letter to Adolph Klein, 1958, MFA.
171 *Most of her ideas seemed*: *WSIW*, 20.
171 *"It is my experience"*: Inez Robb, "She Has Designs on Men," *Charleston Gazette*, April 18, 1953, 2.
172 *A partition separated*: Betty Friedan, reporting notes, BFP.
173 *McCardell hopped a commuter flight*: "Versatility in Women's Clothes: Nine Variations Likes Stripes," *Christian Science Monitor*, September 10, 1941, 2.
173 *"It has been a most happy"*: Ida Lee, owner of Town & Country Clothes in Warrington, Florida, letter to Adolph Klein, 1958, MFA.
174 *Klein further marketed*: "Fashion: Black Jersey with Taffeta: More Taste than Money," *Vogue*, September 15, 1941, 100.
174 *Townley had an additional stroke*: *AF*, p. 240. Over her lifetime, Griswold gave competing accounts of that day. She told Sally Kirkland that she had been the one to call Klein. She told Betty Friedan that Klein had come to her. Whatever the case, she was always consistent about what had happened that day at Townley: She had seen McCardell's clothes and instantly bought several dresses for Lord & Taylor.
174 *And while her colleagues*: *AF*, 240.

174 *In 1941, Griswold*: AF, 240.
175 *Griswold arrived*: GWDD.
175 *At first, Claire McCardell Clothes*: AF, 243.
175 *Help with domestic chores*: For more on the ways in which modernity and household technology increased the workload for women at the time, see Ruth Schwartz Cowan, *More Work for Mother: The Ironies of Household Technology from the Open Hearth to the Microwave* (Basic Books, 1983).
176 *Women's Wear Daily reported*: "Kitchen Culture," *WWD*, October 10, 1941, 3.
177 *Townley survived*: GWDD.
177 *When McCardell sent*: "She Designed Her Career," *New York World-Telegram*, n.d.
177 *"With these dames"*: Osborn Elliott, "The American Look," *Time*, May 2, 1955.
178 *She spent as many weekends*: Nancy Nolf, interview with John Harris, August 1997, Hood Archive.
178 *In time, John came*: Nancy Nolf, interview with John Harris, August 1997, Hood Archive.
178 *He aimed to make*: Author interview with Emily Harris Jones, August 2024.
178 *He would later say*: Author interview with Emily Harris Jones, August 2024.
178 *On September 19, 1941*: Lyn Huntingford McCulloch, "Jean Has a Daughter, Chantal d'Espinay and More Court Cases Make the Lawyers Rich," Fairford, May 20, 2018, lynhuntingford.blogspot.com/2018/05/.
179 *Once there, he began*: McCulloch, "Jean Has a Daughter, Chantal d'Espinay and More Court Cases Make the Lawyers Rich"; legal documents from the court case.
179 *The man's provenance and title*: Transcript Supreme Court Appellate Division, First Judicial Department.
179 *Jean's lawyer wrote to Harris*: letter dated February 28, 1939, from Ernest S. Smith to Irving Harris, Supreme Court Appellate Division, First Judicial Department.
180 *Liz wondered what to call her*: Irving Harris, letter to McCardell, March 11, 1943, MFA.
180 *She welcomed Liz to New York*: Betty Friedan, interview with Peggy LeBoutillier, 1955, BFP.

Thirteen: It's Rather Fun to Have a Limit

181 *By the time the Japanese bombed*: Matthew Dallek, *Defenseless Under the Night: The Roosevelt Years and the Origins of Homeland Security* (Oxford University Press, 2016), Kindle edition.
182 *There was nothing more potent*: Author interview with Robyn Levy, Tory Burch Claire McCardell Fellow, 2023.
182 *One South Carolina congressman*: "Women & Gender," The American Soldier in World War II, https://americansoldierww2.org/topics/women-and-gender, accessed October 13, 2024.
182 *The military forces*: Mattie E. Treadwell, *The Women's Army Corps* (Center of Military History, United States Army, 1991), 38.
182 *The army vetoed*: Hannah Carlson, *Pockets: An Intimate History of How We Keep Things Close* (Algonquin Books of Chapel Hill, 2023), p. 125 of Kindle edition.
182 *She designed a jacket*: Author interview with curatorial staff at the New York History Museum, where there is a Claire McCardell OCD uniform, 2024.

300 ◆ **Notes**

182 *In December 1941*: Virginia Pope, "Civilian Defense Uniforms," *New York Times*, December 14, 1941, 110.
183 *The WPB issued*: L-85 Regulation, 1942.
184 *American women panicked*: "She Designed Her Career," *New York World-Telegram*, n.d., MCHC.
184 *"I think it's rather fun"*: "Style Curbs Seen as Not Excessive," unattributed article, FIT.
184 *She went on a popular*: "Asserts WPB Rules Are No Barrier to Style Ingenuity," *WWD*, May 5, 1942, 19.
184 *When wool became scarce*: Photo archive, FIT.
184 *That summer, she channeled*: "Salvage Sewing Unit of America Bundles Will Open 2-Day Fashion Fair Tuesday," *New York Times*, June 1942, D2.
184 *"Men were favored"*: Joan Gardner, "Skirting New York," The Fashion League, 1943, FIT.
184 *"Amazing it is"*: Jane Driscoll, "Dress Should Reveal Natural Beauty, Maintains Designer Who Emphasizes Curves," *Washington Post*, March 2, 1942, 11.
185 *McCardell, along with designers*: "Trousers of the Times," *WWD*, October 17, 1942.
185 *McCardell took the material*: "Forest and Farm Contribute to Garment Fabrics of Future," unattributed article, FIT.
185 *On one of her routine visits*: *AF*, 250.
185 *As the year progressed*: Winifred Spear, "Dress Designers Surpass the WPB in Effecting Savings," *New York Times*, March 27, 1943, 10.
186 *Ben Sommers of Capezio*: GWDD.
186 *The new shoe design*: *WSIW*, 17.
186 *Women loved them*: *WSIW*, 17.
186 *Sommers thought McCardell*: "Capezio Creates Memorial Tribute to Maryland's Claire McCardell," *Baltimore American*, August 30, 1959.
187 *The problem was best summarized*: Osborn Elliott, "The American Look," *Time*, May 2, 1955.
187 *Lady Levi's had been released*: "A Brief Look at the Origin of Denim in North America," C. C. Filson Co., https://www.filson.com/blog/field-notes/a-brief-look-at-the-origin-of-denim-in-north-america/, accessed June 1, 2024.
188 *Klein walked in*: Betty Friedan reporting notes, BFP.
188 *The patch pocket design*: Diana Vreeland, *D.V.* (Ecco, 1984), 89.
189 *The wrap dress*: *WSIW*, 155.
189 *She explained to*: "Ten Designers Predict," *New York Times*, March 21, 1943, sm18.
189 *Vreeland chose the wife*: "Work Dress: I'm Doing My Own Work," *Harper's Bazaar*, November 1942, 54.
189 *On November 5*: "'Busybody' Work Dress Combines Style and Utility," *WWD*, November 3, 1942, 24.
189 *But it was the creative minds*: Lord & Taylor ad, *New York Times*, November 19, 1942.
190 *Lord & Taylor gave the Popover*: "Sports Got to Work," *WWD*, November 17, 1942, 3.
190 *Klein had encouraged*: "'Busybody' Work Dress Combines Style and Utility."
190 *The denim Popover*: *FIOB*, 90.
190 *Most women wrote*: Various correspondence to Claire McCardell, 1942, MCHC.
190 *A friend of McCardell's*: *WSIW*, 23.

190 *"Her views on fabric"*: "C. McCardell Private Rites in Frederick," *WWD*, March 24, 1958, 1.
190 *"Whee! Look what Claire McCardell's done"*: "Sportswear," *WWD*, April 5, 1943, 10.
191 *By year's end, Townley had sold*: Osborn Elliott, "The American Look," *Time*, May 2, 1955.
191 *"Clairvoyant Claire had"*: Jo Ahern, "Claire and Rudi," *Sports Illustrated*, June 4, 1956.
191 *The winner would receive*: "Vogue's Eye View: Fashion Awards," *Vogue*, March 15, 1943, 37.
191 *McCardell's Popover earned*: Coty Awards photo, MCHC.
192 *Later, Norell confided*: AF, 243.

Fourteen: Mr. Claire McCardell

193 *On March 10, 1943*: Nancy Nolf, interview with John Harris, 1997, Hood Archive.
195 *Eleanor quickly printed*: Wedding announcement in "Society News," *Frederick News-Post*, March 13, 1943, 3.
195 *She also wrote*: Eleanor McCardell, letter to Bishop Helfenstein, n.d., MFA.
195 *McCardell couldn't get a loan*: The Equal Credit Opportunity Act of 1974 finally made it illegal for banks to discriminate against credit applicants based on sex or marital status.
196 *"never approved of her career"*: Mary Corey, "Thoroughly Modern McCardell," *The Baltimore Sun*, October 4, 1998.
196 *"loathed anyone"*: Amy Fine Collins, "The Queen of Yankee Chic," *Vanity Fair*, October 1998, 162.
196 *"Miss McCardell is"*: "Sportshots," *WWD*, March 25, 1943, 8.
197 Mademoiselle, *the fashion magazine*: "The Last Word on Careers," *Mademoiselle*, July 1938, 19.
197 *Test audiences believed that*: Interview with Ring Lardner, Jr., Television Academy Foundation, October 18, 2012.
197 *McCardell's fashion friends*: AF, 237.
198 *Kirkland later told*: Author interview with Katie McCardell Webb, 2018.
198 *John always contended*: Nancy Nolf, interview with John Harris, 1997, Hood Archive.
198 *McCardell's sister-in-law, Sue*: Author interview with Sue McCardell, February 2024.
198 *He rarely traveled*: Eleanor McCardell, letter to Claire McCardell, February 15, 1949, MFA.
198 *Eleanor thought John to be*: Eleanor McCardell, letter to Claire McCardell, February 6, 1952, MFA.
198 *Liz, on the other hand*: Author Interview with Emily Harris Jones, August 2024.
199 *The family of four moved*: Irving Harris was questioned in court over his management of the children's trust fund. After Jean Harris died, each child received $15,000 a year, totaling $30,000 in annual income. Harris testified that he had used the funds responsibly when purchasing housing for them, and he was not found in violation of the trust agreements.
199 *He decorated the interior*: Amy Fine Collins, "The Queen of Yankee Chic," *Vanity Fair*, October 1998, 162.
199 *"Claire seemed content"*: AF, 283.

Fifteen: Make of It What You Will

201 *At night, she entertained*: Sarah Orrick, unpublished family biography of Mildred Orrick, OFP.
202 *It might seem odd at first*: Archival sketchbook notes for Mildred Orrick, The Anna-Maria and Stephen Kellen Archives Center at Parsons School of Design.
202 *"It's a new idea"*: "The Leotard Idea," *Harper's Bazaar*, January 1943.
203 *In July 1943*: "It's Something," *Harper's Bazaar*, July 1943.
204 *To add insult to injury*: Mildred Orrick, letter to Henry Luce, OFP.
204 *"This is a 'leotard'"*: "Leotards," *Life*, September 13, 1943.
205 *Sally Kirkland later noted*: *AF*, 254.
205 *Worse, Kirkland was among*: *AF*, 258.
206 *That year, Orrick invited McCardell*: Correspondence between Eleanor McCardell and Claire McCardell, 1947, MCHC.
206 *Decades later*: Author interview with Sarah Orrick, 2018.

Sixteen: The American Look

207 *McCardell trademarked her name*: Trademark letter, April 17, 1945, MCHC.
207 *One grateful customer*: Letter to Adolph Klein, March 27, 1958, MFA.
208 *Sally Kirkland, meanwhile*: "McCardell Fashions Earned Their Survival," *Baltimore Sun*, May 16, 1976.
208 *The future fashion editor*: Michael Musto, "When 'Absolutely Fabulous' Comes to Breathless Life," *New York Times*, May 16, 1999, ST2.
208 *As a result, a woman's*: Amy Fine Collins, "The Queen of Yankee Chic," *Vanity Fair*, October 1998, 162.
209 *The design, coupled with*: Collins, "The Queen of Yankee Chic."
209 *"Swimsuits are for swimming"*: *RM*, 97.
209 *"Often they were nothing"*: Collins, "The Queen of Yankee Chic."
209 *On Monday mornings*: Collins, "The Queen of Yankee Chic."
209 *I began some years ago*: Claire McCardell, Coty Awards speech, 1944, MCHC.
210 *Dahl-Wolfe said*: Louise Dahl-Wolfe, *A Photographer's Scrapbook* (St. Martin's Press, 1984), 3.
211 Newsweek *later credited*: Lynn Young, "The American Look, "*Newsweek*, June 5, 1972, 87.
211 *In the 1890s, riding a bicycle*: Suze Clemitson, *A History of Cycling in 100 Objects* (Bloomsbury Publishing, 2017), 138.
211 *Even Henry Geiss applauded*: "Claire McCardell: She Designs as She Pleases," *Fashion Trades Magazine*, May 10, 1946.
212 *"We are at last"*: Claire McCardell, Coty Awards speech, February 1944, MCHC.
213 *In the spring of 1945*: This first couture show was really a gallery exhibition. Owing to shortages in fabrics and resources, the French designers showcased their clothes on miniature dolls. The exhibition, called *Théâtre de la Mode*, opened at the Louvre in Paris in March 1945 before traveling through Europe.
213 *"A different kind of battle"*: Dorothy Roe, "Post-War Battle of Fashion—New York Challenges Paris," Associated Press, May 14, 1944.

214 *Shaver welcomed a world at peace*: Press Release, Friday, January 12, 1945, DSP.
214 *The American Look is*: "Predicts One World of Fashion," *The New York Sun*, January 12, 1945, DSP.
215 *As Shaver became*: Newspaper article, no citation, DSP.
215 *When pressed about the competition*: "No. 1 Career Woman," undated article, DSP.
216 *She once said*: AF, 227.
217 *In her shop*: Elizabeth Way, *Ann Lowe: American Couturier* (Rizzoli Electa, 2024), 179.
217 *the store had commissioned*: "A Feather in Her Cap," Winterthur Museum, Garden & Library, https://www.winterthur.org/ostrich-feathers/, accessed June 1, 2024.
218 *"This emancipation of women"*: Transcript of Kenneth Collins speech, February 10, 1941, FGI.

Seventeen: Stay Out of Topeka, You Bum

221 *As Dorothy Shaver promoted*: Carmel Snow, speech on April 18, 1946 at the Biltmore Hotel, April 18, 1946, FGI.
221 *Not long after*: AF, 271.
222 *Kirkland relayed further reports*: Bettina Ballard, *In My Fashion* (David McKay, 1960), 230.
222 *As McCardell's friends*: "McCardell Funeral on Tuesday," *The Frederick News*, December 10, 1945.
222 *"I never want to see"*: *Three Views of the News*, transcript, 1947, MCHC.
223 *Kirkland heartily disagreed*: AF, 271.
223 *She put one of the outfits*: Betty Friedan, reporting notes, BFP.
224 *In the winter of 1946*: Dior, 205.
224 *"In an epoch"*: "Dior, 52, Creator of 'New Look,' Dies," *The Associated Press*, October 24, 1957.
225 *That winter, Dior appraised*: Dior, 237.
225 *Slowly, each toile*: Christian Dior, *Dior by Dior*, translated by Antonia Fraser (V&A Publishing, 2020), 24.
226 *The story of the great couturier*: Dior, *Dior by Dior*, 24–25.
226 *Snow was especially besotted*: Dior, 246. To learn more about the legend behind the coining of this phrase, see Penelope Rowlands, *A Dash of Daring: Carmel Snow and Her Life in Fashion, Art, and Letters* (Atria Books, 2005).
227 *The British news organization*: "New Look Underwear (1948)," British Pathé, https://www.britishpathe.com/asset/78511/, accessed June 1, 2024.
227 *"Are we returning"*: Claire McCardell, handwritten note in notebook, FIT.
227 *A fellow American designer*: Stephanie Lake, *Bonnie Cashin: Chic Is Where You Find It* (Rizzoli, 2016), 45.
227 *Sophie Gimbel, the house designer*: "Fashion: Counter-Revolution," *Time*, September 15, 1947.
227 *Was the painful scaffolding intentional?*: Dior, 393.
227 *American men put it*: Francine du Plessix Gray, "Prophets of Seduction," *The New Yorker*, October 27, 1996.

227 *In the summer of 1947*: Dior, 309.
227 *In protest, a group*: "Resistance," *Time*, September 1, 1947, 14.
228 *Anti–New Look protesters*: "Long skirt hullaballoo! Tell Mr. Dior to go to . . . ," *The Chicago Star*, September 27, 1947.
228 *In Louisville, Georgia*: Dior, 304.
228 *Dior relished every minute*: Dior, 308.
228 *"But Christian is mad, mad!"*: Dior, 291.
228 *McCardell also thought so*: Transcript of the radio interview, MCHC.
229 *McCardell encouraged women*: "Family Counselor" spot, Hemline Debate, transcript, 1947, MCHC.
229 *"prefers comfort to stiff formality"*: Regina Owen, radio editorial release, February 5, 1951, MCHC.
229 *Only two years earlier*: "Fashion: Paris Collections," *Vogue*, April 1947.
229 *With the war over*: "Women and Work After World War II," PBS, https://www.pbs.org/wgbh/americanexperience/features/tupperware-work/, accessed October 1, 2024.
230 *The editors of* Vogue: Tear sheet from *Vogue* in Claire McCardell's scrapbook, 1945, FIT.
231 *They were no longer*: Retail report, 1948, MCHC.

Eighteen: Society Is an Awful Chore, Isn't It?

233 *She attended*: RM, 122.
233 *"Claire, dearest"*: Eleanor McCardell, letter to Claire McCardell, March 17, 1949, MFA.
234 *A letter from John Harris arrived*: Letter from John Harris, letter to Claire McCardell, February 17, 1950, MFA.
234 *Two months later*: RM, 123.
235 *To her, the award*: RM, 123.
235 *After the ceremony*: "Trumans Are Guests as Women's Press Club Presents Honors of the Year," *Sunday Star* [Washington, DC], April 16, 1950, A7.
235 *Liz learned of*: RM, 123.
236 *Or, as McCardell's mother*: Eleanor McCardell, letter to Claire McCardell, undated, 1951, MFA.
236 *At the 1951 Grosvenor Debutante Ball*: "Debutantes Bow at Benefits Ball," *New York Times*, November 25, 1951.
236 *Liz felt deeply uncomfortable*: Betty Friedan, interview with Peggy LeBouttillier, BFP.
237 *"I'm going to have"*: Eleanor McCardell, letter to Claire McCardell, January 1950, MFA.
237 *Her assured television persona*: The care that McCardell put into the scripts for her television appearances can be seen in the many draft edits and handwritten notes between her and producers in the archive at MCHC.
237 *She confessed in letters*: Eleanor McCardell, letters to Claire McCardell, 1951, MFA.
238 *That night, she and Harris*: "Debutantes Bow at Benefits Ball," *New York Times*, November 25, 1951.
238 *He later said*: Author interview with Emily Harris Jones, August 2024.
238 *Some McCardell family members*: Author interview with John McCardell, February 2024.

241 *She went on*: Eleanor McCardell, letter to Claire McCardell, undated, 1952, MFA.
241 *Days before the election*: Claire McCardell, letter to the editor, November 3, 1952, MCHC.
241 *"Although Claire was getting"*: AF, 279.

Nineteen: Ah, Men

243 *I like to have people fall in love*: "Beverly Hills Art Expert is Center of All Art's Big Controversies," Beverly Hills Press, April 22, 1954, Frank Perls papers and Frank Perls Gallery records, Archives of American Art, Smithsonian Institution.
243 *He'd bought a McCardell dress*: Frank Perls, letter to Charlotte Willard of *Look* magazine, January 26, 1953, Frank Perls papers and Frank Perls Gallery records, Archives of American Art, Smithsonian Institution.
243 *Earlier, a reporter*: Phyllis Battelle, "Behind the Label," [unknown publication], April 1, 1953, FIT.
244 *Stanley Marcus had contributed*: Perls Galleries, brochure and publicity material, MCHC.
244 *More than one guest*: Betty Friedan, reporting notes, BFP.
244 *A reporter later asked*: Phyllis Battelle, "Originality Is Trademark of McCardell's Fashions," [unknown publication], April 17, 1953, FIT.
244 *"Only a silly woman"*: "She Has Designs on Men," [unknown publication], April 17, 1953, MCHC.
244 *The following day*: Amy Fine Collins, "The Queen of Yankee Chic," *Vanity Fair*, October 1998, 162.
245 *"Christian Dior, tyrant"*: Ernest O. Hauser, "Will the Ladies Obey M. Dior?," *Saturday Evening Post*, 1953.
245 *Dior put his own fashion*: *Dior*, 385.
245 *"In the minds"*: Phyllis Battelle, "We'll Miss Claire McCardell in Snubbing Parisian Changes," *The Springfield News-Leader*, March 27, 1958, MCHC.
245 *Once again, McCardell became*: "Dior Line Ends that Sweater Look," *Frederick News-Post*, August 27, 1954, 4.
245 *He was a self-taught designer*: Bettina Ballard, *In My Fashion* (David Mackay, 1960), 229.
245 *Christian Dior was still*: Robert Coughlan, "Designer for Americans: Jacques Fath of Paris Sells U.S. Women Wearable Glamour," *Life*, October 17, 1949.
246 *He made women's swimsuits*: Annemarie Elizabeth Strassel, "Redressing Women: Feminism in Fashion and the Creation of American Style, 1930-1960," Dissertation, May 2008, 240.
246 *"Women are poor creators"*: "'Women Designers Inferior'—Fath," *Daily Independent Journal*, December 10, 1953; Also as quoted in correspondence between Claire McCardell and journalist, MCHC.
246 *Johnson hoped that McCardell*: Correspondence between Claire McCardell and journalist; McCardell's typed statement, MCHC.
246 *McCardell, meanwhile*: Betty Friedan, interview with Adolph Klein, BFP.
247 *"Ah, men,"*: Claire McCardell, typed statement to Hope Johnson, January 14, 1954, MCHC.

247 *McCardell titled her essay*: Claire McCardell, *Sports Illustrated*.
247 *Popular opinion in the United States*: Millicent Carey McIntosh, "A Double Life for Mothers," *Parents' Magazine*, October 1948.
248 *After the show*: GWDD.
248 *Orrick and her husband*: Sarah Orrick, unpublished family biography of Jesse Orrick; archival images of Adri Steckling-Coen and Joan Didion during their tenancies at the Orrick house, OFP.
249 *McCardell further encouraged*: Betty Friedan, notes of interview with Mona Roset, BFP.
249 *Of those who did*: Betty Friedan, *The Feminine Mystique*, 2.
250 *The book wouldn't*: Stephanie Coontz, *The Way We Never Were: American Families and the Nostalgia Trap* (Basic Books, 2000), 37.
250 *She equated the swift*: Betty Friedan, *The Feminine Mystique*, 17.
250 *She told a reporter*: AF, 261.
250 *"Whatever his wife did"*: AF, 283.
251 *In it were hundreds of notes*: Joan Crawford, letter to Eleanor Lambert, December 30, 1952, MCHC.
251 *"Dear Miss McCardell"*: Letter written to Claire McCardell, May 8, 1953, MCHC.
252 *Does Dior get letters*: GWDD.
252 *She felt particular ire*: WSIW, 137.
252 *McCardell was designing*: Betty Friedan, interview notes and unpublished drafts, BFP.

Twenty: McCardellisms

254 *Graziani was dubious*: AF, 296.
254 *McCardell's American Look*: AF, 296.
255 *In the spring of 1955*: Osborn Elliott, "The American Look," *Time*, May 2, 1955.
255 *"was a beauty"*: Amy Fine Collins, "The Queen of Yankee Chic," *Vanity Fair*, October 1998, 164.
255 *Her brother Adrian later joked*: RM, 132.
256 *began writing*: Allison Tolman, afterword to the 2022 edition of *What Shall I Wear?* (Abrams Image, 2022).
256 *Heal further gathered*: MCHC houses many of the original documents created by McCardell and used by Heal to create the manuscript, as well as Heal's own notes and writing.
256 *"Fashion should be fun"*: WSIW, p.11.
256 *"People without a sense"*: WSIW, 13.
256 *"First of all, stay firmly you"*: WSIW, 15.
257 *A part of the beauty*: WSIW, 35.
257 *On November 12, 1956*: "'What Shall I Wear' Title of Claire McCardell Book," *Frederick Post*, November 12, 1956.
257 *"One important factor"*: "Claire McCardell," *The Baltimore Sun*, March 24, 1958.
257 *should wear a sleeveless dress*: WSIW, 87.
257 *She encouraged readers*: WSIW, 155.
257 *Your figure*: WSIW, 35.
257 *The book further advises*: WSIW, 56.

257 *In 1953, McCardell told*: Inez Robb, "She Has Designs on Men," [unknown publication], April 1953, MCHC.
258 *Yet in the book*: *WSIW*, 93.
258 *The book became*: As evidenced in the archived manuscript of the book, MCHC.
258 *A later critique*: *RM*, 132.
258 *In the penultimate chapter*: *WSIW*, 146.
259 *McCardell believed above all*: *WSIW*, 22–27.

Twenty-One: The Quiet Genius

261 *"It is the most curious thing"*: Diana Vreeland, letter to Claire McCardell, undated, 1956, MCHC.
261 *He let Marjorie Griswold*: Phyllis Battelle, "Paris Ignored by One Genius," *Texas Sun*, March 27, 1958, MCHC.
261 *Have you ever wondered*: Transcript of radio program, February 5, 1951, FIT.
261 *That year, Adolph Klein*: Gloria Emerson, "McCardell Philosophy of Fashion to Continue," *New York Times*, March 26, 1958.
261 *Become the executive designer*: Gloria Emerson, "McCardell Philosophy of Fashion to Continue," *New York Times*, March 26, 1958.
262 *"I know you make light"*: Eleanor McCardell writes to Claire McCardell, undated 1957, MFA.
263 *In early June*: "Among the Sick," *Frederick News Post*, June 15, 1957.
263 *McCardell began radiation*: Claire McCardell, letter to Eleanor, undated, 1957, MCHC.
263 *"I'm glad my family"*: Eleanor McCardell, letter to Claire McCardell, 1956, MFA.
263 *One of her brothers*: Photo in archive, MCHC.
263 *Back in New York*: Nancy Nolf, interview with Elizabeth Harris, 1997, Hood Archive.
264 *Vreeland was among them*: Diana Vreeland, letter to Adolph Klein, undated, 1958, MFA.
264 *"All these sad months"*: Hope Skillman, letter to Adolph Klein, March 23, 1958, MFA.
265 *Orrick arrived*: *RM*, 135.
265 *"The best friends I've had"*: Dorothy Parnell, "Have You Heard?," *Milwaukee Sentinel*, March 26, 1958.
265 *"Everybody in the fashion world"*: Amy Fine Collins, "The Queen of Yankee Chic," *Vanity Fair*, October 1998, 164.
265 *McCardell then did something*: *RM*, 135.
266 *On March 22, 1958*: Author interview with Sarah Orrick, 2018.
267 *"Even of this service"*: "200 Here Mourn Claire M'Cardell," *New York Times*, March 27, 1958, 33.
267 *"I can't tell you"*: Emilio Pucci, letter to Adolph Klein, March 31, 1958, MCHC.
267 *Obituaries and tributes ran*: Inez Robb, "Fashion's Worm," n.d., MCHC.
268 *"I must tell you"*: Mariana Hiatt, letter to Adolph Klein, March 23, 1958, MFA.
268 *McCardell had not named*: Nancy Nolf interview with Adrian McCardell, 1997, Hood Archive.
269 *Adolph Klein had to bury*: Gloria Emerson, "McCardell Philosophy of Fashion to Continue," *New York Times*, March 26, 1958.

269 *"We decided to let"*: Mary Corey, "Thoroughly Modern McCardell," *The Baltimore Sun*, October 4, 1998.
269 *As the journalist Alice Hughes*: Alice Hughes, letter to Adolph Klein, March 27, 1958, MFA.
270 *McCardell's brother Adrian*: "Claire McCardell Wills Her Estate to Her Kin," *Frederick News-Post*, April 8, 1958.
271 *"Good fashion"*: Mary Corey, "Thoroughly Modern McCardell," *The Baltimore Sun*, October 4, 1998; AF, 307.
271 *"There is one thing"*: Mimi Blaker, letter to Adolph Klein, March 25, 1958, MFA.

Epilogue

274 *"She really invented sportswear"*: Hebe Dorsey, "Designers Suit Themselves," *International Herald Tribune*, February 7–8, 1981, 5W.
275 *"We promised to be"*: Author interview with Emily Harris Jones, September 2024.
276 *As the historian*: Einav Rabinovitch-Fox, *Dressed for Freedom: The Fashionable Politics of American Feminism* (University of Illinois Press, 2021), Kindle edition, 230.
276 *"It wasn't me"*: RM, 16; MCHC, Claire McCardell, handwritten notes for her Coty Awards speech, February 1944.

Selected Bibliography

Books

Arnold, Rebecca. *The American Look: Fashion, Sportswear and the Image of Women in 1930s and 1940s New York.* I. B. Tauris, 2021.
Ballard, Bettina. *In My Fashion.* David McKay, 1960.
Benson, Susan Porter. *Counter Cultures: Saleswomen, Managers, and Customers in American Department Stores 1890-1940.* University of Illinois Press, 1986.
Berch, Bettina. *Radical by Design: The Life and Style of Elizabeth Hawes Fashion Designer, Union Organizer, Best-Selling Author.* E. P. Dutton, 1988.
Blackman, Cally. *100 Years of Fashion Illustration.* Laurence King, 2021.
Bonura, Sandra E. *The Sugar King of California: The Life of Claus Spreckels.* Nebraska University Press, 2024.
Bren, Paulina. *The Barbizon: The Hotel That Set Women Free.* Simon & Schuster, 2022.
Byers, Margaretta. *Designing Women: The Art, Technique and Cost of Being Beautiful.* Simon and Schuster, 1938.
Carlson, Hannah. *Pockets: An Intimate History of How We Keep Things Close.* Algonquin Books of Chapel Hill, 2023.
Coontz, Stephanie. *The Way We Never Were: American Families and the Nostalgia Trap.* Basic Books, 2000.
Cowan, Ruth Schwartz. *More Work for Mother: The Ironies of Household Technology from the Open Hearth to the Microwave.* Basic Books, 1983.
Dahl-Wolfe, Louise. *A Photographer's Scrapbook.* St. Martin's Press, 1984.
Dallek, Matthew. *Defenseless Under the Night: The Roosevelt Years and the Origins of Homeland Security.* Oxford University Press, 2016. Kindle edition.
Dior, Christian. *Dior by Dior.* Translated by Antonia Fraser. V&A Publishing, 2020.
Dreilinger, Danielle. *The Secret History of Home Economics: How Trailblazing Women Harnessed the Power of Home and Changed the Way We Live.* W. W. Norton, 2021.
Ford, Richard Thompson. *Dress Codes: How the Laws of Fashion Made History.* Simon & Schuster, 2021.
Friedan, Betty. *The Feminine Mystique.* W. W. Norton, 1963.

Gabriel, Mary. *Ninth Street Women: Lee Krasner, Elaine de Kooning, Grace Hartigan, Joan Mitchell, and Helen Frankenthaler: Five Painters and the Movement That Changed Modern Art*. Back Bay Books, 2018.

Givhan, Robin. *The Battle of Versailles: The Night American Fashion Stumbled into the Spotlight and Made History*. Flatiron Books, 2015.

Gody, Lou, ed. *The WPA Guide to New York City*. The New Press, 1939.

Gould, Lois. *Mommy Dressing: A Love Story, After a Fashion*. Doubleday, 1998.

Hawes, Elizabeth. *Fashion Is Spinach*. Random House, 1938.

Huber, Melissa, and Karen van Godtsenhoven. *Women Dressing Women: A Lineage of Female Fashion Design*. The Metropolitan Museum of Art, 2023.

Jones, Kevin L., and Christina M. Johnson. *Sporting Fashion: Outdoor Girls, 1800–1960*. Prestel Verlag, 2021.

Kirkland, Sally. "Claire McCardell," in *American Fashion: The Life and Lines of Adrian, Mainbocher, McCardell, Norell, Trigère*. Quadrangle, 1975, 209–315.

Lake, Stephanie. *Bonnie Cashin: Chic Is Where You Find It*. Rizzoli, 2016.

Lewis, Adam. *Van Day Truex: The Man Who Defined Twentieth-Century Taste and Style*. Viking Studio, 2001.

Marcus, Stanley. *Minding the Store: A Memoir*. University of North Texas Press, 1974.

McCardell, Claire. *What Shall I Wear? The What, Where, When, and How Much of Fashion*. Abrams Image, 2022.

Milbank, Caroline Rennolds. *New York Fashion: The Evolution of American Style*. Harry N. Abrams, 1989.

Picken, Mary Brooks, and Dora Loues Miller. *Dressmakers of France: The Who, How and Why of the French Couture*. Harper & Brothers, 1956.

Pochna, Marie-France. *Christian Dior: Destiny, The Authorized Biography*. Flammarion, 2021.

Rabinovitch-Fox, Einav. *Dressed for Freedom: The Fashionable Politics of American Feminism*. University of Illinois Press, 2021.

Richardson, Kristen. *The Season: A Social History of the Debutante*. W. W. Norton, 2019.

Richardson, Nan. *Louise Dahl-Wolfe*. Abrams, 2000.

Rowlands, Penelope. *A Dash of Daring: Carmel Snow and Her Life in Fashion, Art, and Letters*. Atria Books, 2005.

Rubio, Oliva María, John P. Jacob, and Celina Lunsford. *Louise Dahl-Wolfe*. Aperture, 2016.

Ryan, Mary P. *Women in Public: Between Banners and Ballots, 1825–1880*. Johns Hopkins University Press, 1990.

Satow, Julie. *When Women Ran Fifth Avenue: Glamour and Power at the Dawn of American Fashion*. Doubleday, 2024.

Sears, Claire. *Arresting Dress: Cross-Dressing, Law, and Fascination in Nineteenth-Century San Francisco*. Duke University Press, 2015.

Steele, Valerie. *Paris Fashion: A Cultural History*. Bloomsbury Visual Arts, 2017.

Thanhauser, Sofi. *Worn: A People's History of Clothing*. Vintage Books, 2022.

Troy, Nancy. *Couture Culture: A Study in Modern Art and Fashion*. MIT Press, 2003.

Von Drehle, David. *Triangle: The Fire That Changed America*. Atlantic Monthly Press, 2003.

Vreeland, Alexander, ed. *Diana Vreeland, The Modern Woman: The Bazaar Years, 1936–1962*. Rizzoli, 2015.

Vreeland, Diana, *D.V.* Ecco, 1984.

Warner, Patricia Campbell. *When the Girls Came Out to Play: The Birth of American Sportswear*. University of Massachusetts Press, 2006.
Way, Elizabeth. *Ann Lowe: American Couturier*. Rizzoli Electa, 2023.
Weidman, Jerome. *I Can Get It for You Wholesale*. Open Road Media, 2013. Kindle edition.
Williams, Beryl. *Fashion Is Our Business*. John Gifford Limited, 1948.
Woolf, Virginia. *A Room of One's Own*. Harcourt, Brace & World, 1929.
Yohannan, Kohle, and Nancy Nolf. *Claire McCardell: Redefining Modernism*. Henry N. Abrams, 1998.

Dissertations

Robinson, Rebecca. "American Sportswear: A Study of The Origins and Women Designers from the 1930's to the 1960's." Master's thesis, University of Cincinnati, 2003. http://rave.ohiolink.edu/etdc/view?acc_num=ucin1054926324.
Strassel, Annemarie Elizabeth. "Redressing Women: Feminism in Fashion and the Creation of American Style, 1930–1960." Yale University, 2008.

Index

A. C. McCardell, Confectioner, 17
Agee, Alma, 116
Agee, James, 116
Algeria, 114, 164
Algonquin Round Table, 116
Altman, Benjamin, 61
American buyers. *see also* Griswold, Marjorie
   Adolph Klein's message about McCardell's designs to, 171
   going to Paris during wartime, 147, 148–149
   McCardell sketching for, 51–52, 54
   McCardell's Monastic Dress and, 122–123, 125
   on McCardell's separates, 98
   previewing McCardell's fall line, 1955, 248
   questioning female designers, 163
   response to ballet slippers, 177
   stealing designs from Paris for, 52–54
   teaching models how to walk for, 88
   for Townley Frock's previews, 88–89
   Turk's previews for, 81–82, 86
   women becoming, 82
   World War II and, 147, 158
American criticism of Christian Dior, 227–228
American design(ers) and fashion. *see also* garment industry; ready-to-wear clothes/manufacturing; specific names of designers
   The American Look (ad campaign) and, 214–218
   annoyed by European excess and extravagance, 108
   copying French clothes and design, 52–54, 227
   designing uniforms for Office of Civilian Defense (OCD), 181
   on Dior's fashion, 227–228
   fall of France (1940) and, 153–154, 158
   haute couture, 217–218
   influence of Parisian design(ers), 159
   interviewed by New York city mayor (1940), 158–160
   Lord & Taylor "American Designers" window display and, 98–99
   male, on McCardell, 274
   media coverage of, 129–1307
   Rudofsky's negative assessment of, 212
   Vogue magazine defending, 212–213
   during wartime rationing, 185
The American Look campaign, 2, 214–218, 254
The American Mercury (magazine), 62
aprons, 176, 183, 187, 189
art and artists
   commercial art(ists), 40
   contemporary, 37
   exhibition for Three Arts Club board members, 39–40
   International Exhibition of Modern Decorative and Industrial Arts, Paris, 32
   Life's fashion feature on textiles featuring, 253–254

art and artists (*cont.*)
  McCardell on modern, 37–38
  modern art museums, 37
  study of, during college, 31–32, 35–36
Asbury, Herbert, 62
Athenia (ship), 148
athleticwear, 275. *see also* playsuits
Austria, 117, 234
Automatic Continuous Clothing Closure, 93

Bacall, Lauren, 184
Baker, Josephine, 47, 217
Balenciaga, Cristóbal, 228
Ballard, Bettina, 152, 222, 228, 245, 266
ballet, Orrick finding inspiration from, 202
ballet flats/slippers, 3, 177–178, 186
balloon fabric, 185–186
Baltimore Sun, 181, 257, 269
B. Altman and Company, 69–70
Barrymore, John, 143
bathing suit, 20–21, 207–209
Battelle, Phyllis, 245
Battle of Versailles (1973), 274
Beaux-Arts Ball (1938), 113–114, 116
Beecher, Catharine, 25
belts, 114, 119, 131, 143, 160, 183, 188, 248
Bergdorf Goodman, 77, 79, 80, 144, 150, 158
Bernhardt, Sarah, 47, 211
Best & Co., 122–123, 124, 125, 127, 132, 154
Betty Crocker Star Matinee (television show), 238
bias cut, the, 46, 118, 183
bicycles/bicycle outings, 211
Big Pool, Maryland, 20
A Bill of Divorcement (film), 101
Black women, 218
Blaker, Mimi, 271
bloomers, 25
Blumenfeld, Erwin, 213
boardinghouses, all-women, 29–30
body size/weight, 215–216, 257
"bone" color, 185
Bouvier, Jacqueline. *see* Kennedy, Jackie (Bouvier)
Boykin, Angé, 41, 65
Boykin, Mildred. *see* Orrick (Boykin), Mildred
Bradford College, 239–240
Brando, Marlon, 187
bridal attire, 169–170

Brooklyn Museum, 253, 271
Brooklyn Times-Union, 86–87
Budapest, Hungary, 117
Burch, Tory, 5, 275
Bureau of Home Economics, 24, 119
Butterick sewing pattern, 23
buttons, 13, 79–80, 82, 182, 185, 188, 228, 241
buyers. *see* American buyers
Byers, Margaretta, 124

Calder, Alexander, 37
Cannes, France, 254
Capezio Ballet Makers, 177, 186, 271
Capri pants, 211
Carnegie, Andrew, 121, 135
Carnegie, Dale, 120–122
Carnegie, Hattie, 80
  business of, 135–136
  change in name, 135
  early life, 135
  House of Jewels preview (1939) and, 141–142
  job offer to McCardell from, 137–138
  McCardell leaving, 157–158
  McCardell's meeting with, 133–134, 137
  Parisian premieres and, 145–146
  physical appearance of, 136–137
  retail boutique of, 134–135
  trip to Paris during World War II, 147, 148
Carnegie Steel Company, 135
Cashin, Bonnie, 227
cat's eye sunglasses, 207, 236–237
Chagall, Marc, 1, 253
Chambre Syndicale de la Haute Couture, 44, 160
Chanel, Coco, 45, 50, 51, 95, 107, 147, 226, 247
Chanel aesthetic, 136, 137, 144, 145
Chase, Edna Woolman, 84, 131, 192
chastity laws, 110
Cherbourg, France, 41–42
Chez Zelda (boutique), 217
chiaroscuro technique, 35
Christian Science Monitor, 173
Claire McCardell Enterprises, 207, 236, 246, 261, 262
Claire McCardell paper dolls, 262
Clairol hair dye, 237
clairvoyants, 100

clothing. *see also* dress(es); fashion and fashion industry; McCardell, Claire, designs by; sportswear; women's fashion
  bought from society ladies of New York, 36–37
  connection between women's freedom and, 4–5
  custom made, 16–18 *(see also* custom-made clothing)
  depicted in art at the Metropolitan Museum of Art, 35–36
  dress codes for women during McCardell's youth, 13–14
  of Lady Brett Ashley in *The Sun Also Rises,* 43
  McCardell playing in mother's wardrobe, 13, 19
  McCardell's ideas about, 2–3, 247, 256, 276
  McCardell's unique style of, 116–117
  rationing of, 183
  restrictive, 3
  sewing one's own, 16–18, 22–23
  for travel, 96–98
  women's freedom and, 4–5, 22, 110–111
  worn by McCardell, 12–13, 15, 20, 34–35, 83, 117–118, 252
clothing labels
  Best & Co. dresses designed by McCardell and, 123
  of McCardell after her death, 268, 269
  McCardell demanding, of Townley Frocks, 167
  McCardell's aspirations about, 2, 121
Cluny Museum, Paris, 48
Collier's (magazine), 130, 149, 236
Collins, Kenneth, 218
Comstock Act (1873), 110
Conte di Savoia (ship), 102
cooking
  as a hobby for McCardell, 199
  McCardell's Kitchen Dinner Dress for, 175–177
corn fibers, 185
corsets, 13, 14, 15, 25, 146, 227, 245
costume ball (Beaux-Arts Ball), 113–115, 116
costume design, study of, 23, 31, 32
Costume Institute, Metropolitan Museum of Art, 244
cotton calico fabric, 95, 210

Coty American Fashion Critics' Awards, 191–192, 211, 271
Crawford, Joan, 143, 251
crinoline, 14, 15, 26, 238
Cubists/Cubism, 37
custom-made clothing. *see also* haute couture (houses)
  American design moving to ready-to-wear from, 136
  American Look campaign leaving out women designers making, 216–218
  designed by McCardell, 143
  in Hattie Carnegie's boutique, 134
  during McCardell's youth, 16–18
  Monastic dress compared with, 123–124

Daché, Lilly, 146, 255
Dahl-Wolfe, Louise, 116, 210–211, 273
Dalí, Salvador, 108
day dresses, 13, 45, 95
Dean, James, 187
de Beauvoir, Simone, 229
debutante system (1950s), 130, 235–238
decency laws, 15
de Gramont, Count Gabriel, 149
de Havilland, Olivia, 217, 234
De Lima, Edward, 101
denim, 2, 187–191, 265
department stores. *see also* American buyers; specific names of department stores
  American designers featured in display windows of, 98–99
  fake shoppers in, 79
  Fifth Avenue, 61–62
  McCardell's job modeling at, 69–70
  stealing design ideas from, 79
design assistants, of McCardell, 172
Designing Women: The Art, Technique, and Cost of Being Beautiful (Byers), 124
d'Espinay-Durtal, Charles Louis, 143, 179
de Wolfe, Elsie, 42
Dick, Madeleine Astor, 102
Didion, Joan, 248
Dietrich, Marlene, 95
Dior, Christian, 218, 221, 271
  American criticisms of, 227–228
  backlash against, 227–228, 229
  Bar Suit of, 224–225
  Carmel Snow on, 221

Dior, Christian (*cont.*)
  in contrast to McCardell, 245
  death, 264
  early life, 224
  H-Line of, 245
  human models used by, 225–226
  hyperfeminized style of, 3, 229
  Jacques Fath and, 245–246
  McCardell praised by, 261
  McCardell's customers of compared with customers of, 251–252
  McCardell's death juxtaposed against death of, 268
  McCardell's designs in contrast to, 228–229, 245, 251–252
  "New Look" of, 3, 226–230, 245
  reflecting postwar attitude toward women, 229, 230
  starting his own couture house, 224
  use of last name of, 7
  waist size and, 231
  women's waist sizes and, 225, 231
dirndl skirt, 117
divorce, 101–102, 106, 110
dolman sleeves, 94, 188
Draper, Dorothy, 175
dress(es)
  of the 1860s, 13–14
  in 1880, 15
  American haute couture, 217–218
  designed by Dior, 223, 224, 225, 226–227, 228
  designed by McCardell, 1939, 143
  forgeries of Parisian, 53–54
  the Future Dress, 213, 275
  Kitchen Dinner Dress, 175–177
  of Madeleine Vionnet, 45
  McCardell making her own, during childhood, 18
  McCardell taking apart a Vionett, 50–51
  the Monastic, 124–125, 164
  patchwork, 184
  the Popover, 189–191, 201, 205
  Salvador Dalí lobster dress, 108
  Salvage Sally (patchwork), 184
  wedding, 169–170
  wrap dress, 2, 188–190
dress codes, 13, 117, 124, 276
dressmakers, 17–18, 44

Dufy, Raoul, 253
du Pont, Lammot, 240
Duval, Gordon, 66

Edward, King of England, 107, 111
Eisenhower, Dwight D., 150, 240, 241
Ellington, Duke, 99
Elliott, Osborn, 255
entertaining, McCardell's design for women who are, 175–176
Entertaining Is Fun! How to Be a Popular Hostess (Draper), 175–176
Etiquette: The Blue Book of Social Usage (Post), 175
European artists, *Life*'s fashion feature on textiles featuring, 253–254
European designers
  American design *versus* excess and extravagance of, 108
  copying McCardell, 261
  Parsons the New School of Design and, 32
European models, 70
Evangelical and Reformed Church, 12, 86
evening gowns, 14, 44, 96, 132, 160

fabrics
  constructing clothing from discarded, 184
  denim, 187–191
  designs using latest cutting-edge, 185
  for Dior's dresses, 226–227
  excess, from military balloons, 185–186
  featuring motifs from European artists, 253–254
  McCardell's novel use of, 95–96
  in Paris during World War II, 153
  rationing of, 183
  used by McCardell, 160–161, 171
Fairbanks, Douglas Jr., 133
fake shoppers, 79
fashion and fashion industry. *see also* American design(ers) and fashion; garment industry; Paris, France and Parisian fashion; women's fashion
  American sensibility *versus* European extravagance, 108
  copying French designs, 52–54, 72, 79–80
  gendered roles in, 84
  in the late 1940s, 230
  link between freedom and, 22

McCardell's book about, 255–259
McCardell's contributions to, 2, 4, 161–162, 164, 275–276
McCardell's ideas about, 256–257
news coverage about, 129–131
reflected in modern art, 37
Fashion Group/Fashion Group International (FGI), 84–85, 98, 110, 120, 129, 153–154
fashion houses, Paris, France, 43–46, 51–53
Fashion Institute of Technology, New York, 275
Fashion Is Spinach (Hawes), 54
Fashion Originators' Guild of America, 126, 128
fashion shows, 141, 142, 265–266
Fashions of the Times event, 185
Fath, Jacques, 245–246, 271
Federal Economy Act (1932), 110
felt cloche hat, 35
The Feminine Mystique (Friedan), 1, 249–250
feminism, 211, 273–274
Ferris, Jean, 104–106, 143, 179
Fiermonte, Enzo, 102, 106
Filene, Edward A., 61
Filene's department store, 162, 173
fires, New York City, 68
Fishers Island, New York, 208, 240
Fitzgerald, Ella, 217
Fitzgerald, F. Scott, 34, 43, 70, 142
Fitzgerald, Zelda, 43
flapper style, 21, 31, 34–35
Florentine Renaissance painters, 35
Fogarty, Anne, 273
Folies, Bergère, Paris, 47
footwear. *see* shoes
Forbes, Esther, 63
Fortune (magazine), 82, 93, 125
fortune-telling, 100
Franco, Francisco, 107
Franklin, Marjorie, 148–149, 150, 151, 152–153
Frank Perls Gallery, Beverly Hills, California, 243–245
Frederick, Maryland, 2, 11–12, 14, 16–23
Frederick County National Bank, Frederick, Maryland, 11
The Frederick News-Post, 195
Frenchtown, New Jersey, 115, 117, 176, 178, 210, 263, 270

Friedan, Betty
The Feminine Mystique, 1
interview with McCardell, 5
research on women and work, 249–250
second wave feminism and, 273–274
Time interview/article on McCardell, 3
Time interview of McCardell, 1, 3, 250–252
visiting Townley showroom, 247–249
Friedman, Harry, 83–84, 87
Fuller, Dan, 253
Fuller Fabrics, 254
furlough brides, 169–170
Futurama (World's Fair exhibition), 138
Future Dress, 213, 275

"The Gal Who Defied Dior" (Friedan), 3
The Gangs of New York: An Informal History of the Underworld (Asbury), 62
Garbo, Greta, 244–245
garment industry. *see also* American buyers; ready-to-wear clothes/manufacturing; Townley Frocks
anonymity of female designers in, 99
copying of McCardell's Monastic dress, 125–127
fires and, 68
hierarchy in, 72–73
McCardell working for Sol Pollack in, 71–74
New York mayor wanting to learn about, 158–160
New York's Garment District, 59, 70, 265
previews by Seventh Avenue manufacturers, 80–82
problems with mass production in, 79–80
Robert Turk Inc., 78–79
Roy McCardell's concerns about, 67–68
Geiss, Henry
applauding McCardell in the press, 211
Best & Co. order and, 122–123
copying of McCardell's Monastic dress and, 126
on "hanger appeal," 95, 120
on McCardell returning to Townley Frocks, 166, 167
on McCardell's use of fabrics, 95
Monastic dress and, 124, 125, 126, 127, 128
not accepting McCardell's designs, 120, 122
personality, 83

Geiss, Henry (*cont.*)
  on pockets, 91–92, 93
  promoting McCardell as head designer, 89
  reopening Townley with Adolph Klein, 165
  retiring from Seventh Avenue, 241
  sending McCardell to Europe, 101
  on shoulder pads, 94, 95
  Turk's death/funeral and, 87
  wanting McCardell to return to Townley Frocks, 140–141
Genoa, Italy, 148, 151, 153
Gentlemen Prefer Blondes, 143
George VI, King of England, 107, 111
Germany, 70, 153, 159
Gibraltar, Port of, 150
Gilman, Charlotte Perkins, 92
Gimbel, Sophie, 227
Golden Age, the, 15, 61, 104, 139
Gossard Corset, 25–26
government jobs, women working in, 110
Graf Zeppelin, 70
Graham, Martha, 234, 236
Graziani, Bettina, 254
Great Depression, 4, 82, 85, 229–230
The Great Gatsby (Fitzgerald), 34, 142
Great War, the, 103
Greenwich Village, New York, 68, 78–79
Griswold, Marjorie, 197, 209
  Christian Dior and, 261
  lunches with McCardell and Sally Kirkland, 221–222
  McCardell bathing suit and, 209
  on McCardell's idea for longer skirts, 223
  at McCardell's memorial, 266
  visiting Townley showroom, 174–175
  writing to Eleanor McCardell, 271
grocery bag, 188
Grosvenor Debutante Ball, 235, 237–238
Guernica (Picasso), 107
Guernica, Spain, 107

Hall, Jane Harriss, 30
Haller, Thomas H., 25
Hall of Fashion, World's Fair, 1939, 142
Halston, 274
handbags, 188
Harding, Warren G., 24

Harper's Bazaar, 16, 45, 49, 81, 131, 150, 152, 189, 210, 234
  Carmel Snow leaving, 273
  Christian Dior and, 224
  Diana Vreeland and, 144, 186–187
  footless leggings spread in, 205
  Louise Dahl-Wolfe and, 210
  McCardell's designs featured in, 143, 184, 189
  Orrick's leotard idea and, 202, 203, 204, 205
Harris, Elizabeth (Liz), 106, 179, 198, 234, 235, 236, 239–240, 274–275
Harris, Irving Drought
  after McCardell's death, 269–270
  Beaux-Arts Ball and, 115
  countryside home and, 116
  dating McCardell, 108–109
  death of ex-wife, 178–179
  early life, 103
  Fishers Island and, 208
  Jean Ferris and, 104–106
  marriages after McCardell's death, 274
  marriage to Claire McCardell, 193–194
  McCardell meeting, 103, 106
  McCardell's career/professional life and, 143, 196, 197, 199, 235, 250
  military draft and, 169
  moving to New York city, 103–104
  personality of, 143–144
  relationship with children, 178, 179–180
  Sally Kirkland on, 197–198
  tensions between McCardell and, 1950, 233
Harris, John Wakefield
  birth of, 105
  choosing to live with his father, 179
  on Eleanor McCardell, 198
  handling the affairs after McCardell's death, 269–270
  on Harris-McCardell marriage, 198
  on his father, 115, 143–144, 196
  joining the Marines, 238–239
  on McCardell, 178
  on McCardell's death, 266
  McCardell's letters to, 239–240
  McCardell's trip to Austrian Alps and, 234
  in the military, 238–239
  moving to New York with his father, 106
  referring to McCardell as "Mumsy," 180
  relationship with his father, 178, 274

relationship with his sister, Liz, 198, 263, 274–275
writing to Eleanor McCardell after McCardell's death, 270–271
hatpins, 117
hats, 35, 117–118, 200
Hattie Carnegie Enterprises, 135
haute couture (houses). *see also* Dior, Christian
American designers, 217–218
American Look campaign and, 217–218
American press and, 130
copying designs from, 52–54
Hattie Carnegie's boutique and, 80
House of Worth and, 43–44
maiden names for women and, 50
McCardell studying, 42
Normal Norell and, 192
Salvador Dalí lobster dress, 108
World War II and, 147, 152, 213, 222
Hawes, Elizabeth, 53–54, 98–99, 123, 159, 185
Hays Code, 102
Heal, Edith, 255, 256, 258, 262
Hearst, Mrs. William Randolph, 135–136
Hearst, William Randolph, 84
Helfenstein, Edward, 194
Hemingway, Ernest, 43, 112
hemlines, 21, 119, 222–223, 228, 245
Hendrickson's General Store, Frederick, 17
Hepburn, Katharine, 101, 197, 205
Hewitt, Mrs. Peter Cooper, 36
high heels, 3, 83, 177
Hilfiger, Tommy, 374
Hitler, Adolf, 146
Holiday (magazine), 233
Hollywood (stars), 135, 143, 197
home economics, degree in, 24–25, 26
Hood College, 19, 23, 24, 26
hooded peasant's cape, 117–118
hoodies, 2, 211
hoods, 117, 118, 132, 173, 211
hooks and eyes, 170
Hoover, Herbert, 71
Hope Diamond, 143
Horn, Louise, 228
Hotel Astor, New York City, 113, 121, 184
housedresses, 13, 93, 187, 190
House of Jewels (World's Fair exhibition), 141
House of Vionnet, 45
House of Worth (fashion house), 43–45

Hughes, Alice, 123, 269
Hulick, Helen, 124
Hutton, Emma Spreckles, 104

I Married an Angel (musical), 132
Institute of Effective Speaking, 121
International Exhibition of Modern Decorative and Industrial Arts, Paris, 32
International Exposition of Art and Technology in Modern Life (1937), 107
International Ladies' Garment Workers' Union, 84
Ireland, 12, 221

Jackson, Mississippi, 12, 17
Jeakins, Dorothy, 244
jeans, 16, 187
jewelry, 98, 117, 254
Johnson, Hope, 245, 246
Jones, Emily Harris, 275
journalism/journalists, 1, 129–131, 144–145. *see also* specific publications and journalists

Kanengeiser, Henrietta, 135. *see also* Carnegie, Hattie
Keith, Slim, 205
Kellerman, Annette, 20–21
Kennedy, Jackie (Bouvier), 217, 218
Kennedy, John F., 217
Key, Francis Scott, 86
Kirkland, Sally, 192
Fishers Island and, 208
on Irving Harris and Claire McCardell relationship, 197–198, 199, 241, 250
lunches with McCardell and Marjorie Griswold, 221–222
on McCardell's idea for longer skirts, 223
at McCardell's memorial, 266
on Mildred Orrick's leotards, 205
Modern Masters Series fabrics photo shooting and, 253–254
relationship with McCardell, 197
Kitchen Dinner dress, 175–177, 183
Kitt, Eartha, 217
Klein, Adolph, 169, 177, 192, 207, 261–262
brokering endorsements and licensing deals, 236, 255
on continuing McCardell's fashion philosophy, 269

Klein, Adolph (*cont.*)
    denim and, 188
    Irving Harris and, 197
    Marjorie Griswold and, 174–175
    McCardell's cancer and, 264
    on McCardell's fashion ideas, 170–171, 177–178, 209
    at McCardell's memorial, 266
    McCardell's return to Townley and, 165–166, 167
    McCardell's separates idea and, 171, 174
    on McCardell taking an oversight role, 261
    Popover dress and, 189, 190
    trunk shows and, 173
Klein, Calvin, 274
Koogle, Anna (dressmaker), 17–18, 22, 27
Kors, Michael, 5

L-85 restrictions, 183, 185, 186, 187, 188, 222
Ladies' Home Journal, 52
Lady Levis, 187
La Guardia, Fiorello, 33, 158–160, 181
Lamb, William F., 113
Lambert, Eleanor, 129, 191, 203, 255, 266, 274
Lawrence, Gertrude, 136, 145, 157
leather, 2, 114, 131, 153, 262
Le Bourget airfield, France, 55–56
LeBoutillier, Peggy, 215, 236, 266
    debutante culture and, 130
    Hattie Carnegie and, 142
    independent spirit of, 130
    McCardell's friendship with, 129, 137–138
    media stunt with Saks Fifth Avenue, 130–131
    promoting McCardell's work, 131, 161, 162
    wearing McCardell evening gown, 132
LeBoutillier, Philip, 127, 129, 132
Le Corbusier (architect), 37
Léger, Fernand, 253
leggings, 2, 205
Lehman, Mrs. Alan, 141
Lehman Brothers, 85
Léotard, Jules, 202
leotards, 2, 202–204, 205, 206
Leser, Tina, 185
Lessons in Loveliness (radio show), 184
Let Us Now Praise Famous Men (Agee), 116
Leviathan (ship), 41, 57
Lewis, Mary, 154

Library of the Fashion Institute of Technology, 275
Life (magazine), 204, 205, 207, 215, 246, 250, 253, 262
life drawing classes, 32–33
Lindbergh, Charles A., 54–57
Little Women (theater production), 14
lobster dress, 108
London, England, 111
Long, Lois, 129
Loos, Anita, 143
Lord & Taylor, 32, 98–99, 174, 175, 189–190, 197, 201, 203, 209, 214, 254, 273
Los Angeles Times, 124
Louvre, the, Paris, 50
Lowe, Ann, 217–218
Luce, Henry, 204
Luciano, Lucky, 160
Lusitania, 148

Macy's department store, 79, 135, 174, 218
Mademoiselle, 197
made-to-order designers, 217. *see also* custom-made clothing
Maison Dior, 224
makeup, 2, 35, 83
Manhattan (ship), 153
Marcus, Stanley, 227, 230
Marine Corps, 238–239
marriage
    average/median age of, 4, 110, 249
    Friedan's research on, 249
    of McCardell, 4, 193–198, 199
    McCardell discussing her own, 250
    McCardell's lack of interest in, 26, 50, 109
    name changes and, 7
    women grappling with tensions between career and, 196–197
Maryland Center for History and Culture, Baltimore, 275
mass production. *see* ready-to-wear clothes/manufacturing
Matter, Herbert, 131
Maxwell, Vera, 116, 185, 208
May Company department store, 267
Mazur, Paul, 85
McCardell, Adrian (brother), 12, 35, 157, 194, 222, 263, 269, 270
McCardell, Adrian C. (grandfather), 86, 87

McCardell, Adrian LeRoy (father), 11–12, 26, 38
   concerns about his daughter in New York city, 69
   death, 222
   in hospital at age seventy-two, 198
   Irving Harris's letter to, 194–195
   on McCardell's career choice, 67–69
   politics and, 71
McCardell, Claire
   accomplishments and impact of, 4–5, 265, 267–268, 271, 275–276
   Adolph Klein on, 165, 171
   the American Look and, 1–2
   aspiration for her own label, 157–158
   attending Beaux-Arts Ball (1938), 114–115, 116
   attending Dale Carnegie's speech meetings, 121–122
   awards and prizes, 191, 197, 211–212, 230–231, 234–235, 271
   birthday (22nd), 54, 56
   body weight and, 215, 216
   book written by, 255–259
   buying shares in Townley Harris, 241
   cancer of, 262–265
   care package and letter to stepson, 239–240
   clothing worn by, 12–13, 15, 20, 34–35, 83, 117–118, 252
   countryside home of, 115–116
   dating Irving Harris, 108–109
   death and memorial of, 266–268
   dental work of, 64
   desire to change women's fashion, 2–3
   on Dior's H-Line, 245
   on Dior's New Look, 228–229
   endorsements and licensing deals of, 255
   European trips, mid-1930s, 101–103
   family, 4, 11, 12, 14, 17
   the Fashion Group and, 84–85
   at fashion show (1958), 265–266
   grandfather's death, 86
   interior decoration by, 199–200
   interviewed by Betty Friedan, 1, 2–3, 250–251
   letters from customers to, 251
   marriage/elopement of, 193–199
   meeting Hattie Carnegie, 133–134, 137
   meeting Irving Harris, 103, 106
   name usage, 7
   New York apartment of, 65–66, 70–71
   at New York Fashion Week (1958), 265–266
   photographed in *Vogue* story, 213
   physical appearance, 2, 34–35, 83
   presidential election (1952) and, 240–241
   public performances, 236–237, 238
   purchasing clothing in Paris, 36–37, 50
   reacting to Fath's comments about women designers, 246–247
   relationship with stepchildren, 178, 179–180
   religion and, 38–39
   seeing an astrologer, 100
   silence between Mildred Orrick and, 206
   spending time in Frenchtown, New Jersey, 178
   Sports Illustrated article by, 247
   supporting her stepdaughter for debutante ball, 237–238
   trademarking her name, 207
   travel to Europe during wartime, 147–153
   vacations, 233, 234
   will of, 270
McCardell, Claire, designs by
   in 1957, 262
   Algerian-inspired costume for ball, 114, 118
   Baby McCardell line, 250
   bridal attire, 169–170
   Diana Vreeland and, 144–145
   displayed in Frank Perls Gallery, 243–245
   dolman sleeve, 94, 188
   European designers copying, 261
   exercise suit, 133
   fabrics used for, 95–96, 160–161, 226–227
   the Future Dress, 213, 275
   for Hattie Carnegie's ready-to-wear sportswear, 141–143
   in Hemingway's novel, 43
   hoods/hoodie, 117, 118, 132, 173, 211
   impact of wartime rationing on, 183
   innovations of, 2, 3, 164
   inspirations for, while traveling, 117
   interview by Helen Wulbern on, 163–164
   Kitchen Dinner Dress, 175–177, 183
   leggings, 205
   leotards and, 203–205
   media coverage of, 131–132, 161–162
   mix-and-match separates, 96–98, 108, 171, 172–174

McCardell, Claire, designs by (*cont.*)
  the Monastic dress, 122–128
  for Office of Civilian Defense (OCD), 181–182
  originals *versus* fashion-trend iterations, 205
  playsuits, 209–211, 212
  pockets and, 91–93
  Popover dress, 188–190, 191, 201, 205
  red dress based on Beaux-Arts Ball costume ("the Monastic"), 118, 119
  samples of, 172
  side zipper, 93
  simplicity in style, 93–94
  spring dress silhouette, 1947, 222–223
  swimwear, 207–210
  that could last for years, 119–120
  three-piece denim suit, 190–191
  for Townley Frock preview, 88–89
  unpadded shoulders, 95
  using art-inspired fabrics, 253–254
  for Vera Zorina, 132–133
  during wartime rationing, 184–186
  for Win-Sum, 158, 162–163
McCardell, Claire, work by
  as assistant designer to Sal Pollack, 71–74
  assisting Robert Turk for Townley Frocks, 83–84, 85–88
  for Hattie Carnegie, 138–141
  head of design department at Townley Frocks, 88–89
  looking for, after graduating from college, 59–62
  modeling at B. Altman and Company, 69–70
  modeling for Robert Turk, 78, 81, 82
  painting parchment lampshades, 64–65
  returning to Townley Frocks, 164–167, 169
  sketching job in the Garment District, New York, 70
  sketching Parisian clothing for American buyers, 51–52, 54
  for Townley Frocks, 83–84, 85–89
  working for Robert Turk, 77–80, 82
McCardell, Claire, youth of
  childhood nickname of, 11
  clothing worn by, 12–13
  college, at Hood College, 23–25, 26–27
  college, at New York School of Fine and Applied Arts, 31–33, 35–36, 37–38
  custom paper dolls made by, 16
  dates/dating by, 33–34, 49, 50
  education, 18–19, 23
  graduating from Parsons, 59
  at Le Bourget airfield, France, 55–56
  making her own dress, 18
  Parisian social/street life and, 46–49
  playing in her mother's wardrobe, 13
  relationships with boys, 20
  sewing her own clothes, 22–23
  sleepaway camp, 20–21
  study in Paris, 40, 41, 43–46
  swimming without stockings, 21–22
  walking to general store with mother, 17
McCardell, Ela, 13, 14
McCardell, Eleanor (mother), 11–12, 14, 67, 206
  after McCardell's death, 270–271
  encouraging her daughter for her television appearance, 237
  on grand stepson joining the Marine Corps, 238–239
  on her daughter moving back to New York city, 69
  on McCardell returning to New York, 69
  McCardell's cancer/death and, 263, 266
  McCardell's elopement and, 195
  on McCardell's potential, 19, 27
  on McCardell's travel to Austria, 234
  sensing tensions between McCardell and Irving Harris, 233
  stepgrandchildren of, 198
  wardrobe/clothing of, 13, 15, 17–18
McCardell, John (Max) (brother), 12, 157, 194, 198, 222, 263
McCardell, Robert (brother), 12, 157, 194, 222, 258, 263
McCardellisms, 256–257
McLean, Evalyn Walsh, 143
media, 129–132
  after winning prize for House of Jewels preview (1939), 141–142
  on Dior's New Look, 228–229
  Hattie Carnegie and, 140
  interview with Helen Wulbern, 163–164
  McCardell promoted in the, 161–162
  McCardell's *Sports Illustrated* article, 247
Mellen, Polly, 208
Men at Arms (Waugh), 239

Mencken, H. L., 62
mend-and-make-do aesthetic, 184
men's fashion, McCardell finding inspiration from, 95, 184
Merit Award *(Mademoiselle* magazine), 197
metal fasteners/hooks and eyes, 93, 170
Metropolitan Museum of Art, New York, 35–36, 191, 244, 271, 273, 275
Mi-Carême ball, 113–114
midinettes, 44, 49–50
military, women in the, 182
military draft, 169
Miró, Joan, 243, 253
A Mirror for Witches (Forbes), 62–63
mix-and-match separates, 3, 96–98, 108, 171, 172–174
models/modeling
  American Look and whiteness and social standing of, 215
  for Christian Dior, 225–226
  for McCardell's new silhouette, 1947, 223
  McCardell's work, 69–70, 81, 82
  McCardell writing about comparing oneself to, 257
  for ready-to-wear clothing, 118
  by ready-to-wear designers, 131
  slouching, casual manner of, 70, 88
  wearing McCardell's art-inspired clothing, 254
modern art, 37–38
the "Monastic" dress, 124–125, 126–128, 134
Mount Olivet Cemetery, Frederick, Maryland, 266
Museum of Modern Art, 37, 191
museums, 244

Nada label/line, 123, 126, 127
Nast, Condé Montrose, 84
Nazis/Nazism, 107, 148, 153, 159, 212, 222
Neiman Marcus Award, 227, 230
New Deal, the, 109–110
New Hackensack, New York, 86
"New Look" (Dior), 3, 226–230, 245
New York City. *see also* American design(ers) and fashion; garment industry
  Beaux-Arts Ball in, 113–114
  Bergdorf Goodman, 77–78
  debutante system of, 235–236
  Dorothy Parker writing about, 69
  Fifth Avenue department stores, 61–62
  Garment District, 59, 70, 265
  McCardell going to school in, 30–33, 35–36, 37–40
  McCardell looking for work in, 59–61, 62, 64–66
  McCardell returning to, 69
  number and influence of women designers in, 218
  Seventh Avenue manufacturers, 80–82, 218
  single women moving to, 29–30
  Three Arts Club (house) in, 29, 30, 36–37
  Turk family in, 78–79
New York Dress Institute, 160
The New Yorker, 123, 129, 202–203
New York Fashion Week (Press Week), 203, 205, 265
The New York Herald, 54
New York Hospital, 263, 266
New York School of Fine and Applied Art. *see* Parsons the New School of Design
New York Times, 42, 100, 116, 129, 131, 142, 149, 184, 189, 241, 269
New York World-Telegram, 123, 132, 245
Nineteenth Amendment, 21
Noguchi, Isamu, 129
Norell, Norman, 136, 139, 140, 145, 191, 192
Normandie (ship), 106, 112, 146
Norwood, Reverend Robert, 38–39, 264–265, 267
nylon hosiery, 142, 183

Office of Civilian Defense (OCD), 181–182
O'Keeffe, Georgia, 104, 190
Olympic (steamship), 106
Order L-85. *see* L-85 restrictions
Orrick, Jesse, 100, 109, 201, 248, 273
Orrick, Martha, 31
Orrick, Sarah, 206, 266
Orrick (Boykin), Mildred, 47, 50, 60
  after McCardell's death, 273
  friendship with Joset Walker, 48, 138
  friendship with McCardell, 30–31, 48, 205
  helping Townley Frocks after McCardell's death, 269
  House of Vionnet and, 45, 46
  interest in the mystical, 100
  leaving Paris, 57
  at Le Bourget airfield, France, 55–56

Orrick (Boykin), Mildred (cont.)
  leotard idea of, 202–204
  McCardell exploring Parisian social life with, 48
  McCardell's cancer and, 264, 265
  McCardell sharing apartment with, 70–71
  at McCardell's memorial, 266
  Mi-Carême ball and, 114
  moving to rural Virginia, 109
  in Paris with McCardell, 41
  secondhand Paris clothing and, 37
  secondhand Paris outfits and, 37
  sketching job in Paris, 51, 52, 53
  St. Catherine's Day, 49
  study in Paris, 41, 42
  supporting women pursuing fashion careers, 248
  during wartime, 201–202
  while studying in New York, 33, 38
  working with Natacha Rambova, 65
overalls, 16, 185, 223

Pacific Lumber Company, 185
Paley, Babe, 143
pants, women wearing, 124, 184, 185, 205, 211
paper dolls, 16, 262
Paris (ship), 103, 106
Paris, France and Parisian fashion. *see also* Dior, Christian; haute couture (houses)
  after the Nazi occupation, 221, 222
  American designers display featured by department stores and, 98
  American students in, 42
  buyers at couture houses in, 51–53
  Carmel Snow on travel to, 1946, 221
  comeback after Nazi occupation, 213
  expat Americans in, 42–43
  Fashion Group discussing American fashion and, 153–154
  Hattie Carnegie and, 134, 135
  Jacques Fath and, 245–246
  McCardell exploring and attending events in, 46–49
  McCardell's 1937 trip to, 106–108
  McCardell's study in, 41–42, 43–44
  Nazi occupation in, 153, 212
  Robert Turk Inc. and, 78
  shoulder pads, 94–95
  St. Catherine's Day in, 49–50
  stealing and copying from, 52–54
  visiting fashion houses of, 43–46
Paris clothes, bought from society ladies of New York, 36–37
Park Avenue Social Review, 66
Parker, Dorothy, 69
Parnell, Dorothy, 265
Parsons, Frank Alvah, 31–32, 36, 40, 42
Parsons the New School of Design, 23, 26–27, 31–33, 172, 233, 271
patch pocket, 127, 182, 188–189
patchwork dress, 184
patents, 127, 189, 205, 207
Pathé (news organization), 227
patterns, clothing, 16, 18, 207
pedal pushers, 211
perfume, 262
Perkins, Frances, 110
Perls, Frank, 243–245
Phony War, the, 152–153
photos/photography, 31, 131, 162, 204, 210–211, 213, 253–254, 263
Picasso, Pablo, 1, 37, 108, 253–254
Pilates, Joseph and Clara, 216
Pilates exercise program, 216
playsuits, 133, 207, 209–211, 212
pockets, 2, 13, 61, 91–93, 124, 164, 182, 184, 188. *see also* patch pocket
Pollack, Sol, 71, 72, 73–74
Pollock, Jackson, 129
pop art, 262
Pope, Virginia, 129, 185
Popover, the, 189–191, 201, 205
Post, Emily, 175, 257
pot holder, Popover dress and, 189, 201
Potter, Clare, 185, 255
Practice Houses, the, 25, 26
première, 44, 225
presidential election (1928), 71
presidential election (1952), 240–241
Press Week (New York Fashion Week), 203, 205, 265
Prohibition, 33, 48
Pucci, Emilio, 174, 267, 271
Pulitzer, Lilly, 174
purses, 91, 92, 182
push-up bra, 252

Queen Mary (ship), 101, 102
Quinn, Billy, 47

Rabinovitch-Fox, Einav, 276
Rambova, Natacha, 65, 68, 100, 202
rationing, wartime, 170, 182–184
ready-to-wear clothes/manufacturing. *see also* American design(ers) and fashion; garment industry; McCardell, Claire, designs by
   American Look campaign and, 217
   Christian Dior and, 261
   design challenge with, 118
   at the Frederick, Maryland general store, 16–17
   Hattie Carnegie and, 136, 137
   job at Bergdorf Goodman and, 77–78
   men in second-wave, 274
   problems with replicating made-to-measure clothes, 79–80
   sizing system and, 118–119
   spectator sportswear, 78
   Zorina line, 132–133
Rebel Without a Cause (film), 187
Rebstock, Mildred, 235
reticule, 92
Reuss, Edith Marie, 98–99
RKO Pictures, 101
Robb, Inez, 267
Robert Turk Inc., 78, 82–83
Roddy, Gay, 71–72, 73, 77
Rogers, Ginger, 237
romper, one-piece, 133, 210
A Room of One's Own (Woolf), 63
Roosevelt, Eleanor, 84, 110, 181, 182, 236
Roosevelt, Franklin D., 84, 109–110, 142, 148, 180
Roset, Mona, 249
Rosie the Riveter, 230
Roth, Rose, 135
Rubinstein, Helena, 35, 84
Rubinstein, Ida, 47
Rudofsky, Bernard, 212

sailing, 207, 208
Saint Laurent, Yves, 264
Saks Fifth Avenue, 130–131, 227
Salvage Sally dress, 184
San Antonio, Texas, 103

San Francisco Chronicle, 92, 104
sashes, 143, 163, 234
Saturday Evening Post, 245
Schiaparelli, Elsa, 95, 108, 162
seamstresses, 44, 49, 53, 68, 225
second-wave feminism, 273–274
sewing one's own clothing, 16–18, 22–23
Shaver, Dorothy
   the "American Look" campaign and, 214–215
   death of, 273
   on a dress worn once, 108
   living with her sister, 196
   Lord & Taylor "American Designers" window display and, 98–99
   Marjorie Griswold and, 174
   on McCardell's designs, 175
   at McCardell's memorial, 266
Shelton Hotel, New York, 103–104
shoes, 49, 83. *see also* ballet flats/slippers
shoulder pads, 94–95
Simpson, Adele, 98–99
Simpson, Babs, 204, 209
Simpson, Wallis Warfield, 107–108, 111, 112, 145
Singer sewing machine, 18
sizing system, 118–119
Skillman, Hope, 160–161, 185, 264, 266
Slack, Chester, 33, 71
sleeveless dresses, 213, 257
Smith, Al, 71
snood, 170
Snow, Carmel, 64, 131, 149, 150, 151, 187
   Christian Dior and, 221, 226, 228
   leaving *Harper's Bazaar,* 273
   at McCardell's memorial, 266
   postwar trip to Paris, 149
   trying to draw New Yorkers back to Paris, 221
Sommers, Ben, 177, 186
spaghetti ties, 143, 188, 256
Spain, 107, 150
Spanish Civil War, 107
Spectator Sports, 136, 137
spectator sportswear, 78
Spirit of St. Louis (plane), 55
sports culture, American, 216
Sports Illustrated, 247

sportswear
   athletic clothing before, 25
   for bicycling, 211
   in early twentieth century, 2
   impact on women, McCardell writing about, 247
   McCardell's job modeling, 69–70
   photographing, 210
   playsuits, 207, 209–211
   Seventh Avenue previews for, 81–82
   spectator, 78
   swimwear, 207–209
   women's freedom and, 110–111
   Workroom Originals (Hattie Carnegie), 137
Spreckels family, 104–105, 274
standardized sizing, 118–119
St. Bartholomew's Church, New York, 38–39, 264
St. Catherine's Day, 49–50
steamer trunks, 96–97
Steckling-Coen, Adri, 248, 269
Stein, Gertrude, 43
Stieglitz, Alfred, 104
St. James' Church, New York City, 266
stock market crash (1929), 82
St. Paul's Episcopal Church, Baltimore, Maryland, 193–194
The Studio Boys, 33
suffragists, 4, 92
Sui, Anna, 5
suitcases, fitting women's clothing into, 97
The Sun Also Rises (Hemingway), 43
SunSpecs, 236–237
Surrealists, 37, 108
Sustersic, Bessie, 83, 93, 120, 172, 249
swimwear/swimsuits, 2, 207–209, 246

tasseography, 100
tea dresses, 13–14
Teen-Age Manual: A Guide to Popularity and Success (Heal), 258
television, 237
temperance, 33, 48
Théâtre de l' Odéon, Paris, 47
Three Arts Club, New York City, 29, 30, 36–37, 59
Three Views on News (radio show), 228
Time (magazine), 1, 255
toddlers, McCardell's line for, 250

Toklas, Alice B., 43
Tolman, Allison, 275
The Town Journal, 1, 247
Townley Frocks. *see also* Geiss, Henry; Klein, Adolph
   after McCardell's death, 269
   Claire McCardell Enterprises and, 207
   closure of, 141
   denim Popover dress, 188–190, 191
   disagreements about pockets in, 91–93
   Kitchen Dinner Dress and, 175–177
   Klein and McCardell team/relationship at, 170–171
   Marjorie Griswold and, 174–175
   McCardell first working for, 83–84, 85–88
   McCardell leaving, 138
   McCardell's disagreements over design choices in, 91–96
   McCardell's office and staff at, 171–172
   Monastic dress and, 122–123, 127–128
   reopening of, 1941, 165, 169
   Robert Turk Inc. and, 83
   success of McCardell's Monastic dress and, 125
Tracy, Spencer, 197
travel, McCardell's ideas about clothing for, 96–98
Triangle Shirtwaist Factory fire, Greenwich Village (1911), 68, 73
Truman, Harry, 235
trunk shows, 173, 264
Turk, Abraham, 78–79
Turk, Bernard, 86
Turk, Robert, 77–78, 79, 81, 82, 86–87, 265
Turkish-style trousers, 25
tweed, 95, 164, 171, 205, 221

undercover shoppers, 125–126
uniform(s), 118–119, 124, 181–182
Union Manufacturing company, 16–17
US Department of Agriculture, 24
US Department of State, 32

Valdes, Zelda Wynn, 217, 218
Van Alen, William, 113
Vanderbilt, Mrs. Frederick, 36, 135–136
Vanity Fair, 196
velocipede, 211
vice laws, 110

Villager Clothes, 273
Vionnet, Madeleine, 45–46, 50, 147
Vogue, 16, 22, 45, 62, 64, 81, 84, 108, 152, 171, 197, 222
   "American Issue" of, 123–124
   applauding Dior's design, 229
   ballet flat on cover of, 186
   Cubism-inspired fabrics showcased in, 37
   defense of American contemporary fashion, 212–213
   Harper's Bazaar and, 150
   McCardell described in, 162, 169
   McCardell's designs/clothing in, 143, 170, 174
   postwar portrayal of women in, 230
   shoulder pads and, 94
Vogue Pattern Book, 17
Vreeland, Diana, 144–145, 186–187, 202, 262, 264, 266

Wald, Connie, 145, 265
Waldorf Astoria, New York, 106, 141, 176, 236
Walker, Joset, 47, 48, 101, 138, 167, 206, 255, 266, 273
Walker, Mary, 15
War Production Board (WPB), 183
wartime (World War II), 4, 146, 147–154, 180, 181–186
Washington (ship), 148, 149, 150
Washington, DC, 234
Washington Post, 184–185
Waugh, Evelyn, 239
wedding dress(es), 169–170, 218
Weissmuller, Johnny, 102
West, Mae, 217
Wharton, Edith, 42, 236
What Shall I Wear? The What, Where, When, and How Much of Fashion (McCardell), 255–259, 275
White Sash (perfume), 262
Wife Dressing: The Fine Art of Being a Well-Dressed Wife (Fogarty), 273
The Wild Ones (film), 187
Williams, Beryl, 118
Winnie award, 191–192, 211
Win-Sum, 158, 162–163, 166
witches/witchcraft, 62–63
Woman of the Year (film), 197

women. *see also* marriage
   absent from professional artistic life, 63
   as buyers during garment industry previews, 82
   debutante system (1950s) and, 130, 235–236
   discrimination of unmarried, 195–196
   Fashion Group (professional organization) for, 84–85
   fashion media coverage by, 129–130
   fiscally beholden to men, 64
   grappling with tensions between career and marriage, 196–197
   Hays Code and, 102
   hourglass shape of, 3, 170, 223, 224, 245
   Kitchen Dinner Dress for working, 175–177
   in the military, 182
   military volunteers, uniforms for, 181–182
   modern clothes and freedom of, 110–111
   moving to New York, 29–30
   in New York's garment industry, 84
   postwar backlash to autonomy of, 229–230
   prejudice against single, 110
   pressures to maintain a certain body weight/size, 215–216
   right to vote, 71
   shifting gender roles in Hollywood, 197
   standardized sizing for, 119
   waist sizes of, 3, 225, 231
   witches and, 62–63
   working, 24, 84, 109–110, 124, 247–248
   working on McCardell's design team, 248–249
"Women Are What They Wear," 247
women designers. *see also* American design(ers) and fashion; specific names of designers
   American Look leaving out group of, 216–218
   Dale Carnegie and, 120–121
   high-profile cross-promotion of, 254–255
   Jacques Fath on, 246
   self-promotion by, 120–121
   wartime, 184–185
women of color, 218
women's fashion. *see also* American design(ers) and fashion; clothing; fashion and fashion industry; McCardell, Claire, designs by; Paris, France and Parisian fashion
   in the 1860s, 14–15

women's fashion (*cont.*)
  in 1920, 21
  in the 1930s, 93
  after wartime, 222–223
  backlash against Dior's designs for, 226–227, 229
  bathing suit, 20–21
  Christian Dior and, 3
  decency laws and, 15
  flapper style, 21, 31, 34–35
  by Madeleine Vionnet, 45–46
  McCardell's ideas and impact on, 2–3, 4–5, 96–98, 276
  pants and, 124, 184, 185, 205, 211
  pockets and, 91–93
  shoulder pads and, 94–95
  at turn of the nineteenth century, 15–16
  during wartime rationing, 183–185
Women's Press Club, 234–235
Women's Wear Daily, 81, 82, 85, 99, 117, 118, 123, 138, 163, 176–177, 189, 190, 196, 255
Woolf, Virginia, 63

wool fabric, 95–96, 118, 171, 183, 184
wool jersey, 21, 97, 170, 173, 202, 203, 205, 208, 211
Woolman, Edna, 150
work clothes, 117, 132
workplace, women in the, 24, 84, 109–110, 124, 247–248
World's Fair (1939), 138, 141, 142, 183
World War II. *see* wartime (World War II)
Worth, Charles Frederick, 43–44
wrap-around skirt, 133
wrap dress, the, 2, 188–190, 205
Wulbern, Helen, 163–164

"The Yellow Wallpaper" (Gilman), 92
Young, Marian, 132, 133, 158
Young, Roland, 238
The Young Executive's Wife: You and Your Husband's Job (Heal), 258

zippers, 93, 161
Zorina, Vera, 132–133, 136, 177